Exploring Ethics

through
Children's Literature

Book 2

Elizabeth Baird Saenger

© 1993
CRITICAL THINKING PRESS & SOFTWARE
(formerly Midwest Publications)
P.O. Box 448 • Pacific Grove • CA 93950-0448
Tel# 800-458-4849 • Fax# 408-372-3230
ISBN 0-89455-486-7

ABOUT THE AUTHOR

Elizabeth Baird Saenger grew up in Houston, Texas, where she graduated from Rice University. She holds an M.Ed. from Tufts University and has completed courses at Teachers' College, Columbia University, and at Bank Street College of Education. She has taught at almost every level, from pre-kindergarten to post-graduate, and in both public and private schools. She has taught ethics to elementary-age children at the Fieldston Lower School of the Ethical Culture-Fieldston Schools in New York since 1983. Elizabeth and her husband Robert have lived in Mamaroneck, New York, for many years. They have two adult sons.

FOR

BOB

AND FOR

DAVID AND MICHAEL

ACKNOWLEDGMENTS

First of all, I thank my students, the children at Fieldston Lower School, the Ethical Culture-Fieldston Schools, Riverdale, Bronx, New York, who have taught me so generously and inspired me so happily.

The Director (now retired) of those schools, Howard R. Radest, gave me freedom within a structure of support and encouragement. His successor as Director, Jeanne E. Amster, has been wonderfully supportive as well. And especially, my principal, Helen Halverson, has been continually involved and helpful. I am very grateful to all three.

The professional expertise of my colleagues at Fieldston Lower School has been a source of inspiration as I strive to teach well.

Mark Weinstein contributed early ideas. The Council for Religion in Independent Schools provided a first grant, followed by several from the Ethical Culture-Fieldston Schools. All of these were essential to my development of this work.

Tom Lickona and Michael Schulman, each well known in the field of moral education, have been extremely kind in their encouragement of my efforts, and I am grateful.

I thank the writer Clyde Robert Bulla for his enthusiastic interest and help. Also, I thank Sheila Garrigue, Marion Dane Bauer, and Adrienne Su for their art and their interest in this book.

Several distinguished educators took the trouble to read early drafts of this work and offer thoughtful comments. I am especially grateful to Marilyn Watson of the Child Development Project in San Ramon, California, to Jo Anne B. Stack of the Mamaroneck Public Schools in Mamaroneck, New York, and to Cary Page of Springside School in Philadelphia. Margery R. Bernstein contributed suggestions for evaluation, and I particularly thank her. Librarians in the children's sections of public libraries in New Rochelle and Mamaroneck, New York, were particularly helpful in their suggestions as well.

During the entire period I have been teaching ethics, I have been part of the Columbia University Moral Education Seminar. That experience has been stimulating and important to me. In addition, I have attended several annual conferences of the Association for Moral Education, to which I belong, and found them a vital source of information and ideas.

I appreciate the patience and good humor of Michael Baker of Critical Thinking Press & Software. Bonnie Baker gave me wise, astute editorial guidance. My editor, Gaeir L. Dietrich, asked questions, suggested organization, and gave wonderful help, page by page.

David and Michael, my adult sons, were most supportive, as were my mother-in-law, Lucie Saenger, and my sisters, Nancy Baird and Joan Glover, and I am deeply grateful. Robert Saenger, my husband, was simply superb, as always. And as always, I thank him most of all.

E.B.S.

CONTENTS

INTRODUCTION

In every culture, we share certain basic values. We all try to treat each person with respect and with kindness. We try to be honest and trustworthy. But it is rarely obvious what the right thing to do may be in particular situations, and ethics are lived in particular situations. In this book, I hope to show how children's literature can be used to help children develop their own strength as independent ethical decision makers.

GUIDING VALUES

Each individual person is of infinite worth, to be treated with absolute respect and kindness. This is the precept orienting ethics and guiding these lessons. In children's terms, ethics is *the study of how people SHOULD treat each other.*

WHAT ETHICS IS AND ISN'T

An explicit, clear definition of ethics is important because children are likely to think that any difficult decision is an ethical decision (once they've heard the word "ethical").

"I have an ethical problem," a child may proudly say. "I want to go to my friend's house today, but if I do, I'll probably end up missing my favorite television program. I don't know what to do!" Such a statement is an opportunity to help the whole group understand the distinction between any difficult decision and an *ethical* decision.

This child's choice is almost certainly not an ethical one at all, but simply a choice. You might help illustrate this by asking the children what could possibly *make* it an *ethical* choice. For example, if the child had promised to go to the friend's house and the friend was counting on the visit, that could make the problem ethical. Or if going to the friend's house could cause some hardship for the child's mother or younger sibling, for example, that could also make the problem ethical. A decision becomes ethical when it involves some conflict in how people should treat each other.

Or, a child may say, "The sun is unethical! It's shining right in my eyes!" Use such an opportunity to say, "Wait a minute. Can the *sun* be either ethical or unethical, ever?" Help your children understand that only human beings can make *ethical* choices and decisions. Some will argue that non-human animals can make ethical decisions, but I say no. Animals behave according to instinct or training, but not in accordance with ethical values.

Children may assume that anything "nice" or pleasant is ethical. Even among adults, there can be a tendency to confuse ethics with a kind of vague and sweet sentimentality. For example, using phony politeness to fool someone in order to get your own way is hardly ethical, although it seems nice. Children understand this.

Say to the children, "*Ethical* is not the same as *nice*. Something could be ethical but not nice, or nice but not ethical, or it could be both nice and ethical." (A child will invariably interject, "Or it could be not nice *and* not ethical!") Ask the children for examples that demonstrate the distinction between nice and ethical. I've had children answer:

> "Well, when my dog smells chicken, he begs me for a chicken bone. But I know it would splinter and hurt him, so I can't be nice to my dog, but I am being ethical to him."

> "Last year, before we moved here, I had a teacher who was really, really strict! She sure didn't seem that nice. But she was fair and we all worked hard, and I think she was ethical."

Another confusing area is intention. In spite of the outcome of what we do (or say), the intention with which we do (or say) something makes our action ethical or unethical. For example, a person can intend to do harm, but the result could turn out to be lucky for the intended victim, in which case the act was unethical, even though the victim was glad it happened. Or a person can try sincerely to, say, help another, but end up hurting him, in which case the act was ethical, even though no one is smiling about it. My students, even second graders, enjoy thinking of specific examples of this importance of intention, once some of them grasp it.

Finally, as "how people should treat each other" implies, ethics is mostly about action. You will need to state this and repeat it from time to time. We can't help our feelings, but we can help our behavior. Of course this can be reassuring (bad *thoughts* aren't punished) as well as salutary (good intentions are not enough). But do say it: ethics means how we act towards one another.

OBJECTIVES OF THIS COURSE

The goal in teaching ethics is to improve the rigor and clarity of children's reasoning about ethical issues without forgetting either the emotional content or the experiential context.

Emotions like love, fear, shame, loyalty, and anger constantly shape both small and large ethical choices. For example, how many of us have said, "I was afraid to do what I thought was right," or, "I wanted to forgive her, but I was just too angry"? Caring and concern, trust and hope, courage and commitment, sharing and forgiving are all ethical values whose emotional dimension is inescapable.

In ethics class, we can try to provide a safe forum for sharing both feelings and ideas. Children need help to grow in appropriate self-confidence as independent ethical decision makers. You can offer them guidance as well as support and encouragement in this noble effort.

A fifth-grade boy, on the first day of ethics class, remarked, "If someone hurts you physically, even badly, after you get well, you can't really *remember* the pain. Somehow your brain just isn't hooked up that way. You may remember that it hurt, but not how it felt. But if someone says something that hurts your feelings, you can think of it a long time after and *feel* the same hurt. That's part of why ethics is important! Hurting someone's feelings is important." His classmates agreed.

We can hope that ethics class does indeed serve to improve children's behavior. At the least, it can make them better listeners, clearer thinkers, and more reflective, articulate speakers.

CLASSROOM PROCEDURES

CLASSROOM ENVIRONMENT

This course of study works best with small groups (about twelve) so that everyone can participate readily. The time period for each session should be about forty minutes. Sessions might be once a week. The chairs should be arranged in a circle so that everyone can see everyone else's face easily, and so that everyone is on an equal basis. (Occasionally, some children find the eye contact with peers too distracting or exciting for this circular arrangement to work well. You might experiment with more traditional children-facing-teacher set-ups as needed.)

Certain standards of decorum are helpful to the atmosphere of ethics as a serious class rather than a sort of "rap session." These include

- no feet allowed on vacant chairs

- no lying on the floor

- no two children in one chair (unless of course there aren't enough chairs)

It is important to keep the ethics lessons distinct from other, "regular" lessons. If you are teaching these lessons with your regular class, take pains to set them apart from other classroom work, using a special time, place, and arrangement. If you are not the classroom teacher, you need your own time and space for this class.

It may seem paradoxical for the one subject which permeates every aspect of life to be deliberately separated, off in its own realm. But this separation is important because children (like adults) need a safe, separate arena in which to consider the ethical aspects of their own behavior. They need to (and will) make the connections between principle and action themselves.

Children already know what they are "supposed to say" about ethical issues. *The purpose of ethics class is the deeper understanding and integration into their lives of moral principles by the children themselves.*

Listening to peers and discovering that others have many of the same concerns, the same scruples, the same conflicts as they do are vital ingredients to children's forging and keeping their own standards. They need experiential space to accomplish this.

I especially remember an incident from a sixth-grade group discussing the need to resist peer pressure and do the right thing, and how hard it is to have that kind of courage. A girl remarked, "Usually, you say what you don't mean and don't want to say because you'd rather feel bad about it afterwards and have the wrong people like you for the wrong reasons than just be yourself and do what you know is right." The forum of an ethics class provides a place where such urgent struggles are respected and encouraged.

USING CHILDREN'S LITERATURE

I have found the strong need for an involving context in which to "see" moral issues, both for students and for teacher. Mere paragraph dilemmas on the one hand or overladen "story-vehicles" on the other are both unsatisfying for most children and teachers, and wear thin very quickly, in my experience. Real literature has its own intrinsic rewards and, carefully chosen and used, sparks many more good ethics discussions.

The basis for these ethics lessons is the reading aloud of the literature by you. Do not relinquish this role! Children should not take turns reading aloud. These are not reading lessons, and there should be no perception by the children of peers' different reading abilities to distract from or pollute the focus on moral issues.

Also, no child has the facilities for oral expression, occasional word substitution or definition, timeliness of pausing, and choice for emphasis of the adult. Everyone in the group should share the same story at the same pace in as much the same way as possible. And, incidentally, you should certainly "ham it up" as much as is comfortable, affecting different voices for different characters in a story, and acting things out with gestures and body language for fun and effect.

YOUR ROLE AS ETHICS DISCUSSION LEADER

SETTING THE TONE

We must assume that children arrive at school with a basic framework of ethical values from home and from society. Children are passionately concerned about understanding right and wrong, and eager to discuss ethical problems. These problems are no less urgent or difficult than the problems any of us face. The difference is in the context and in the "newness" for the children, but not in the essence. Therefore, remember to take your children's issues seriously and to be warmly receptive to the (sometimes tentative, sometimes awkward) voicing of them in discussion.

Basic to this sort of discussion is the clear and free acknowledgment by you that you frequently make ethical errors and do things which you deeply regret. When I say this in my ethics classes, the children quickly ask, "Like what?" I simply answer that I'm too embarrassed to tell them, which is true, and which they readily accept. At other times, I've related specific incidents from my experience, especially when they serve to illustrate a particular issue under discussion.

For example, in a story (such as Estes' *The Hundred Dresses*) of peer-group pressure to reject someone who seems different and to disregard that person's feelings, I relate a painful incident in my memory of a girl who came to my school in the middle of the year. She wore the same dress (actually, a jumper, with different blouses) every day and didn't speak to anyone, and none of us spoke to her. I remember feeling bad for her. I remember thinking she must feel shy and alone and scared. But *I* wasn't going to be the one to take the risk of befriending her, even just a little. After some weeks, she left my school.

When I tell this true story, my remorse is so evident that the effect on children is usually great. Some even exclaim, "And she could have turned out to be the best friend in the world!"

In any event, a confession of your own ethical shortcomings, past or present, is obviously ethically appropriate. It is partly a model. Also, it serves to clear the air and set the tone for less inhibited thought and words about real-life ethics within the group.

DISCIPLINE ISSUES

While it is important to avoid a "preachy" or unrealistic role, you still must guide the discussion and maintain order. Some rules of the ethics class should be made very clear:

- When one person is speaking, everyone else must listen respectfully to that person.

- People who are not present may not be spoken about by name (since they may object and can't tell their side of the story).

- People who are present should be addressed directly (not referred to in the third person).

The fewer and simpler the rules, the better. This will depend on your own style and previous relationship with the children.

If there is a breach of civility or ethics right in front of you in ethics class, of course you must react. You may need to say to the children, "Maybe you meant that as a joke, but if you had been talking about me, I would have felt terrible when you said that! I really care about the person you made your 'joke' about and I don't like it *at all*! Don't ever say something like that in this class!"

This makes your indignation clear, it affirms standards of ethical behavior, and by offering the explanation of "joke," it affords a dignity-preserving "out" for the offender. Also it defends the victim with minimal embarrassment. But notice that it does *not* invoke *ethics*, certainly not explicitly. This is extremely important.

Although it is always tempting to try to use ethics class for solving behavior or discipline problems from the class itself, or from the whole school, don't do it! If, for example, you remind children in regular class that just that sort of unkind remark was what the child had proclaimed wrong yesterday in ethics lesson, or say, "Today we'll be talking about teasing in ethics class because of what some of you did at recess," the whole atmosphere becomes oppressive (in the manner of "Big Brother" who is always watching and judging) for the children, and they'll simply "clam up."

Despite all your efforts, some children will continue to misbehave, to say and do unkind, unfair, or unethical things to each other. (Alas, just as you and I will!) Do not confuse the roles of ethics teacher and school disciplinarian or even school standard setter. Such a mix is beyond the capacities of any human being. More to the point, it gives ethics a bad name with the children and just makes them feel they must be more careful in hiding their mistakes. It hardly promotes honest reflection, much less soul-searching change.

Teaching ethics requires a delicate balance of humility and leadership. This is doubtless achieved only sporadically, but it is an especially important goal for an ethics teacher.

GUIDING THE DISCUSSION

Good discussion requires intensive planning and attention. Make written notes of good questions and points to make ahead of time, and keep notes after discussions (children have reminded me, "You asked us that two weeks ago," or "You said that example").

Although we have become firm enough in our values to be able to offer ethical guidance, we are still struggling with everyday issues just as the children are. In this spirit, discussion questions are indeed shared by you. *Beware of slipping into "guess what I'm thinking" modes rather than genuinely sharing questions or simply stating clear goals.*

Help the children by

- articulating particular objectives

- referring to important principles

- offering specific examples

- providing interesting alternatives

- suggesting significant consequences

Children also need help and training in discussion techniques:

- listening carefully to one another

- responding to one another rather than only to the teacher

- avoiding "put-downs"

- asking appropriate questions which seek clarification

- defining terms

- waiting one's turn to speak

Such skills require constant practice and patience. They are intrinsic to both means and ends of ethics discussion.

Summary of Do's and Don'ts for Teaching Ethics

Do...		Don't...
Do react to what you see happening in class.	...	Don't be "Big Brother."
Do affirm the values of respect for each person.	...	Don't use ethics class as a discipline lesson.
Do honestly share questions of ethics.	...	Don't hesitate to be in charge of the class.
Do probe for ethical principles.	...	Don't probe for psychological motivation.
Do read the literature vividly, dramatically, and with a sense of humor.	...	Don't let anyone but yourself read aloud an ethics story.
Do be optimistic about children's capacity for goodness.	...	Don't expect the impossible.
Do listen to the children and remain open-minded.	...	Don't play "guess what I'm thinking."
Do think hard about your own ethical values.	...	Don't be afraid of discussing difficult ethical issues.
Do admit your own failings and doubts.	...	Don't think you have to present yourself as a paragon of virtue.

ETHICS VS. PSYCHOTHERAPY

Ethics class is not a psychotherapy group. (It is presumed that you have neither the competence for nor the immediate goal of improving your children's mental health.)

In discussion, keep the focus on ethical justification and conceivable consequences and alternatives. Avoid probing psychological motives or relying on such popular psychology terms as "guilt trip" or "dysfunctional family."

Saying, "I think the real reason you said that is because you feel mad about what happened to you this morning" is beyond the sphere of ethics class. Each person is entitled to respect and to the privacy of his or her own motivations, at least in the rather "public" forum of class discussion.

One of the great advantages of using situations from literature is detachment. But similarly, with literature, keep the discussion away from consideration of whether this character's neglectful mother or unhappy family may be the real source of the problem. *Stick to the ethics.*

Each person is responsible for his or her own behavior, and that is the subject of ethics class. Say this, and try to follow it.

ETHICS ISSUES

SHARING PERSONAL ETHICAL ISSUES

As the year progresses, children might be invited to share or present to the group ethical issues from their own experience. These issues are sometimes so rich, vivid, and universal that the whole group spends quite a lot of time discussing them.

But there must always be the strict rule that no one can be mentioned by name, since that person is not there to tell his or her side of the story, or may simply object to its being shared. My children are extremely respectful of this particular ethical rule of ethics class.

At other times, you might need to interrupt politely, explaining that a particular incident (too personal, too off-the-track, too difficult) is not a proper issue for ethics class. Clearly, some matters require prompt and private attention, perhaps by a school counselor or with a parent or proper authorities.

In class discussion, focus needs to stay on children's realms of ethical responsibility and decision making. When children want to bring up incidents of unethical behavior by adults, I explain, usually without challenging the child's assessment of the incident, that our purpose in ethics class is to talk about issues of *children's* ethics. Although we may not like or approve of everything we see happening, our job is to work on what we *can* work on: our own ethics. I include myself as a member of the class community and remain willing to discuss issues of my own fairness or ethics.

Some children may perceive ethics class as a kind of grievance center. There can be a contagion of children announcing, perhaps in a "tattle-tale" tone of voice, "I have an ethical issue: today, at lunch, a certain person...." Although no names are mentioned, the other children know what this issue is about, most are uncomfortable, and some are directly involved (and angry!).

I made a rule for my classes that any personal ethical issue had to be brought to me, privately, before class. I would describe it to the group, if appropriate, in a form disguising identities or, depending on the incident and the child, invite that child or children to present it to the group. Alternatively, children could bring an "unscreened" issue to the group as long as everyone understood that I reserved the right to interrupt and close the discussion at any point that it seemed inappropriate.

Ethical issues experienced by the children themselves can be invaluable sources of discussion. Recently, we had an intense discussion about teasing, and how to resist joining in, especially if your best friend is one of the teasers and you don't like the person being teased anyway. There was rapt attention when a girl earnestly advised her peers to "think very hard how *you* would feel if it was you being teased." And there was also quick agreement when someone pointed out that "you could get in trouble yourself!" Both high-minded and self-protective reasons deserve to be heard and evaluated together because both are valid.

Sometimes, children explain their own ethical problems with such force and clarity that the whole class time is spent struggling with that one incident and how best to deal with it. I remember a fourth-grade girl describing her dilemma at summer camp. A certain counselor told her children that if they would vote for her as best counselor, she would make sure they got a special reward from the camp director. But this particular counselor had not been a good one at all, in the sincere judgment of this girl: "She had yelled at the kids all the time and just talked to the other counselors instead of helping us." The others campers shared this view but wanted the reward and put great pressure on this girl to "vote right." If she voted her conscience, her fellow campers would be hurt by not getting the reward they wanted, and they had done nothing wrong. What should she have done?

Ethics is often simply a matter of appreciating another's perspective, and ethics class can provide for this. A fifth-grade girl came into class and said she had an ethical problem that she couldn't solve. She had an older brother, college age, who was always extremely nice to her, and she was crazy about him. But when he had his friends over to the family apartment, this brother acted differently, and seemed not to even want her around. She was confused and upset about it because he seemed almost like two people to her—one when his friends were around, another with her alone.

Another child raised his hand and said, "I have an ethical problem with *my* little sister!" He really liked his sister a lot, he explained. She was in kindergarten and he'd always kind of looked out for her and enjoyed her company. But the problem was that, when he had friends over (one of whom was in the class and could confirm his story), this beloved little sister just wouldn't leave them alone and give them the privacy they felt entitled to. "I try to tell her to leave us alone, but she just doesn't get it," he earnestly said. "I don't want to hurt her feelings, but what should I do?" A third child in the class said, "Hey! Isn't this really two sides of the same problem?" All agreed, with some surprise and amusement, that it was. And all were helped a little by seeing things from different perspectives, especially the first girl with the older brother.

Also, I have very occasionally brought up ethical issues from my own experience in an ethics class and been surprised at the strong and memorable effect it had on the children. Once I mentioned my intense frustration at having to choose for that very evening between a meeting I *should* go to and a party I *wanted* to go to, partly because it was to celebrate hard work

I'd shared in. The children discussed the ethical ramifications with me very seriously. And they, *and* their friends and parents, were still asking me about it months later! (One girl suggested earnestly, "Can't you take a cake or something to the meeting so it will *seem* like a party?" I did go to the meeting, but without a cake.)

AGE-APPROPRIATE ETHICS ISSUES

Such topics as truth telling, obedience, and hurting back deserve special attention. These are the ethics that the children are *living*, after all.

TRUTH TELLING

Children often are confused about recognizing deliberate partial truth telling as lying. A child may tell *part* of the truth, omitting the part that could cause the child trouble. (For example, this occurs with Alan and his friend Shaun in Levoy's *Alan and Naomi*—see the suggested lesson for that book.) I explain that, since the child knew the other person was misunderstanding, this actually is lying, even though what was said was technically true.

Many children get quite agitated about this, and the argument can become intense. How can it be lying if it was the truth? Eventually they grasp that intentional deception is what constitutes lying, not simply correlation with (partial) reality. This concept needs and deserves reiteration, and it becomes a memorable lesson.

On the other hand, even young children can be both principled and resourceful in their devotion to truth telling. One autumn day, a second grader in my class raised her hand and proclaimed earnestly, "I have a big ethics problem!" When asked what this problem was, she explained, "This person that I really don't like came right up to me and asked me, 'Do you like me?'" The other children instantly, and with some emotion, agreed that certainly was a big ethical problem.

"Why?" I asked.

They explained, "Well, if you tell the truth, it would hurt the person's feelings, but if you try not to hurt the person's feelings, you'd be telling a lie." Although these children were rather new to ethics class, it was clear they had already pondered such problems seriously.

Some offered suggestions. "You could say, 'I'd rather not answer that question right now,'" but others pointed out that such an evasion really made the answer all too clear. None of us had a good solution. Finally, I called on a boy who had not raised his hand or participated in the discussion.

He answered, Solomon-like, "I'd say, 'Well, there are some things about you I do like and some things I don't like,' because I could say that honestly about everyone I know." I was as grateful for his wisdom as his peers were.

OBEDIENCE

Closely related is the matter of obedience. By about third grade, most children have figured out that they can disobey many rules with impunity. Then why follow them, especially if the rules seem silly or onerous? Children like to talk about this problem, and especially to hear what their peers have to say about it. They are well able to understand and articulate the importance of maintaining *trust*. Also, they can understand and express the fact that there may be important reasons, such as safety, for the rules, reasons which they simply don't know about.

As a third grader recently told her peers in my class, "You should obey anyway because, like, it could be a cactus." When I looked confused, she explained that, for example, "Your parents could have told you not to go into a plant store, and you didn't know why, and so you just thought you should do it anyway. But maybe there was a *cactus* in that plant store, and it could hurt you!"

Another child agreed with her, but offered his own reason. He pointed out that new privileges may also come from such obedience and proven trustworthiness. The others were quite interested in this benefit they apparently had not considered. The value of ethics class as a safe forum to air such real issues is great.

One year, a distressed parent approached me, saying, "My daughter really needs ethics class!" A few days later, she explained that her third-grade child, against strict family rules, had "conned" a new baby-sitter and left their city apartment together with a visiting child, walked up and down two blocks, entered several stores, and returned. The mother was upset by the breach of trust between herself and her daughter, the more so because the child seemed quite unconcerned.

Many weeks went by. I didn't mention the incident to the child or even refer to a similar example in class. But issues of trust and obedience arose in class discussion about stories from time to time. At last, children did an ethics play about obedience and trust. In the discussion afterwards, this girl suddenly raised her hand. Speaking in such serious and heartfelt tones as to command the rapt attention of her peers, she said, "It would be more seriously unethical if, for example, a child would fool her baby-sitter and go outside her apartment with her friend and walk along two blocks, because she would be breaking her parents' trust in her if she did a thing like that."

I caught my breath, suddenly remembering the long-ago incident. The child had obviously been struggling with issues of her own ethical responsibility, perhaps more than even her own mother realized, and her role as instructor was powerful.

HURTING BACK

Finally, there is the thorny ethical issue of "hurting back." If someone (a peer) does something bad to you, *on purpose*, should you do something bad back?

Everyone in class will have wrestled with this problem, but may be unaware of its universality, and hence, especially grateful for the discussion opportunity. Further, this is an issue for which their own experience is likely to have been at variance with the advice and preachments (as distinguished from behavior) of most adults.

After some discussion, it might be most effective to write two big headings on the chalkboard: REASONS YOU *SHOULD* HURT SOMEONE BACK and REASONS YOU *SHOULD NOT* HURT SOMEONE BACK, and then ask for suggestions. (Many children have difficulty distinguishing between *reasons* and *consequences*. Depending on the group and on the emotional heat of this topic for them, it might be just as well at this point simply to include consequences with reasons.)

Typical *should* reasons might be as follows:

- It could teach the person not to bother you again.

- It could show other people not to bother you.

- It could be a sort of punishment.

Typical *should not* reasons might be these:

- It could really hurt the person.

- It could set a bad example.

- It could start a bad cycle going.

- It could get you in trouble.

- It could be misunderstood or give the wrong message.

- You could get hurt worse than before.

The class could then be asked to decide which are the *best* or *most ethical* reasons for each course of action, and *why*.

It is very important for children to see that the problem is one shared by many others, and it is especially important for them to be able to listen to the different reasons offered by their peers. In developmental terms, this brings the sort of dissonance that produces accommodation (or synthesis) and growth in thinking.

Sometimes the discussion on this issue can be very moving and sometimes very practical. Children will say quite emotionally, "I know that I *shouldn't* really hurt the other person back, but I know that I *would* really try to hurt him (her)." (Although this may be changing, with boys, the hurting is usually physical, with girls, verbal.)

Once in my class, a boy said, "If I didn't get him back, I know it would just eat at me and eat at me inside until I couldn't stand it any more!"

Another boy had a practical suggestion: "When I get really mad at someone like that, I write their name and some bad stuff on a piece of paper, and

I keep doing that for a few days, and then finally I just crumple the piece of paper all up! The person never knows, but I feel better!"

Of course, every teacher is familiar with children's tendency to neglect or misconstrue *intention*. Much can be accomplished by sorting out whether a particular offense was actually an accident or a simple misunderstanding. This too is an important ethics lesson, especially if children are provided with appropriate language to organize and clarify it.

On the first day of ethics class, a child new to our school had a very good question: "Why should I be ethical to someone I hate? I don't care about the person anyway!" One child answered, "Because the person could hurt you! It's safer to at least try to be nice." A different child said, "You should be ethical anyway because *you* would know about it yourself! You're the one who has to keep on thinking about how you treated that person, and it's *much* harder to get up the courage to set things right later, after more time has gone by and you know how wrong you've been. Believe me, I know!" A third child commented, "Anyhow, you don't have to *like* someone to be *ethical* to him or her!"

CHILDREN'S ISSUES

Occasionally, you should be ready to stop everything in order to explain and briefly discuss some of the important issues of medical and legal ethics which bombard children through the news media, and which nobody else may be helping them to clarify or begin to understand. Many times, these issues are disturbing or confusing to adults just as they are to children. I think you should acknowledge this deep uncertainty, explain or answer questions as best you can, and return to the regular lesson. These kinds of ethical issues are not the stuff to be "force fed"—wait for the children to bring them up. But be ready to help when they do.

"WIDER WORLD" ETHICS ISSUES

Depending upon schoolwide philosophy, important issues such as world hunger or the need for peacemaking or helping those in need in our own community can be given special attention in ethics class. In my opinion, such issues are most effective when they are few and reflect your own special ethical interests (but also your clear willingness to entertain opposing views).

Though all the most universal causes become controversial as soon as specific remedies or programs begin to be discussed, fear of controversy hardly seems ethically admirable. Democratic respect for opinions with which one disagrees is a great ethical model here! So also is deep concern for problems of the world beyond the classroom.

TEACHING SUGGESTIONS ————————————

ORGANIZATION OF THIS BOOK

Most of us teachers think in terms of units, especially in planning. When I first began to teach ethics, I thought perhaps I could do a unit on truth-telling or a unit on compromise and sharing. Not so with ethics!

Ethical issues and ethical decisions arise unpredictably, from a particular context, and in surprising combinations. Children experience them that way, just as we do. The precepts and principles that we can all recite acquire meaning only when we are striving to live by them, often in apparently small or unexpected choices, too often only in retrospect.

Accordingly, you will notice that the basic organization here is *by story*, and that there are many different ethical values and issues (perhaps overlapping or conflicting) in each story. That is how ethics happens, and that, in my opinion, is the best way to try to teach it.

THE STORIES

Children thoroughly enjoy hearing these stories. They are quick to see the ethical issues, even if they have never had ethics class before. Allowing the children to see the issues for themselves in the context of stories is vital to their gaining self-confidence as worthy participants who recognize ethical issues from their own experience.

The stories are arranged in order of age appropriateness and effectiveness, starting with early fourth grade and proceeding through to late sixth grade. The stories I have chosen for this guide have worked well with many children over many years, and I still enjoy using them and admire their art.

THE LESSONS

The lessons I offer reflect years of my own classroom experience, but of course, they should be taken as suggestive, depending on the verbal or intellectual sophistication and interest of any particular group. I have tried to offer more discussion questions and suggestions than would be needed, and therefore too much for any one group at any one time. Selection and adjustment of the parts of these lessons are expected and invited.

Some of the lessons in this book are for stories furnished with the book, and some are for stories that are readily available through your school or public library. The lesson plans are somewhat different depending on whether or not the story is included here.

For stories included in this book:

- Points for discussion are indicated in the story by a pointing hand and a roman numeral.

      ☞   I

- In the lesson plan, a pointing hand with a roman numeral identifies the questions that go with the discussion pause of the same number in the story.

☞   I

- Questions for the children are indicated with an asterisk.

    ✸

- The lesson plan includes suggested pauses, to allow children time to assimilate and react to what they have heard, and other comments which may be helpful.

For stories not included in this book:

- In the lesson plan, page numbers are provided to show where suggested discussion points are located.

- A pointing hand in the lesson plan indicates the paragraph just preceding the spot for discussion.

    ☞

- Questions for the children are indicated with an asterisk.

    ✸

- Suggestions to aid you in reading and discussing the story are included.

Finally, of course, the questions provided are meant to be guides. Be sensitive to your children's mood and attention span. Anyone gets frustrated when a good story is interrupted too often, no matter how interesting the discussion questions.

Some children listen better if they are simultaneously drawing pictures or fiddling with clay. At other times, you can have a quick vote (with eyes closed, so nobody feels unduly pressured by peers) between reading or another appropriate ethics class activity such as debates, or even a combination, with thirty minutes for reading and discussion followed by ten minutes of freeze game (see Other Activities). But remember that literature and discussion are the real heart of ethics class.

PREPARATION

Before any story is read aloud, you need to read it and think about it. If you don't like it yourself, it's best to use one of the other stories. Your own enthusiasm and regard for the story will be clear (and contagious) to the children, but so will your negative feelings. Further, you need to think about your own questions for the story, and decide which parts or issues deserve the most emphasis. Plan ahead so you can not only enjoy the stories yourself, but be ready for unexpected points the children will raise.

HOMEWORK

Homework assignment questions should be given either before class discussion on a topic or after this discussion. Both strategies have advantages and disadvantages. Most children need the prior discussion to clarify expectations for ethical issues in homework, but the challenge of struggling independently with an issue before sharing ideas with the whole group is also a worthy one. Accordingly, the homework questions included in the lessons are both "application" and "starter" types, mixed with regular class discussion questions.

Of course these written assignments are important for revealing to you the depth and clarity of your children's comprehension as you go along. On some crucial objectives, such as identifying ethical reasons on both sides of an issue, you may want to use both types of assignment. Let them work on their own, then have a good discussion with the whole group, then use an assignment in which they apply new understandings to the same topic.

It is my habit to insist on complete sentences for most written work, for the clarity of thinking as well as the skill in written expression. Following the practice of my school, I make comments on the children's homework papers (rather than letter grades), but award the sixth graders' work with my own system of check, check-plus-in-parentheses, check-plus, check-double-plus (rare). This seems to work reasonably well for this age. Any child whose paper shows a real lack of comprehension gets prompt individual help (rather than a check-minus). I explain to the children that I am looking for how clearly, completely, and well they explain their ideas about ethical issues we are working on. Certainly, originality gets special praise too, especially in the application or recognition of ethical principle. (I correct spelling, but don't "count off" for misspellings on ethics work.)

Depending on the practices of the school and the particular classroom, as well as on the difficulty of the assignments, ethics class homework assignments should be given perhaps once a month for fourth graders, more frequently for fifth graders, and probably every week for sixth graders.

DEVELOPING YOUR OWN LESSONS ───────

CHOOSING STORIES

In general, I would say that ethics class literature needs to center on ethical problems, to be full of ambivalences rather than answers, and to be moral in its point of view. Also, literature works better if it is unfamiliar to most children, so there is the "hook" of wondering how the story will be resolved. Appropriate stories are suggested in the supplemental bibliography. (See Recommended Discussion Books in the Bibliography section)

DEVELOPING DISCUSSION QUESTIONS

As you read a story, think about the ethical issues that interest you. If there could be at least two perspectives on a given incident or decision, both of them ethically defensible or understandable, then it may be a good ethical issue for class discussion. Even after years of practice, I still sometimes pick issues that turn out to be "duds," of more interest to me than to the children. That's why you need a surplus of possibilities.

For any incident in a story, try to imagine, sympathetically, the perspectives of various characters. Write down questions expressing these various perspectives on the issue. These will lead to others. Write as many as you can. Think about what decision you would choose and *why* an incident makes you mad. Once you get started, it's hard to stop!

There is great value in the children's moral outrage in response to breaches of ethics in stories (like the first, Garrigue's *Between Friends*), because it helps them see that they already do have some strong ethical views. It's easier to recognize a value when the value is violated. Children need that learning experience in the fresh context of unfamiliar stories.

As you formulate your questions, remember that often they are true questions whose "answers" should be as unknown to you as to your children. The class discussion will be better for being the more truly open. It will also be more fun, and more stimulating for you and the children. Although you have your own strong ethical values, you can still question how they work out in particular situations.

It's not necessary to resolve every question or issue. Some ethical problems will just be left "hanging" for the children to ponder.

Possible starting questions include:

- What exactly was wrong about what that character did?

- How do you suppose the other person felt? Why?

- What else could she have said that would not have hurt his feelings?

- Do you think he would have done the same thing if...? Why?

- If the results had been different, would she still have been wrong to do it? Why?

GETTING STARTED

Whatever the grade level, it is important to begin with activities that set the tone of acknowledging and affirming each individual person. Sitting in a circle, ask the children to say their names and tell the group something about themselves that they would like the others to know, for example, something they have recently learned to do, something they really like, something special that recently happened to them, etc. (If the group already knows each other's names, just have them tell something special about themselves.)

Each child has a turn reciting what the other children have said and then his or her own name and introduction. The repetition can be fun, and of course it serves to help everyone (especially you, the teacher) get acquainted as well as affirmed. "This is Dorcas and she has a new baby sister; this is Abdul and he likes to draw cartoons and he also is learning to swim; and my name is Jessica and I just love to play soccer!"

Now say that this is *ethics* class, write the word on the chalkboard, and ask whether anyone knows what ethics might mean. After a few guesses, explain simply that ethics is the study of how people *should* treat each other. Mention that we all realize that nobody does what he or she should do all the time, but that we all try. Often it's hard to know exactly what we should do. Ethics class is a place where we can work together to try to decide what we should do in different kinds of situations.

Such words of introduction should be kept quite brief because they won't mean much to the children until they begin to become involved in specific examples of ethical issues, through the stories you'll share. Without more ado, therefore, plunge right into the reading.

LESSON PLANS AND STORIES ——————

BETWEEN FRIENDS

by Sheila Garrigue (abridgement and revisions by Elizabeth Baird Saenger)

STORY SYNOPSIS — In the story, nine-year-old Jill moves with her family from California to Massachusetts and is anxious to make friends. As she gradually gets to know and care about Dede, a Down's syndrome girl who lives nearby, she faces more and more conflicts because the "popular kids" would be friends with Jill but want nothing to do with Dede. There are subplots, to do with her mother's pregnancy and strange ambivalence about Dede, the death of an elderly neighbor, and the privileges of a spoiled peer. The story is rich in appeal for children, and very rich in topics for good ethics discussion.

OBJECTIVES — Children will share and analyze the ethical choices of the lead character, Jill, as she deals with friendship and peer pressure. They will distinguish ethical reasons from other reasons, and they will learn to identify ethical reasons on two sides of an issue.

Further, students will grow in appreciation of the humanity of retarded people, while being given the chance to air and compare their own attitudes about those who are really different.

TIME — Reading aloud and discussing this book can easily extend over many weeks.

HOMEWORK — Homework assignment questions should be given either before class discussion on a topic or after this discussion. Both strategies have advantages and disadvantages. Most fourth graders need the prior discussion to clarify expectations for ethical issues in homework, but the challenge of struggling independently with an issue before sharing ideas with the whole group is also a worthy one. Accordingly, the homework questions below are both "application" and "starter" types, mixed with regular class discussion questions. Depending on the practices of the school and the particular classroom, as well as on the difficulty of the assignments, ethics class homework assignments should be given perhaps once a month for fourth graders.

PROCEDURE — When reading aloud, take care to "ham it up." Give Dede a lower, slower voice, the adults distinct voice tones, and so on, as much as you can. It vastly helps children to comprehend a long read-aloud story.

Remember that you will be selecting from the suggested questions and points for discussion. Don't try to use them all!

DISCUSSION AND HOMEWORK QUESTIONS

Chapter 1

☞ I

Wait for the children's reactions, if any.

☞ II

Children may want to voice their experiences with retarded people or any people who seem very different. Allow for this, but wait until later for more careful attention to this topic.

☞ III

✳ Why does Jill's mother want to leave?

✳ Is it understandable to feel uncomfortable around retarded people? people who look strange?

> Children instantly perceive the mother's real reason for leaving, and generally express outrage because she's an adult and therefore should behave better. This matter of their different expectations for the ethics of children and adults might be probed a little.

> More importantly, they might want to express their own feelings from experiences when confronted with really different people. They need to realize that these reactions, particularly fear, are pretty universal.

> The ethical issue of how we respond to these feelings, how we actually treat people who are very different, should be introduced, and, depending on class reaction at this point, discussed in a preliminary way.

> What "different" people want, most of all, is to be treated as much as possible as if they were the same as everyone else! They want acceptance as equal members of the human community, no more, no less. And, in fact, this is the most ethical, respectful, and appropriate way to behave towards them. You should be clear and explicit about this, but give the children room for airing and discussing their experiences and qualms.

Chapter 2

☞ IV

Pause to give children a chance to react and to be sure they understand the various characters in the story.

Chapter 3

☞ V

* What do you notice already about Dede?

   She's very sensitive to others' feelings.

☞ VI

* What do you notice about Dede's mother?

   She's very eager to help Dede have a friend.

☞ VII

* Do you think a retarded person can be bored?

* What's wrong with referring to Dede as a "retard" (pronounced with the accent on "ree")? What's wrong with calling anyone a "retard"?

   This generally generates very heated discussion.

You might take a little time here to discuss and list on the chalkboard the kinds of insults or teasing that are never acceptable. These include comments about

   • physical appearance

   • race or ethnicity

   • family

   • handicapping condition(s)

   • religion

You can elicit such a list readily from most groups of children. The commonality is that these are qualities that we either can't help or shouldn't be expected to change (because they are a deeply personal part of ourselves). Therefore insults which refer to these qualities are always very wrong and hurtful. Such references or insults are assaults on human dignity.

☞ VIII

* Does she "know the difference"?

☞ IX

* Why do you think Jill started defending those boys? Why did she feel confused?

Homework Assignment

Jill had several opposite feelings and attitudes about Dede, the retarded girl, and about her brothers' friends.

1. Using complete sentences, explain at least two reasons why Jill felt so confused.

2. In your opinion, which reason is most *ethical*, and why?

> Children might say something like, "Jill couldn't stand to see Dede getting hurt," and "Jill liked her brothers' friends and wanted them to like her." This is a rather obvious assignment, but it's a beginning.

Chapter 4

☞ X

Pause to allow for children's reactions.

☞ XI

* What do you notice about Dede? about Jill's mother?

> Dede, again, is sensitive to Jill's feelings. Jill's mother is behaving strangely.

Chapter 5

☞ XII

* What do you notice that is already better (or more ethical) about Jill?

> She at least says "retarded" instead of "ree-tard." I had a child say recently, "At least Jill is beginning to treat her like a person instead of an 'it'."

☞ XIII

* What do you think about Jill's mother's reaction?

☞ XIV

* What would you have done in Jill's situation? Why?

> Recently, a child in my class summed up Jill's problem succinctly, "She'd like to be good, but she wants to be 'cool'."

☞ XV

Pause to allow for reactions.

☞ XVI

  ✳ Has Jill's mother got a point? Why or why not?

    Again, most children will strongly disapprove of Jill's mother's behavior. But it's helpful to explore the reasons why and also to try to imagine her point of view—that she wants her daughter to have friends, for example.

☞ XVII

Pause for any reactions.

Chapter 6

☞ XVIII

  ✳ Do you understand how Jill feels?

☞ XIX

  ✳ Who does Jill's mother remind you of now?

    She is behaving like Dede's mother, over-anxious for her child to make friends.

There is an ongoing theme of Dede's mother's obvious over-eagerness for Jill to be Dede's friend and Jill's mother's obvious over-eagerness for the "popular" girls to be Jill's friends. Children are very sensitive to these particular nuances and will want to discuss the ethics of who chooses friends at some time in the story.

  ✳ What, if anything, is wrong about the way she's acting?

    Kids deserve to make their own friends!

    I had a child say recently, "Dede may feel embarrassed about the way her mom is acting too, but she's just not able to express it."

☞ XX

  ✳ What do you think about Marla so far?

☞ XXI

Pause to allow for children's reactions.

Chapter 7

☞ XXII

Pause. Children will react with outrage and concern for Dede's feelings.

☞ XXIII

Pause to allow for children's reactions. By now, there will be accumulating outrage among children hearing the story about Jill's mother's attitude towards Dede. You can share this, and even add rhetorically:

✳ Can you imagine *your* mother acting this way?

☞ XXIV

I act out Dede's rocking and saying "ah...ah."

☞ XXV

✳ What is the most ethical thing for Jill to do now? Why?

✳ Might Dede just forget about it? If she does, is it right for Jill to "forget" about it too?

✳ Would it be right for Jill to have a sort of fake party for just her and Dede?

✳ Was telling Dede about the nonexistent party an acceptable sort of lie?

This discussion is usually very intense. It might be finished with the following assignment.

Homework Assignment

If you were Jill, what would you do about Dede and the party? Why? Is there a difference between what you think you *would* do and what you think you *should* do? Why? Please explain, using complete sentences.

Chapter 8

☞ XXVI

Pause to allow for children's reactions and to be sure they understand.

When the reason for the mother's behavior is now revealed, it needs to be handled delicately. The tragedy was the death of the earlier child, not the retardation. As the rest of the story makes clear, retarded people deserve the same respect as anyone else, and can lead very worthy lives. If the coming baby should turn out to be other than "perfect," he or she will be welcomed and cherished by the family.

Chapter 9

☞ XXVII

✳ Can you understand Karen's point of view?

Dede *is* different after all.

☞ XXVIII

* Can friends owe each other like that? Are they really friends if they do?

☞ XXIX

* Why not? How and why is it different now?

Issues of responsibilities in relationships might be discussed here.

Chapter 10

☞ XXX

* How can you tell the difference between "sharing excitement" and bragging?

Jill was hurt by Marla's bragging, but Marla was unaware of Jill's feelings. Marla probably just thought of herself as sharing excitement. Often, it is easy to tell when someone else is bragging, but hard to realize it about yourself.

* Why is bragging unethical?

This issue is familiar to children's experience, and important to them. Usually, they are able to explain that bragging is wrong because it is inconsiderate of the other person's feelings.

These questions can also be used well for homework.

☞ XXXI

Illustrations of Dede's sensitivity or response to Jill's feelings have been deftly presented at several points, and may or may not be emphasized, depending on the group. The contrast here is with Marla's insensitivity about Jill's new jacket.

☞ XXXII

Pause to allow for the children's reactions.

Chapter 11

☞ XXXIII

* Can you understand how Jill feels?

Notice that Jill slipped back to saying "retards," at least to herself. Point out that we all have unworthy *feelings*. It's what we *do* that counts.

☞ XXXIV

Pause to allow for children's amazement.

Chapter 12

☞ XXXV

✳ What should Jill do?

Homework Assignment

In the story, *Between Friends*, Jill has a very tough decision to make.

1. In complete sentences, name at least three reasons why Jill *should* go to Boston. Which of these reasons is *ethical*? Why?

2. Name at least three reasons why she *should not* go to Boston. Which of these is ethical? Why?

    There are several variations on this assignment, but the main idea is to get clarification of the difference between ethical reasons (for examples, Marla's feelings would be hurt if Jill didn't go to see her at this very important time, Jill already had a commitment to Dede) and reasons which are perfectly good reasons but not particularly ethical or unethical (Jill wanted a chance to go to Boston, Jill was curious to see Dede's school) and finding ways to weigh them realistically as well as ethically.

    In general, an *ethical* reason takes more account of another person's feelings or follows some rule of fairness. Children find this difficult, but interesting. It is very important for them to understand this clarification of ethics.

    Although our hearts may be with Dede and her school party, we must fully respect the perspectives of children who will argue that this is a more important event for Marla, that the ethical reasons for her side are just as urgent as Dede's. Remember that there are ethical (as well as ordinary) reasons for *both* sides of Jill's decision.

    You can use the chalkboard to list reasons on both sides as a class activity, either after the children have had a chance to work on it themselves, or before, to clarify the assignment if you prefer.

Chapter 13

☞ XXXVI

✳ What do you think of Jill's behavior?

☞ XXXVII

✳ How does Jill feel? *Should* she feel upset or ashamed of herself?

☞ XXXVIII

⁕ Have you ever seen someone smile with his or her mouth but look angry at the same time like that?

☞ XXXIX

⁕ Why is Jill so happy now?

Chapter 14

☞ XL

Pause for children's questions.

☞ XLI

Pause for children's reactions.

☞ XLII

Children may be shocked or just curious. Pause if explanation is needed.

At Dede's school, there is much instruction about practicalities of people with handicapping conditions. My students are often offended when the teacher explains about different children's problems to the group of visitors. "But that's none of their business! That's *private!*" they protest. I agree with them, but explain that this is the author's way of "getting in" important information.

☞ XLIII

Pause for children's reactions to the change in Jill.

Chapter 15

☞ XLIV

Pause for children's reactions.

☞ XLV

⁕ What do you think about Jill's father's behavior here?

Adults also are sometimes uncomfortable around retarded people.

☞ XLVI

⁕ What is one reason for Dede's progress?

Chapter 17

☞ XLVII

Be sure children understand that a few weeks have passed.

☞ XLVIII

Pause for children's reactions. Be sure this sinks in.

☞ XLIX

The last sentence about friendship really "hits home."

Writing Assignment

In class, children might be asked, perhaps anonymously, to write on index cards what they consider to be the most important ethical rules of friendship. These could be read aloud, ranked, and discussed.

Or have children work in small groups, deciding together the ethical rules for friendship. Then the groups can combine into a larger one, sharing their lists. The best agreed upon rules can then be written on the chalkboard and ranked. Or a bulletin board display can be made.

Examples include:

✳ You should like friends for themselves.

✳ Trust and be trustworthy.

✳ Be caring.

✳ Help each other.

✳ Be honest with your friend.

✳ You must both be ready to compromise.

✳ Stick up for your friend.

✳ Be sensitive and considerate of your friend's feelings.

✳ Be a good listener.

✳ Respect your friend.

✳ Be forgiving of your friend.

✳ Don't take your friend for granted.

BETWEEN FRIENDS

by Sheila Garrigue* (abridgement and revisions by Elizabeth Baird Saenger)

CHAPTER ONE

"There's a place!" Jill threaded her way through the sunbathers at the York Falls town pool. Mom followed with the beach bag. "Now," Jill said, as they spread their towels on an empty patch of grass, "aren't you glad we came?"

"No. There's too much to do at the house. We shouldn't be wasting time here."

"It's not wasting time. We've been unpacking and putting stuff away ever since the weekend. Everyone has to have some time off once in a while."

"Okay. You're right," Mom said. She lay down and closed her eyes against the August sun. "This does feel good!"

Jill looked at the families sitting on the grass with their sandwiches and the groups of teenagers playing cards under the trees. It was good to see people again. We must've moved on to the quietest street in York Falls, she thought.

She got up. "I'm going in the water." She strolled toward the pool, trying to look as if she belonged there. Who can I talk to? she thought. There were a couple of girls over to one side, throwing a Frisbee. As she watched, the Frisbee took a wild curve in her direction and she fielded it. "Here!" She sailed it back to them, but they didn't ask her to play.

She joined the line at the diving board and grinned at the kids jostling in front of her. "Is it a good board?" she asked.

"If you're a diver, forget it!" a redheaded boy said. "It's dead as a...yeow!" Another boy pushed him in.

"You're docked, Kelleher! You, too, Parker!" the lifeguard yelled. "Get over here!"

Shoot, Jill thought. Just when I was getting a conversation going. She dove in. The water exploded against her head and cooled her skin as she arrowed down to the bottom.

Climbing out, she sat on the edge and swung her feet, watching what was happening. Then she stared, fascinated, at a group down at the far end. Gross. Retards. "Gross!" She clamped her hand over her mouth. People'd think she was a weirdo, talking to herself.

☞ I

What're retards doing at the town pool? she wondered. She didn't know they could swim—they didn't even have swim bubbles or kickboards or anything. There were about a dozen of them with a couple of counselors. Some were learning strokes and some were jumping in and swimming across. Funny seeing so many all together. You usually only saw them when they were out with their families. Once she'd seen a grown man holding his mother's hand to cross the street.

* Reprinted by the permission of Bradbury Press, an Affiliate of Macmillan, Inc. from *Between Friends* by Sheila Garrigue. Copyright ©1978 by Sheila Garrigue.

☞   II

Jill looked over at Mom. She was lying flat as a shadow on the grass, asleep in the sun. She'll get another burn, Jill thought. I'd better wake her. But she didn't. She'd only start nagging about having to leave and it was too soon.

There was a pickup game going on in the ball field beyond the fence. Jill walked over. Maybe she could get on one of the teams. The kids looked at her for a moment, standing there, then went back to their game. Jill joined a girl in a bikini who was watching on the sidelines. The left fielder dropped an easy one. I could've caught that, she thought, and when the inning ended, she yelled, "D'you need any more players?"

"No," the catcher yelled back.

"What's the score?" Jill asked the girl in the bikini.

"Who knows?"

"Looks like a pretty good game," Jill said.

The girl stared at her. "I guess. Baseball bores me," she said. She waved at the pitcher and strolled away.

"Oh."

It was hot standing there and Jill went back to the pool. She did a racing dive and swam underwater to the other side. It was a good dive—she'd been on the junior swim team in San Diego. Hey, she thought, suppose someone notices and asks me to join the team here! She came up and looked hopefully at the faces around the edge. But nobody said anything.

Well, the retards are having fun anyway, she thought. Okay for them. They all know each other. They haven't just moved to a new town.

She climbed out of the pool. I might as well write to Susan now, she thought. Nothing else is happening, that's for sure. She pulled her pad and pencil out of the beach bag.

> *Dear Susan,*
>
> *We've been in York Falls for a week and so far it's Dullsville. Larry and Tom have gone camping with some guy at Dad's new office. Dad got sent upstate right away and it looks like he's only going to get home on weekends for a while.*
>
> *Mom and I have done just about all the unpacking. The house is okay. There must've been a sale on brown paint a while back because the whole inside is brown. Mom says we have to do it over.*
>
> *Massachusetts is sticky hot and the only place to cool off is the town pool, which is where we are right now. Nobody speaks to you here. I wish we were still in San Diego.*
>
> *Write and tell me what the gang's doing.*
>
>   *Love,*
>
>   *Jill*

Mom's shoulders were turning red.

"Mom. Hey, Mom!"

Her mother lay there as if a steamroller had gone over her.

"Mom, you're getting a burn."

"Mmmph...."

"Wake up. Your shoulders are red."

"Darn! I didn't mean to fall asleep. Put a little lotion on, would you, honey?"

Jill squeezed some lotion onto her fingers and began smoothing it over her mother's shoulders. The closest to a tan Mom ever got were big orange freckles sprinkled all over. But she always kept trying, lying out for hours as though some miracle were going to turn her golden brown. Jill ran a track of gel down Mom's backbone. Sometimes she felt like the mother.

"Mom—there are retards at the pool. Look!"

"Don't stare at them, Jill. It's rude."

"Don't you think it's weird having them come to the pool with everyone else?"

"No." Her mother spoke shortly.

"They can swim, some of them."

"Can't we talk about something more cheerful?" Mom turned on her back. "I'll just do my front a bit," she said. "Vitamin D. Good for the baby."

You'd never imagine that Mom was going to have a baby. She was so skinny, every knob on her shoulders showed, even the pattern of her ribs. There wasn't a bulge to show where a baby might be. Jill kept thinking, funny there should be a new baby coming nine whole years after me. That's a long time between.

Jill remembered that both her parents had seemed really upset about the new baby when they found out. She'd heard arguments through the door when they were still in California. The trouble was, maybe, because Dad had lost his job at about the same time. That was why they'd moved to Massachusetts, because Dad had found a job here and...

"Watch out!" Jill looked up. A beach ball came rocketing toward them. It bounced and knocked over someone's soda can. "Hey!" a woman cried angrily.

Jill jumped up to catch the ball. A girl in a red bathing suit was chasing it. She ran clumsily, breathing hard through her open mouth. She stopped when she saw Jill and stood a little way away, waiting.

"Those mongols! Shouldn't be allowed here, upsetting everybody!" the woman yelled.

"Here," Jill called to the girl. She threw the ball carefully into her outstretched hands.

"Thank you." The girl's voice was low and kind of rough. She turned and walked back to her friends.

"You're welcome," Jill said.

As soon as the girl turned, Mom sat up. She had a funny, stiff look on her face. "Let's get out of here," she said. She began stuffing the towels and lotion into the beach bag.

"It's still early. Why do we have to?"

"It's getting...too crowded," Mom said. "Anyway, we've got a good twenty-minute walk home and there's so much to do—we shouldn't waste a whole afternoon here."

☞   III

"Oh, Mom..."

"I mean it. Don't give me a hard time, Jilly. Dad'll be coming home tonight and I want to be able to show him we've made some real headway while he's been gone. I'd like to get started on those porch chairs."

Jill picked up the beach bag. "That's right! I forgot it's Friday!"

CHAPTER TWO

Jill and Mom were working hard, moving in and painting things in the old house they'd moved into. It was hot and Jill was tired of all the jobs. "When're the boys coming back?" she asked. "They're getting out of all the work!"

"There'll be plenty left for them, don't you worry. They'll be home Sunday."

"I wish I could've gone camping."

"I know. I'm sorry there wasn't anything for you, Jilly. But it seemed such a great chance for them to make some friends."

"Well, I sure would like to get to know someone around here! Where is everybody? I haven't seen one girl on this whole street all the times I've been up and down it. And when I talked to a kid at the ball field, she looked at me as if I were from Planet X or something!"

"We just have to be patient, honey. I've always heard people take a while in New England. But when they finally do make friends, they're good ones. It's hard in summer with people away. You'll find some friends when school starts, you'll see." She ran a finger softly down Jill's cheek. "Anyway, I'm glad you didn't go camping. I'd have looked pretty funny rattling around in this place all alone." She threw down her paint brush. "Ugh! This smell's getting to me." Sweat stood out on her upper lip and her face looked like putty. "I...I think I'll lie down for a while."

"Are you okay?"

"It's just the paint."

"Do you want me to keep going?"

"No. Put the stuff away. We'll finish tomorrow. Maybe it'll be cooler. Tell you what—why don't you walk down to Main and get a pizza for supper? I'll throw a salad together when you get back."

She got up and walked in from the porch. There was a heaviness to her these days, even though she was so skinny. I guess she's missing her friends too, Jill thought, as she pressed the lid onto the white paint and stuck the brushes in a can of turpentine.

In the kitchen, Jill took the money her mother'd left on the counter and headed for the door. Upstairs, in the bathroom, Mom was throwing up. It sounded awful.

"Maybe I shouldn't go?" she called up the stairs. "Can I do anything for you?"

"No. Go ahead." Mom's voice was muffled.

Jill started up the street, trying to guess who lived in the houses. Someone was playing one-handed piano and Jill stood on her toes to see. It was a girl about sixteen. Too old. Outside another house was a tricycle and the sounds of little children coming from inside. Then there was an old man sleeping and a big black cat, just watching. She crossed another street.

"Hey! You girl! Come up here!"

Jill jumped. At first she couldn't see where the voice was coming from. Then, in the shadows at the back of a porch, she saw a hand beckoning, bony and white. Squinting, Jill saw that it was an old woman.

"Yes. You. Come up here a moment." The voice was raspy.

"Well...I..."

The voice softened. "Oh, I won't bite you, girl. Just for a minute. I want to ask you something."

"I have to go to the store..."

"I know, I know. I won't keep you."

Jill let herself in the gate and slowly climbed the porch steps. The old woman motioned her forward.

"What's your name?"

"Jill. Jill Harvey. I...we just moved in last weekend."

"So that's it. Thought I knew everybody around here." The old woman nodded, satisfied. "See everyone sooner or later from my porch. Want a glass of my lemon- ade?"

"Well, I don't..."

"It's all right. Won't poison you. You can pour me some, too. Hotter'n Hades today!"

Jill poured the lemonade. As she went toward the old woman, something soft moved under her foot. There was a yelp and whatever it was scuttled under the couch. "Oh!" she said, startled. "I'm sorry. I hope I didn't hurt..."

"That's Squeak. No sense at all. Always getting underfoot." The old woman sipped the lemonade and then set it down with a shaky, old hand. "Name's Mrs. Lacey. Easy to remember on account of the lacey curtains in my front windows."

"Yes, ma'am."

"Now. You look like a good girl to me. I've watched you come down the street a time or two and I've taken to you. Do that sometimes. So I asked you up here to see if you'd like to tackle a little job for me. Sit down, girl." Mrs. Lacey patted the couch beside her. "It's Squeak. Got to do something about him. Don't like walking him in this heat. Makes my heart beat a mite too fast. So how'd you like to walk him a couple times a day for me? I'd pay a quarter a day."

"Okay."

"Good. Are you used to dogs? Do you have one at home?"

"No. We used to...Jess. He got killed by a car."

"Too bad! Animals and traffic don't mix. Well, Squeak's no trouble—stays right on the leash. Here—come out of there, Squeak!" Mrs. Lacey leaned down and hauled a small dog from under the couch. He was low to the ground and had longish blond hair and a tail like a plume that curled over his back. His face looked as if someone had put his hand against it and pushed.

"Oh, he's cute! A Pekinese," said Jill.

"Yes. Squeak and I have lived together a long time. And before him, I had his mother. His leash hangs on that hook by the door and you can come once in the morning and once about this time of day and take him up and down the street. Good for him. He's getting fat."

Jill squatted down and let the dog sniff at her hand, then stroked him softly between his small, round ears.

"I'll start tomorrow," she told Mrs. Lacey.

"Good. Do you live on Maple?"

"Yes. Number 94."

"Oh, that was Augusta Miller's place. Well, you have a pal next door, don't you?"

"I..."

"That Marla Burns lives at 96, doesn't she? Must be about your age."

"I don't think so. I haven't seen a girl there."

"Yes, she does. She and her mother. Mother's divorced. Oh...now I recall...Marla goes to her grandma's in August."

Jill leaned forward. "I thought I was the only girl around here."

"Bless you, no. Let me see...there's Connie Ward. She lives around the corner on Main. She'd be about the right age. And Karen McCluskey lives somewhere in the sixty block. Nancy Cohen—she plays the cello right nice—and her sister Jean is learning piano, I hear. None in the Kelleher family—all boys...Can't think of any more at present, but that's a start."

"Thanks, Mrs. Lacey!" Jill got up. "I'd better be going. I have to get a pizza for supper. Thanks for everything." She hurried down the porch steps. "I'll come for Squeak in the morning."

Jill ran down the block to Main. It'd be fun to walk that little dog every day. Now she'd have something else to write Susan about.

Coming back down Maple with the pizza in its white box warm in her hands, Jill was surprised to see a car parked in front of her house. She hurried to see who'd come to visit, but as she got to her gate, a woman backed out of the car hauling a big suitcase. They almost had a collision.

"Oh!" the woman said. "Jeez, I'm sorry, honey. I didn't hear you coming up behind me. Is the pizza okay?"

"Yes, fine." Jill stared at the woman. She was middle-aged. She had hair a kind of silver color in a long pageboy, and she was wearing a black-and-white striped pantsuit.

The woman clapped her hand to her head. "Oh, for heaven's sakes, do you live here?"

"Yes," Jill said.

"Then you're the new people...I mean...well, isn't that great..." She laughed. "You don't have a clue who I am, do you?"

"No."

"I'm Mrs. Burns, honey. I live next door to you. I'm sorry—I'll move my car. But this is great—I've a kid just about your age. Marla's ten—she'll be tickled pink when she finds out you've moved here."

Jill grinned. Mrs. Burns was nice. "I'm Jill Harvey. I'm going to be ten in October...Is Marla home yet?"

"No, hon. She's still at her grandma's. But she'll be back in time for school. Then you two'll have to get together."

The pizza was cooling off fast.

"I'd better go in. Mom's waiting for the pizza."

"Okay. Bon appetito, as they say!" Mrs. Burns waved gaily and began dragging the suitcase toward her house.

☞   IV

"Who's that?" Mom asked, as she closed the front door. She was looking better.

"It's Mrs. Burns from next door. And Mom! She's got a kid my age. She's away at her grandmother's, but she'll be back in time for school."

"What's she like, Mrs. Burns?" Mom asked, putting the pizza into the oven to heat up again. "She certainly has wild-colored hair...."

"Oh, she's nice, Mom. Really. Very friendly. I bet you'll like her." Jill started setting the kitchen table. "Hey, Mom, I forgot to tell you about Mrs. Lacey...."

CHAPTER THREE

Over the next couple of weeks, Jill's father settled into his new job, although he still had to be away except for weekends. Her brothers Tom and Larry did a lot more of their share of the moving-in work, and Jill worked out a comfortable routine with walking Squeak.

Sometimes she could hear Mrs. Lacey fussing around inside the house. Sometimes she'd be outside, snoozing on the couch. And sometimes she'd beckon Jill over into the shade to try some of the tart lemonade from the pitcher on her table. It was good up there on Mrs. Lacey's porch. A lot of the time they'd just sit without saying much at all—they'd become friends enough for that. But other times, Mrs. Lacey was in a talking mood and then she told Jill about the families up and down the street, or how it'd been in the old days, when there was iceboating on the river below the falls and a big town picnic every Fourth of July. And Jill told her about California and the orange tree in their garden.

Mom laughed when Jill told her Mrs. Lacey's stories about the neighbors and the town. "Mrs. Lacey did the whole family a favor when she gave you that job! I'll bet we know more about York Falls than some people who've lived here all their lives!"

Now Squeak was pulling Jill along the sidewalk, taking a slightly different route. Suddenly, a big red dog jumped the fence and came up to them. He stopped short, his tail waving gently from side to side, and greeted Squeak, first touching his nose and then sniffing him thoroughly all the way around. The big dog looked a lot like Jess...

"Hi."

A girl stood at the top of the porch steps. She was plump, with a different sort of look to her face. She started down the steps. "Hi," she said again. "That's my dog."

Jill thought, she looks like one of those retards at the pool. "Yeah?" she said.

"That's Barney. He's my dog."

"Oh. Er...he's a nice dog." Jill looked around. Suppose someone saw her talking to a retard. She pulled at Squeak's leash, but now it was his turn to sniff. "Come on, Squeak..."

"Barney l-likes him," the girl said. "What's your name?"

"Uh...Jill. *Squeak*...um, what's yours?"

"Dede."

"Uh-huh." Jill stroked Barney's broad head. His tongue lolled out happily. She scratched him under his chin and he stretched his neck for her, just the way Jess...Jill stooped quickly and hugged him, hiding her face against his solid warm body. After a moment, she felt an awkward pat on her shoulder. "Don't cry. B-Barney likes you."

☞ v

"Dede?" A woman's voice called from the house. "Who're you talking to out there? Dede?"

Dede's mother came down the steps. "Who...oh. Hello. I'm Dede's mother."

"Er...I'm Jill...Jill Harvey. We moved in at 94. I was just passing by."

"Our name is Atkins. Well, now. How would you like to come in for a while? I bet I can find some cookies..." Mrs. Atkins was smiling brightly.

"Oh, no, that's okay. I have to go now. I can't stay. I'm sorry. I have to take Squeak home to Mrs. Lacey's."

Mrs. Atkins' smile faded. "I see. Well. Maybe another time."

☞ VI

"Yes. Maybe." Jill yanked Squeak away from Barney and hurried along the sidewalk.

"You were longer than usual," Mrs. Lacey said. She looked closely at Jill. "You look a mite flustered. What's the matter?"

"Nothing. We went to the dime store. And then Squeak wanted to make friends with the dog near the corner. That's why we're late. I'm sorry I worried you."

"Oh, I know Squeak's always in good hands with you. That must've been the Atkinses' dog…"

"It was. Mrs. Atkins came out…and…and…her daughter…"

"Ah…She's a good girl. Helps her ma around the place. Lonely, though. Both of them." She shook her head.

"Does the girl…Dede…does she have any sisters?"

"No. There's just her and her ma, now."

Jill started down the steps. "Oh, I almost forgot, Mom said she and Dad would like to visit tomorrow night…"

"I'll be here!"

Jill walked home slowly, remembering how quiet it'd been when she and Mom had been all alone in the house. It must be pretty boring for that girl Dede. Only, she thought, maybe if you're a retard you don't notice things like that.

☞ VII

Next morning, the heat lay heavily over everything. You could see it, shimmering up off the sidewalk, steaming out of the dewy grass. The leaves of the trees hung down. Nothing moved. Even the birds weren't flying.

Squeak's tongue hung out as he panted up the porch steps after their walk. Jill ran the water till it was cold and Squeak lapped at it as if he'd never stop.

"I'll be back around five," she called to Mrs. Lacey. "We're going to the pool for the day."

Mrs. Lacey waved limply from the couch.

Mom had packed cold cuts and hard-boiled eggs and lemonade and apples for lunch, so they could stay at the pool. They staked out a spot for themselves on the grass and Mom lay right down and closed her eyes. Dad jumped into the pool with such a splash you'd have thought he'd empty it. The boys went off to look for Ed Kelleher and his friends. Jill slid into the water and floated on her back. Cool, cool. It felt so good to be relaxing for a change.

Later, as they sat around eating, Larry said, "Hey, Jill. Ed says he saw you talking to a retard yesterday."

"So?"

"So how come you're so friendly with a retard?"

"I'm not so friendly. I was only there because Squeak and her dog liked each other." Jill stopped peeling her hard-boiled egg.

"She can't find anyone else to be her friend, Lar." Tom grinned.

"She's not my friend, dummy. I told you."

"I'd say it was a perfect match."

"Shut up."

"Cut it out, all of you," Dad interrupted. "This conversation's going nowhere." He glanced at Mom, who had eaten her sandwich and lain back down again. "Anyway, I don't want you disturbing your mother." He got up and dove into the pool.

Suddenly, there was loud laughter nearby.

"It's Kelleher," Tom said.

"And Parker and Rusty what's his name."

The three boys were throwing a beach ball around in a circle. Dede Atkins was running heavily from one to the other as she tried to catch up with it.

"Come on, old Dede. Try harder!" Ed jeered.

Dan and Rusty were chanting: "Deedee-dum, deedee-dum, deedee-dumb dumb dumb!"

"That's mean," Jill said. "Mom? Tell them."

"I don't want to get into it," Mom said, without opening her eyes. "Where's her mother? She ought to be watching."

"Aw—they're not doing anything that bad," Larry said. "She doesn't know the difference anyway."

☞   VIII

"How do you know?" Jill felt her face getting hot as she watched Dede stumble around the circle. Just then, Dede tripped and sprawled on the ground.

"That's it!" Jill jumped up and gave Ed Kelleher a push that sent him barreling into Dan.

"Hey!" he yelled.

She snatched up the beach ball and bent over Dede. "It's okay. I got your ball back. Come on."

Dede got up slowly. There were tears in her eyes. She wiped her nose with the back of her hand. "Hi."

"Show me where your mother is. I'll take you back to her."

"Goody-goody!" Ed shouted.

Jill turned her back on him and walked Dede away.

Dede pointed to a shady spot near the fence and Jill recognized Mrs. Atkins. She was sitting in a beach chair reading a magazine. She looked up as they came near.

"Oh, Dede, there you are. I lost sight of you for a moment or two. I see you've found a friend..." She peered at Jill. "You're the girl with the dog."

"Yes. Jill Harvey. Mrs. Atkins, some kids were being mean to Dede. That's why I brought her back to you."

Mrs. Atkins' face tightened. "Are you all right, Dede?" she asked quickly.

"Yeh."

"Thank you, Jill. I...I only lost sight of her for a very short while. I wasn't worried because she knows how to swim...You'd think these kids could find something better to do. I should have been paying closer attention, but it's hard to watch all the time. I'm very much obliged to you." Her voice was sharp.

Jill talked quickly. "I'm sorry, Mrs. Atkins. They were...you know...just teasing. They weren't thinking, they didn't mean..." I must be crazy, she thought, sticking up for Ed Kelleher and the others. A moment ago she'd been so mad at them. But, in a way, she could see what made them do what they'd done. "Dede's okay now," she told Mrs. Atkins. "I have to go back...but I'll try to watch out for her. I'm...sorry."

She went back to the others and finished peeling her hard-boiled egg.

☞ IX

CHAPTER FOUR

Everything was very quiet up and down the street. The paint on Mrs. Lacey's gate stuck in the heat and she had to give it a shove.

Mrs. Lacey was sitting on her couch with her eyes closed.

"Come on, Squeak," Jill whispered. "Time for your walk. Let's go."

They went up the street as usual and back down the other side. They turned at Main and, when they got to Dede's house, Barney was waiting in his yard, and he and Squeak greeted each other through the fence pickets. Dede was on her steps, shelling peas into a bowl.

"Want one?" She held out her hand.

"No, thanks."

"Want a cookie?"

"No." Jill pulled Squeak away from the fence. "I have to go."

Mrs. Lacey was still asleep. Jill filled Squeak's bowl as quietly as she could so as not to wake her. Then she tiptoed down the path to the gate and turned to wave. But Squeak hadn't curled up in his basket the way he usually did. He was standing at the top of the steps, whining.

"Ssh! Lie down, Squeak!"

The little dog started down the steps toward her; then he retreated into the porch, whimpering.

"Be quiet!" Jill went back up the steps. Squeak was trembling. His tail was tucked between his legs, dragging his little body down against the ground. "Are you sick?" Jill bent to touch him. "Do you have heat stroke?"

Jill tiptoed along the porch. "Mrs. Lacey..." Mrs. Lacey was fast asleep. "I think Squeak's sick. Could you wake up for a moment...Mrs. Lacey?"

Mrs. Lacey stayed the way she was, in the corner of the couch, her hands folded in her lap, her head resting a little sideways on the cushion.

Jill looked at Squeak uneasily. The dog was shivering from one end to the other. "Mrs. Lacey, please wake up." Jill touched her hand. It was cold.

A slow pounding started in Jill's chest. "Mrs. Lacey," she breathed. "Please..." She pulled a little at the old woman's sleeve. "Oh...please..." Nothing. Mrs. Lacey didn't move. "Oh...do-on't..." Jill begged. But she knew. She looked at the still face and she knew. Mrs. Lacey wasn't there anymore. Squeak had known right away.

☞ X

Fleeing then. Fleeing down the steps. Away from Mrs. Lacey sitting so quietly. Home...Dad would know what to do...No. They'd gone to the supermarket. Oo-oh...where? Dede. She'd seen Dede. Fleeing back to Dede's. Everything a blur...calling it out as she flew up the path. Then running. Mrs. Atkins and Dede and Jill, running back to Mrs. Lacey's so that the quiet, quiet figure shouldn't be left alone.

Mrs. Atkins went right away to the telephone.

Jill stayed close to Mrs. Lacey. She shivered next to her on this sticky hot evening. She stared at Mrs. Lacey, as if by doing so she could make an eyelash flicker or a smile spread over that peaceful face. Nothing.

She didn't cry. There was a wall across her throat and the tears dammed up behind it. Little dry gasps came instead, as if she couldn't quite catch her breath. Then she felt the warmth of Dede's body at her side. And Dede's hand on hers, patting her gently over and over.

"It's okay," Dede said. "It's okay. It's okay."

And Jill clutched her hand and held on hard until the ambulance came.

Suddenly Mom and Dad were there.

"Oh, Momma! She's dead, Momma. She was alive this morning and now she's dead..." Jill felt Mom's arms go around her. She leaned into her. Across Mom's shoulder she could see Dad shaking hands with Mrs. Atkins. The gesture seemed all out of place.

"Mom...the Atkins are here...I thought you weren't home...I..."

"Oh, honey...I'm sorry. But we're here now."

Dad brought the Atkins over. "Peg, this is Mrs. Atkins. She called us."

Mom shook her hand. "Thank you so much," she said stiffly. "It was very kind..."

Dede held out her hand, too, but Mom didn't see. Jill took it.

☞ XI

"Mrs. Lacey told us where her family lives," Dad was saying. "We'll be glad to..."

The ambulance men brought up their stretcher and lifted Mrs. Lacey onto it. Gently—as if she could feel what they were doing. Very carefully, they carried her to the ambulance, and it took her away.

"That's very good of you," Mrs. Atkins said. "I think I should get Dede home now, if there's nothing you need us for..."

"No. Nothing." Mom said. "We can manage. Thank you."

Jill sat on the edge of the couch listening to Mom on the telephone inside, calling Mrs. Lacey's family. It didn't seem right for them to be poking around in Mrs. Lacey's house and looking in her address book. Tremors like little waves breaking on hard sand ran through Jill without stopping. Squeak pressed close against her leg.

After a while, Mom came out. Her face was sharp with strain. "We'll go soon, honey," she said. "Just a couple of people calling back and then we'll go home."

She rubbed Jill's rigid back. "Oh, honey. Poor baby. I...I wish I could..." She turned away and went back inside.

Dad appeared in the doorway. He stood there for a moment, then came and lifted Jill off the couch as if she were three instead of almost ten. And he sat down and folded her into his lap the way he used to when she was little. He didn't say anything. Just held her.

After a while, he spoke. "Jilly," he said softly, "I want to try to explain...It's something I think will help you now...There are a lot of things people have to deal with in their lives. There's a kind of pattern, you know. You see it as you get older. I mean...well, all through your life, wherever you are in it, you...you're already getting ready for the next stage...not even realizing, most of the time." He stroked her shoulder. "You're my Jilly, right? Nine years old and still my little girl? But, inside, you've begun getting ready to grow into a woman. And then...well, how about your mother? All set with our family—and now all of a sudden getting ready to bring a new baby into the world. And that baby! Well, I guess he's got a whole lot of things to get ready for!" He laughed softly. "Me, too!" His voice rumbled against her back.

Jill began to relax against him. The thought of Mrs. Lacey so still, so still...the jangling telephone inside the house, the passersby pausing on the sidewalk—all blurred into the background as her father talked. "That's how it was with Mrs. Lacey, honey. She knew she was going to die. Everyone old knows that...know it's something they must get ready for, just like everything else they've ever done. Of course some are better at it than others. But they all know it's coming...The way I see it, Mrs. Lacey had herself all set, except for one thing, Squeak. You see, she had to figure out what was going to happen to Squeak..."

Jill's heart jumped against the wall in her throat. She leaned down and touched Squeak's silky back. He whimpered and snuggled closer.

Dad took her face in his hand and turned it so he could look right into her eyes. "Honey...I think Mrs. Lacey had held on for quite a while...looking for someone. She must've seen a lot of people come and go past her porch, but none of them was quite what she was looking for. Then she spotted you, and I can just imagine her watching you going up and down the street doing errands for Mom...And maybe she liked your face. And after she'd talked to you, maybe she liked you more, and she decided to see how Squeak would take to you. Well, you know how well you two hit it off—she could see that right away—and I think she figured she'd found the person who'd look after Squeak for her when she was gone."

"She never said."

"I know, honey. She wouldn't have wanted to scare you. Or make you sad. But I reckon in her heart she knew she could count on you and...and...once she got the two of you matched up, well, that was the last thing she had left to do. Then she could let go."

They locked up Mrs. Lacey's house and went home in the warm darkness. The boys met them on the porch. "We made supper," Tom said. The first stars were twinkling overhead. Mrs. Lacey had pointed out the constellations a few nights before. Jill looked for them. Then she picked up Squeak and went in.

A long time later, with his live little body warm against her, she finally knew they would not see Mrs. Lacey again, and the tears came at last.

CHAPTER FIVE

Dear Susan,

I hope you know it's YOUR TURN TO WRITE!!! But since you haven't and I have a few more things to tell you I'm writing AGAIN.

You know I told you about Mrs. Lacey. Well, on Saturday when I took Squeak home, she was dead. It was awful, I mean, we didn't say good-bye or anything. And I never told her how much I liked her.

Now I can't.

Mom and Dad said I could keep Squeak and yesterday at the funeral her relatives said it would be okay. He's a neat dog.

We had some people back to the house after the funeral. I know it sounds weird, but it was like a party. Dad stayed home from work and it was the first time we got to meet the neighbors.

Most of the kids here are still gone on vacation. Marla from next door won't be back till school starts. There was one girl at the funeral—Karen McCluskey—but I didn't get to talk to her. The only other kid around is Dede Atkins, only she's retarded.

That's all for now. What are you doing? You'd better write or I'm going to be really mad.

Love,

Jill

☞   XII

Jill sat on the porch steps brushing Squeak. She felt quiet inside. The sad feeling was still there but she was all cried out.

"Hi." Dede and Barney stood at the gate.

"Hi. What're you doing?"

"W-we're taking a walk."

"Yeah? Does your mother know you're out by yourself?"

"Sh-she lets me if Barney's with me."

"Where're you going?"

"F-for a walk."

Squeak's tail was going like sixty. Jill laughed. "Look at him! Do you want to go too, Squeak?"

Squeak yapped, his eyes begging.

"Well, is it okay if we come with you, Dede?"

"Yeh."

"Wait a second." Jill ran inside. "I'm going for a walk with Dede," she called upstairs.

"Who?" Mom answered.

"Dede Atkins."

"Oh, honey, I wish..." Her voice sounded funny but Jill didn't feel like stopping to figure it out. "Well...okay..."

☞   XIII

On Monday, Jill and Dede and the dogs headed out on their usual walk. They did it every morning now. Today they were going to the variety store. The dogs sensed they were heading toward Main, with all its fascinating smells, and pulled them along faster.

But the store was crowded.

"The dogs'll have to stay out here. Can you hold the leashes, Dede? I won't be long."

"Okay."

As she was paying for a folder, someone said to Jill, "Hi. Are you Jill Harvey?" It was Karen McCluskey.

"Yes."

"I saw you at Mrs. Lacey's funeral."

"I saw you too."

"What are you doing?"

"I just bought a folder for school. How about you?"

"I was just looking at the tapes and stuff. Hey—want to go to Charlie's and get a cone?"

"Sure!" Finally she'd met someone! "I'll get Squeak."

"You got to keep Mrs. Lacey's dog?"

"Yes. Her family said okay."

"You're so lucky! My sister's allergic. It's a pain. We can't have anything with fur, ever."

Outside, Jill called, "Hi, Squeak!" and the little dog jumped against her, yelping a welcome. Jill pulled the folder out of its bag. "I got it, Dede. See?"

"I like it." Dede stroked the smooth cover.

"We're going up the street to get an ice-cream cone."

"I like ice-cream cones."

"Got any money?"

"No," said Dede.

Jill dug into her pocket to count what she had left. "Karen—do you have any extra?"

"No."

Jill looked up. Karen's voice was flat. "I'm not paying for her," she said.

"Oh...er..." Jill shuffled the coins in her hand. "It's okay. I've got enough."

"I'm not going into Charlie's with her," Karen said. She spoke as if Dede wasn't even there. The words hung between them like skywriting in the air.

☞　XIV

"Well...but...she walked here with me..." Jill glanced at Dede. She was staring at the ground. Shoot! Jill thought. Dede being along is wrecking everything, but I can't just leave her here on Main. You'd think Karen could see that! Why was she making such a big deal out of it, anyway?

"Well, then...I guess we don't have time for a cone right now," Jill said. "Um...I forgot I told my mom I'd be right back."

Dede's face clouded. "No ice cream?"

"Maybe tomorrow." She took Squeak's leash from Dede. "Come on, Dede. I'll see you, Karen."

"See you," Karen said.

Jill dropped Dede at her house. Mrs. Atkins looked up from weeding the flower bed. "I just think it's lovely you two girls are getting together all the time."

Jill said, "Oh...I have to take Squeak out anyway." That sounded mean. She really did enjoy their walks. It was just she always felt she had to be holding Mrs. Atkins off.

☞　XV

On the way home, Jill looked back a couple of times, thinking she might see Karen. But she didn't. Karen was probably sitting in Charlie's right now with another friend. I bet she's got a million, Jill thought. She doesn't need me.

Mom was on the front porch, repairing a chair seat.

"I met Karen McCluskey, Mom."

"Great! Where?"

"In the store. She's nice. She came up and talked to me. She wanted to go for a cone."

"Did you have enough money with you?"

"Yes, only I was with Dede and Karen didn't want her along..."

"So you didn't go?" Mom looped the rush through the hole in the center of the chair seat and yanked it tight. "You know, Jill, you're really handicapping yourself, spending all your time with that girl." She frowned at the chair, undid what she'd just done and started over.

☞　XVI

"It's not all my time. Anyway, up till now, I didn't know anyone else. You want a soda?"

"No. I'm watching what I eat. Because of the baby." A shadow passed across her face. "You never know what's in that stuff...chemicals, additives, who knows what..."

Jill shook her head. "They wouldn't be allowed to sell it if there was anything wrong with it. Think of all the millions and trillions of sodas people drink every day!"

"I'm just being extra careful, that's all."

Jill laughed. "Well, since I'm not having a baby, can I just go ahead? Hey, maybe I'll call Karen—see if she's home yet."

"You do that. I'd like to see somebody...else around here once in a while."

☞   XVII

Jill looked up Karen's number and dialed. Karen answered.

"Karen? It's Jill."

"Oh. Hi."

"I just wanted to say...well, it was too bad...about just now, I mean. The thing is, I couldn't dump Dede. She's not used to being on Main."

"Oh. Well, the thing is, that kid gives me the creeps—the way she looks and the way she talks. I mean, when you're with her, doesn't everyone stare all the time?"

"Maybe they do, a little. I guess I've gotten used to being with her and I don't notice. Anyway, you want to do something after lunch?"

"Sure. How about the pool?"

"Great. We can ride our bikes."

"Okay. I'll see you about two at your house. Bye."

Jill hung up and hugged Squeak.

CHAPTER SIX

"Why don't you wear that nice green skirt and a white blouse?"

"Mo-om. No one wears skirts to school!"

"I just think it's silly to wear long pants on a hot September day."

"Well, I'm going to."

Mom headed for the door. "I give up!"

Jill had laid everything out on the bed ready for the morning. Blue jeans, soft and faded just right. A blue plaid shirt which matched. Shoes. Folder. Pencils. Assignment notebook. She was ready.

She and Mom had been to the York Falls Elementary School two weeks before to register for fifth grade. The hardest thing for Jill was that her brothers' school, unlike in California, was way across town instead of being on the same grounds. She felt lonesome, just thinking about it.

The telephone rang. Too early to be Dad.

"Ji-ill. It's for you."

"Who is it?"

"Karen, I think."

"Hello?"

"Hi. It's Karen."

"Oh. Hi!"

"Do you want some company walking to school tomorrow?"

"Sure. Thanks. Will you pick me up? What time?"

"Oh yeah. About eight-thirty. See you."

"See you."

Jill found Mom in the kitchen. "Karen's picking me up in the morning."

"That's good. She seems like a really nice girl. I'm glad you've made friends with her." She laughed. "I'd begun to think you'd never spend your time with anyone but Dede!"

Jill went back upstairs. Tom was getting his school stuff together. He zipped a couple of pens and a pencil inside his big blue folder.

"Got everything?" Jill asked.

"Guess so," Tom said. "I'll find out soon enough." He grinned. "How about you? It's going to feel pretty funny, being in a new school, huh?"

"I guess so." Jill fidgeted in the doorway. "Tom...have you noticed the way Mom acts around Dede?"

"What way?"

"Well, she acts weird. Stiff, kind of."

"Yeah?"

"And she's always harping at me about getting some other friends. I'm going to...I mean, it's not like Dede's the only kid I'll know around here...I already know Karen. But Mom seems to have some kind of hang-up about Dede."

"I hadn't noticed. I don't know...maybe she thinks you'll start acting like her."

"Well, that'd be pretty dumb! But I don't think that's it. No...it's almost as if she was...scared of her. You'd think she could see there's nothing scary about Dede."

"Maybe you're imagining it. If you want to know, I don't get why you hang around with Dede myself."

Jill wiggled herself into his beanbag chair. "Well, now I'm used to the way she is, she's sort of...comfortable to be with. She's quiet. She never wants anything. And she's never mean. I never heard her say one mean thing about anybody. And...well, I know it sounds funny...but she listens when I talk. But supposing I don't want to talk, say, just walk along...that's okay with her, too."

☞   XVIII

"I see what you mean," Tom said. "Well, maybe it's just a question of Mom getting used to her, too."

"She never will, the way she's going," Jill said.

At eight-thirty the next morning, Karen rang the doorbell.

"Hi, Karen!" Mom had combed her hair out as if this were some big social occasion. And she kept smiling. "How nice of you to take Jill along with you. How thoughtful!"

Karen looked embarrassed.

"We have to go, Mom," Jill said quickly. "Don't forget to walk Squeak."

"I won't. I need the exercise as much as he does. Have a good day!" Mom was being pretty charming, considering how she usually acted in the morning. Though, as Jill thought about it, Mom was looking better at breakfast lately. The baby must be settling down.

☞   XIX

When they got outside, Karen said, "We'd better stop for Marla."

"She's back?"

"Yes. She called last night to be sure we walked to school together."

"What's she like? Her mother's sort of glamorous—like some movie star or something."

"Yeah. Well...Marla's pretty, I guess. She has naturally curly hair. My mother says her mother used to be a dancer. Laraine Marshall, that's her stage name. Marla calls her Laraine, if you can believe it! And her grandma, the one in Boston, was a Rockette at Radio City Music Hall, and pretty famous, Marla says."

"They sure don't sound like the York Falls type!" Jill laughed.

"They came to York Falls after Mrs. Burns got married to Mr. Burns, and then Marla and her mom just stayed on after the split."

"Did you ever see him?"

"No. He went away ages ago. My mother says he was nice. But he decided to live in Nebraska, and Mrs. Burns wouldn't go because of her career. Only as far as I can see she doesn't have one!"

"She didn't go back to being a dancer?"

"No. Maybe it was hard to do, with a kid. I think she works sometimes."

They climbed Marla's steps. The door flew open and Marla ran out and hugged Karen.

"Oh, Karen, I've missed you absolutely dreadfully!" she cried. "Of course it was fabulous in Boston. But it's even more fabulous to be back with my friends!"

Nobody talks that way, Jill thought. She's not for real. She stared, fascinated. Marla was small and pretty. She chattered on at Karen, holding on tight. It's...like she rehearsed it, Jill decided. Karen rolled her eyes and waited for Marla to let go.

She did finally and turned to Jill. Jill backed up a couple of steps.

"And you're Jill," Marla said in a whispery voice. "Laraine told me she'd met you. And she's seen your cute brothers in the yard. I think it's just great you're next door. Much more fun than that old drag, Mrs. Miller." She made a face. Then looking straight into Jill's eyes, she said, "I guess you and Karen have been doing just everything together while I've been away." Funny the way she said it, almost threatening.

☞   xx

"Oh, no," Karen said quickly. "We only met a few days ago."

Mrs. Burns appeared in the doorway. She leaned against it, her pink chiffon robe floating around her. She waved a glass of orange juice at the girls. "Bye, sweets," she said huskily to Marla. "Don't be late home. Al is taking us out to dinner."

Marla didn't answer. She went down the steps without looking back. Karen and Jill hurried to catch up. She was looking mad.

"What's the matter, Marla?" Karen asked.

"She always makes him take me. And I know he doesn't want me along. Why would he? I have to sit there and watch him making eyes at her all through dinner. I hate it!" She marched along.

Jill glanced at Karen, who shrugged. Better change the subject, Jill thought. She said, "That's a neat skirt, Marla." It was made of white pleated nylon and Marla had a navy and white polka-dotted blouse to match.

Marla slowed down. "Do you like it? My grandma got it for me. She likes skirts on me. She says I have to show my legs to advantage if I'm going to be a dancer."

"Are you?"

"I guess so. Our whole family dances."

"She takes tap and ballet and modern and lots of other stuff too," Karen said.

"My grandma says she's going to see me center stage one day," Marla said. "She says that's all she's living for, to see me center stage, the way she used to be..."

A school bus passed them. The kids inside were knocking on the windows.

"It's the retards' bus," Karen said. "Going to Pearson."

Each window framed a face. Some were grinning. Some were ugly. Some were...empty. Dede was waving in the back window. Jill waved back.

"Ugh!" Marla said. "How can you wave at them? I can't even look at them, they're so gross."

Dede didn't look so gross to Jill any more.

"They can't help the way they look," she said.

☞   xxi

CHAPTER SEVEN

A few weeks later, Jill and her brothers were still helping with painting rooms of their new house. It was Saturday.

Jill stood back to look at her work. No smudges, no spots. The October sun warmed her through the glass. Marla was out in her backyard, watching Leroi, her poodle, smooshing through the fallen leaves. Boy, she thought, if that were me I'd jump right into those leaves and fall down so they covered me up and no one would even know I was there. I wouldn't just stand around letting Leroi have all the fun. But she knew why Marla wasn't jumping in the leaves. She was dressed in her red skirt with the anchor on it and a blue blazer with a gold crest on the pocket. She'd be leaving for her ballet lesson at eleven. After that, she had to go to her creative drama session. Later in the afternoon, she had a piano lesson.

"I'm being groomed," she'd told Jill. "I need to know all these things if I'm going on the stage." Being groomed didn't seem like much fun. It used up every Saturday.

Jill knocked on the window. Marla looked up and waved.

"Wait," Jill mouthed through the glass. She ran down the stairs and out into the yard. "Marla! Hey, Marla?"

Marla came over to the fence. "What?"

"Do you know yet if you can come to my slumber party Friday?"

"I asked Laraine, but I didn't really get an answer yet."

"What do you mean?"

"Well..." Marla looked embarrassed. "She wouldn't say yes and she wouldn't say no. But I do want to come, Jill."

"It's going to be fun. Just you and Karen and Connie and me. And we'll have pizza and popcorn and listen to tapes. It's what I asked for instead of a birthday party. I'm too old for birthday parties."

"I'll ask again. I should've known not to ask her in the evening. She's always...tired in the evening. I'll let you know later today for sure."

"Okay. I have to get back to painting. We're finishing the baby's room."

"That's so neat—your mother having a baby—you're lucky! Isn't your mother absolutely thrilled?" Marla's eyes shone.

"I guess so. She doesn't talk about it much."

"I think it's fabulous! What do you hope it'll be?"

Jill smiled. "Just a baby. I don't really care if it's a boy or a girl. Oh—I guess I'd rather have a baby sister."

"That's what I'd want. I've always wanted a sister...only there's no way I'm going to get one unless my mother marries again..."

"Marla! Marla, did you tie Leroi up?" Mrs. Burns beckoned from the door. "Let's go! Grandma wouldn't like you to be late for your lessons."

"Oh...okay," Marla called. "I'll let you know about the party," she told Jill.

* * *

"It's beautiful," Mom said from the doorway.

"And it's finished," said Dad. "Except for that radiator. I'll do that one." They all stood admiring the sunny yellow walls and white trim. "Okay, boys, wash your brushes and take the afternoon off."

Jill said, "I'm going to rake up leaves and make big jumping piles."

"Fine, honey," Mom said. "But take Squeak for a walk, first, will you? He hasn't been out today."

"Okay. We'll go down to Charlie's for a cone."

Charlie's was crowded, but the only people Jill knew were Mrs. Atkins and Dede, who were having a milk shake at the counter.

"Jill! How are you?" Mrs. Atkins said. "We haven't seen much of you since school started."

Jill was embarrassed because it was true. "I know," she said. "I've been pretty busy…" There was homework. And watching TV at Karen's. And working out on Marla's trampoline…Mrs. Atkins kept smiling. Jill said, "Uh…want to walk back to my house now, Dede? I was planning to make some leaf piles and jump in them."

"Yeh." Dede beamed. "Let's make some leaf piles and j-jump in them."

"Okay, Mrs. Atkins?"

"It's a lovely idea, Jill. A lovely idea!"

Jill thought, She doesn't have to pat my shoulder like that.

At Dede's house, they called Barney and then walked up Maple together, the way they used to, Barney and Squeak leading the way.

"I'll find the rakes," Jill said. "You let the dogs loose out back."

They piled the leaves high and Jill took the first jump, swooping stomach first. Leaves flew around her, then showered down like golden rain from the blue sky. Barney plunged in after her and licked her face anxiously, while Squeak yapped from the edge.

"Yuck, Barney!" Jill pushed him off and he bounded away. She lay on her back in the leaves and stared at a bird planing slowly above her. "This is great. I could stay here for a hundred years…a hundred years…"

"Yeh." Dede leaned on her rake. Her face was red from her hard work and her nose was running. She never noticed when her nose ran.

"You know, I didn't think I'd like it here, Dede. I thought I'd always want to go back to California." She laughed. "Do you know, I just thought of something. My friend Susan never wrote to me once and I was really mad…I mean, she'd been my best friend…but just now I realized I haven't thought of her for weeks!"

"Yeh?"

"Yeah. And do you know something else? I'm even beginning to like this dumb town. I mean, school's not bad…I know most of the stuff…and I'm in the power group in spelling."

"Th-that's good."

"Jump into the leaves, Dede. It's fun."

Dede put down her rake, took a run and landed heavily beside Jill. She sneezed as the leaves fountained up around her. Jill fished in her pocket for a tissue.

"Here. Blow your nose. I get to sit next to Connie Ward in science. She's my lab partner. Marla's partner is Tommy Williamson—of course she gets a boy! I wish Karen was in our room so we were all together. I wish we had her instead of that creepy Mary Poletti who always copies over my shoulder. Karen's in our gym class, though…"

Dede listened to her and smiled up at the sky, wheezing a little from the dust in the leaves. Jill thought of the things they did in gym. Dede wouldn't be any good at gym. Too fat. She'd get out of breath right away.

"Do you ever have gym, Dede?"

"Yeh."

"Like—what do you do?"

"W-we run…and walk backward. Sometimes we j-jump." Dede's face was serious. "W-we're training."

"Training? What for?"

"Special Olympics."

"Olympics! That's crazy. How could you guys be in the Olympics?"

Dede shook her head in puzzlement. "I don't know."

Jill thought, she gets some pretty weird ideas into her head sometimes. "Tell me some more, Dede," she said. "What do you do when you're not in gym? Do you do arithmetic? Stuff like that?"

"Yeh." Dede smiled. "I know my numbers up to ten. I can wr-write them. And I can write Dede. D-E-D-E."

"That's good! You'll have to show me."

"Yeh."

"Anything else?"

Dede frowned, thinking, "We play store. And we c-cook." She sat up. "And we g-grow things."

"What? Vegetables, flowers?"

"Yeh. I like that best. I l-love flowers." Dede smiled. "They're just seeds in the beginning. I water them and I water them and then th-they grow into flowers for me."

It was the longest sentence Jill had ever heard her say. Dede shut her eyes and lay back in the leaves. Jill did too.

The sun filtered down through the trees. It felt good on her closed eyelids. She listened to the sounds of the autumn afternoon.

"Let's try and fool old Barney, Dede. I'll cover you up and we'll see if he thinks you've gone home without him."

"Okay."

Jill hollowed out a place in the leaf pile and Dede got into it. "Keep still now," Jill said, as she raked the leaves, "or Barney will figure it out."

Soon she couldn't see Dede at all.

"Hey, Barney!" Jill called. "Where's Dede? Where's she gone?"

Barney wagged his tail. "I don't think we've fooled him," Jill said out of the corner of her mouth. The leaf pile stirred a little. Barney's tail wagged harder. He started sniffing around the edge of the leaves, playing the game.

"Jill! Hey, Jill!" Marla waved over the fence.

"Hi. You're home early."

"I know. I forgot my piano music. Laraine's so mad!"

"Can you come over?"

"Yes. Only I still have to have my piano lesson. I thought I'd get out of it. But I wanted to tell you…I asked her and I can. Come to your party, I mean. Well, I'd better go. I'll come over as soon as I get…"

The leaves exploded as Barney plunged into the middle of the pile, his tail swishing them in all directions. Dede popped up like a jack-in-the-box. Marla's smile froze on her face.

"We'll see you when you get back," Jill called.

Marla said stiffly, "I didn't know…I mean…I forgot—I have to do something important…" She stared at Dede and said loudly, "Anyway. All I wanted to do was tell you I can come to your party." She turned and walked into her house.

"Party?" Dede said.

☞   XXII

Why'd she have to say that? She knows I haven't asked Dede, Jill thought. "Dede! Your hair is all full of leaves and twigs and junk," she said.

"What party?" Dede asked.

Marla's so mean, Jill thought angrily. "Oh…it's not a party really…just a…sleepover…you know…"

"Can I come?"

"Well, the thing is, Dede…well. I can only have just a couple of kids and…well, you can't…this time, I mean…"

"I never w-went to a party," Dede said, pulling leaves out of her hair.

"Never?"

"N-nobody asked me."

"Oh." Jill felt rotten. She tried picturing Dede at her slumber party. No. She'd be so out of it, it wasn't funny.

"Let's go inside and see what there is to eat," Jill said.

"Yeh! I'm h-hungry!"

Mom was peeling potatoes in the kitchen.

"What's to eat, Mom?"

"You'd better think about your weight, Jill. You're always eating these days." She turned. "Oh. Dede, uh…hello." She put down the half-peeled potato, wiped her hands dry and headed for the door. "Make yourselves a sandwich," she said. "I'll get out of your way. I'll be upstairs…"

"Hi," Dede said to Mom's back.

☞   XXIII

"Here, Dede," Jill said, handing her a can from the refrigerator. They made tuna fish sandwiches and Jill poured some apple juice. "Let's go back outside," she said. She thought: Mo-om, it's safe to come down now.

The girls sat in the sunshine with the dogs stretched out beside them.

"I l-like tuna," Dede said, taking a bite out of her sandwich.

"Yes, it's good. And I like steak…"

"Yeh."

"…and French fries…and cheesecake…"

"Yeh…and-and b-brownies…" Dede grinned, taking another bite. As she did, a blur of white shot between them. The sandwich vanished from her hand.

Jill jumped. "Leroi! Bad dog! How did you get over here?" Barney and Squeak barked furiously at Leroi, but he just stood there, licking his lips. "I don't believe it!" Jill turned to Dede. "He must've dug a hole under the fence. I'd better…" She stared. Dede's face was scrunched up. She was rocking. Backward and forward. Backward and forward. "What're you doing?"

☞　XXIV

"Ah…ah…ah…"

"What is it? Leroi didn't hurt you, did he? Let me look."

Dede's hand was held tightly against her body as she hugged herself and rocked and rocked. Jill peeled it away. One of the fingers was a bit red.

"Bad Leroi! Bad dog!" Jill rubbed Dede's finger gently. "It's just grazed a little. It's not bleeding. Look…Dede…"

Dede wouldn't look. "Ah…ah…ah…"

"He didn't mean it. He's really a nice dog. I guess he just saw that sandwich and he wanted it…Maybe Marla forgot to feed him or something…" Jill talked fast. She had to make Dede forget her finger—think about something else. "Dede, stop crying. I guess I'd better take him back. Dede…hey, do you want to put a Band-Aid on it? Come on…we'll take Leroi home and tie him up and…Dede…"

"Ah…ah…" Dede was going on and on as if she'd cry forever. Jill ran inside the house.

"Mom!" she called up the stairs. "Leroi snapped at Dede's finger and she's crying and I can't make her stop. Can you come out?"

"Oh, honey…I just lay down…Can't you try to…?"

"No. I've been trying."

"Daddy'll come. I'm undressed…Get her a Band-Aid. They're in the bathroom cabinet."

"I am getting her a Band-Aid. But I guess she really got scared or something…"

"Daddy's coming."

Dad came, wiping his hands on a rag. "What's going on?" He frowned. "What's the matter?"

Jill pointed at Dede, rocking in the grass. He stopped looking mad and ran outside. "Poor kid," he said, hugging Dede.

"Ah…ah…"

He pulled her up gently. "We're going to put something on it, honey."

"Ah…ah…"

Jill put her hands over her ears. She couldn't stand it. "Hey, Dede. Shall I make you another sandwich?"

Dede shook her head. Tears were pouring down her face. It's so weird, Jill thought, she didn't cry this way when the boys were being mean to her...

"Do you want me to call your mother?"

Another shake. "Ah...ah..."

"Dede...hey, listen! You know what? I'm going to tell you something I was keeping for a surprise..."

"Ah...ah..."

"Listen! How can you hear me if you keep crying! You know what's coming to you in the mail pretty soon?"

"Ah.... ."

"An invitation to my birthday party in a couple of weeks!"

Dede looked at her. "...Ah...a...p-party? M-me?"

"Yes. You!"

"A p-party?"

"I mean it!"

Okay, Jill thought, great! What do I do now? I'm not even having a birthday party in a couple of weeks!

☞   xxv

CHAPTER EIGHT

Jill walked Dede home.

"Mama!" Dede called before they'd even opened the gate. "Mama!"

Mrs. Atkins ran outside, looking worried. "What's the matter?"

"I'm going to a p-party!"

"Party?"

"J-Jill's having a party. She asked me."

Mrs. Atkins looked at Jill. Jill nodded. "You did? How wonderful!"

Jill was embarrassed. "Oh, it's just a little..."

Dede said, "It's a b-birthday party!"

"Oh, Jill!" Mrs. Atkins took her hand. "That's lovely of you. Dede'll be so excited. When is it?"

"Er...in a couple of weeks. Dede'll be getting an invitation in the mail." Jill wanted to get off the subject, so she told Mrs. Atkins about Leroi. Dede's finger wasn't even red any more. Why didn't I keep my stupid mouth shut, she thought.

She walked slowly home, trying to figure out what she was going to do. It was quiet on Maple, and Jill was halfway up her porch steps when she heard her parents' voices.

"I don't understand you at all, Peg. At least you should explain to the kid why you're acting this way. You're confusing her. She can't figure you out and neither can I!"

"I can't...I know I'm being silly, Joe. But I don't even want to put it into words. It might bring bad luck!"

"That's plain stupid, Peg. You should know better!" Dad's feet drummed down the stairs and out onto the porch. "Oh." He stopped short. "Jilly. Did...? Yes, you did."

Jill wished he hadn't found her there. It looked like she was eavesdropping and she wasn't.

"Dad...I just got..." But she knew her face was giving her away. She'd heard enough to guess they'd been fighting about her.

"Okay. This settles it. Come inside, Jilly." Dad put his arm around her shoulders. "Mom's going to have to face up to a few things."

Mom came down the stairs in her bathrobe. She'd heard. You could tell. "I'm sorry, honey," she said. Jill didn't know if she meant her or Dad. She had a sort of wary look, as if she expected to be hurt.

"Now we're going to sit down and talk this whole thing out," Dad said.

"What whole thing?" Jill wondered.

"Where are the boys?" asked Dad.

"At Dan's," Mom answered.

"Oh. Well...This concerns Jill more than them, anyway, because of Dede."

"Joe, I can't."

"Then I will. Sit down, Peg."

Jill sat on the edge of a chair. Something important was happening. She watched them carefully.

"You've been puzzled by your mom's behavior toward Dede, haven't you, Jill?"

Mom had shrunk back into her chair. Like a child in trouble, Jill thought. "It's okay, Dad," she said.

"No. It's not okay. I want this out in the open, where it always should have been. I'm going to tell you what's bothering your mother. You've a right to know. Dede's our neighbor and your friend and she's going to be around. We've got to stop avoiding this issue." He looked at Mom and spoke quickly. "There was another baby once, Jilly—a long time ago when you were still a baby yourself. Even the boys don't remember. Well...maybe Tom..." Mom was staring down at her hands, clenched together in her lap. "Anyway, the baby was a girl—your sister—but, when she came...well, you could see something had gone wrong somewhere along the way..." His voice shook. "It wasn't fair...such a little thing...she didn't live..." He cleared his throat. "Just as well. She'd have had no kind of life..." He broke off. He got up and walked abruptly to the window and stared out.

Jill sat very still. She felt oddly relieved. It was as if at last she was hearing something that had been there unspoken from the beginning. She looked at her parents. Mom pinned down in her chair like a butterfly on a board. Dad with his back turned. The silence was smothering. She had to say something.

"I guess Dede reminds you, Mom..."

Mom shook her head. "It isn't that, Jilly. It's...it's because of the new baby coming. I'm older this time and that makes it risky. I'm...really spooked about it, I guess. So scared the same thing will happen...again."

"Was...was that baby retarded, like Dede? Is that why you don't want to have her around?"

"No. Not like Dede." She stared at Dad's back. "It's so silly, really."

Jill said, "I don't get it, then. What happened? Do you know what happened?"

"No." Mom's voice was cool as stone.

Dad turned at the sound of it and his face softened. He sat on the arm of Mom's chair and held her. "We don't know," he said. "She...her body wasn't properly formed. She would have been retarded, only it would've been much worse. Blind...deaf. Dede's retardation is due to what's called Down's syndrome. With our baby, we could only guess at the cause—the doctors said it might have been a virus your mother had..."

"Oh. You think maybe our baby will catch what Dede's got?"

"No, no, honey. You can't catch Down's syndrome. What our baby's trouble was, was different. And it might have been caused by a virus Mom had while she was pregnant...nothing to do with Dede's retardation."

"But you haven't been sick!" Jill burst out. "It would never happen twice! God wouldn't let it happen twice! Whatever it was, that was nine whole years ago—why don't you ask the doctor? Maybe he can find out ahead of time and then you'll know."

"I don't want to know!" Mom's voice was shrill.

"Oh Mom. Oh Mom." Jill knelt beside her and held on tight, and realized it was more of a stretch than it used to be. That baby really was there. "It'll be all right. I know it, Mom. Everything's different now from then. You're in a new place. You and Dad are even different people from the way you were nine years ago. And I'm big now. I can do a lot of things and we'll all help so you don't get tired. And I'm going to keep Dede out of here, so you won't have to see her."

"Oh, honey, there's no need for that now..." Mom gestured helplessly. "You see, all these years I've tried to forget what happened. It was too sad to think about. And I'd just about done it. Even when the new baby started, I could blot out what had happened the last time. But, seeing Dede all the time, well...it was like a little voice nagging at me, saying, 'You see what can happen, you see what can happen.'" She laughed and the tears brimming in her eyes spilled onto her cheeks. "Your father's right. I was being superstitious. Seeing Dede's not going to affect the way things turn out." She smiled at Dad and Jill felt herself relax.

☞ XXVI

"The boys should know, too," Mom said quietly. "Now we must tell them."

CHAPTER NINE

"No way!" Karen said, plumping her pillow. "She gives me the creeps!"

Marla got up and lurched around the room, imitating Dede. They all hooted with laughter.

"You're too much, Marla!" said Connie.

Marla bowed and climbed back into her sleeping bag.

"Come on, you guys. Quit fooling around. You've got to help me out. I've invited her to a nonexistent party," Jill said.

"Forget about it. She won't remember."

"Yes, she will. She's talked about it every day since, and her mother told Mom how wonderful it was of me to ask her. So I've got to come through."

"Well, count me out!" Karen said, grinning.

"Come on, Kar. What're you afraid of?"

Karen's grin faded. "I don't know. But I am. I'm not kidding. She does give me the creeps. Maybe it's because I don't know what she's going to do. I mean, it's not like with a normal kid who acts the same way you do. Then you can kind of look ahead and...be ready. I mean, you know they think the same way you do. Like, supposing I say to you, 'Are you going to watch the soccer game after school?' I know you're either going to say 'Yes, I want to,' or 'No, I have too much home-work,' or anyway something that makes sense to me. But if I ask Dede that, she'll say 'Yeh' and all the time not even know what soccer is. Her saying 'Yeh' wouldn't mean anything. How can you talk to a person like that? I don't have any idea what she knows and what she's thinking...if she's thinking anything. She lives in a different world from us...you know what I mean?"

☞ XXVII

"I know. But she has feelings, that's for sure. Even if she doesn't understand everything, she knows when someone's unhappy. And she knows when someone's being mean to her. She can get scared, too, just like us. She's sort of the same, only different. I mean, a lot of stuff goes right over her head. But then something that wouldn't bother one of us really gets to her. Like...well, the way I got this party idea was because she got scared when Leroi grabbed her sandwich. He didn't really hurt her, but she started crying and she couldn't stop. I tried every-thing to make her stop and that's when I ended up telling her she was being in-vited to a party. And that worked. Do you guys realize she's never been asked to a party in her whole life? That's why she's so excited about it...There's no reason to be scared of her, Kar. I'm not scared of her and I see her everyday."

"I know and I don't get it. I'd be so bored!"

"Well—it's not like it's for hours and hours. I like company when I take Squeak out. And she has to walk Barney. So it just...works for both of us. And she's nice. I mean, I never heard her say anything mean. And she gets fun out of little things."

"I don't see how you can stand being seen with her," Marla said. "You know, the way she looks and the way she walks..."

"Well, it's not catching, for heaven's sakes."

"And the way she talks!" Marla went on. "I can't understand her half the time!"

"Well, you don't listen half the time!"

"What do you talk about?" Connie asked quickly.

"Oh...school...and people...the dogs..."

"Duh-duh. Duh-duh..." Marla pulled down the sides of her mouth.

"She doesn't talk like that," Jill said. "You're so dumb, Marla. What it comes down to is—are you supposed to be my friends or aren't you?" Jill glared at all of them. "Mom says we can have the party in a couple of weeks. You're already having the sleepover. So, are you going to come or not? I figure I'll ask all the girls in 5B."

"Well," Karen said slowly, "maybe. If everyone else says yes."

"I'll come," Connie said.

"Okay." Marla had stopped making faces. "Okay. I'll come, too. Only because it's you, Jill Harvey. And you owe me!"

☞   XXVIII

* * *

Jill wrote out her invitations. She printed Dede's in big letters and drew a bunch of balloons with happy faces, so Dede would know right away that it was the party invitation.

"I hope it goes all right," she said to Mom. "What if the other kids are mean to Dede?"

"We'll tell them to cut it out!" Mom said. "But I think it'd be a good idea to warn the others what to expect."

Twelve girls accepted their invitations and Jill explained that there'd be someone retarded at the party.

"Retarded? But I've never...How? I don't think...I couldn't..." they said.

"Don't get uptight," Jill said. "She's nice and she's friendly and it's just she's sort of slow picking things up. It'll be okay. I'm figuring out some games that won't be hard for her. Some of them will seem stupid for kids like us, but if we all go along, it'll be fun. How about it?"

Two of the girls suddenly remembered something else they had to do on that day, but the rest said it was okay with them.

On the day, Dede and Barney were the first to get there. Mom's face froze, just for a moment, when she came out of the house and saw them. She seemed to shiver a little, as if shaking off a spell. Then she hugged Dede around the shoulders, saying, "Good to see you!" Jill let her breath go.

Jill had told Tom and Larry to get lost, but of course they didn't. They hung out of the bedroom window and made dumb remarks as the kids arrived. "Aren't you guys supposed to be some place else?" Jill called up to them. They grinned. "Nope," they said.

She turned back to her friends in the yard. There was something wrong already. Karen and Connie and Marla, Ayisha, Maria, Kyanna, and Lisa, Inez,

Jackie, and Jennie were all standing together. Dede was standing by herself. She was smiling at them. But they weren't smiling back. They were just staring. Maria whispered something in Inez's ear, and Inez laughed.

Jill said quickly, "Hey, let's go out back. Dad's hidden peanuts all over. Whoever finds the most gets a prize."

"I like peanuts," Dede said.

"I like peanuts," Marla mimicked.

"Shut up, Marla" Jill glared at her.

"Okay, you guys," Marla said, with a look. "Remember peanut hunts?"

The others giggled.

Dad distributed paper bags and they spread out.

"I call, the toolshed's mine," Lisa said.

"No fair!" Jennie shouted.

"Everyone can look everywhere," Dad said.

"Any up in the tree?" Jackie asked.

"Nothing is higher than you can reach from the ground," Jill answered.

They hunted for five minutes, then Dad blew a whistle. "Time to count them up!" Everyone spilled her peanuts out on the grass. Each pile was different. Dede's was nothing but shells. Ayisha and Jennie snorted with laughter.

"That's okay, Dede," Dad said. "I should've told you not to eat them until after I'd counted them."

"I like peanuts!" Dede said with a big smile.

"Well, I guess you do!" Dad smiled back. Good old Dad! He walked around, counting. "Looks to me as if Lisa's found the most, so she gets the prize." (Jill had found some good prizes at the thrift shop.) "There you go, Lisa," handing her a little ring in a box. "But I've got to hand it to Dede. She's way ahead of the rest of you in the eating department!"

Dede beamed.

Dad pulled four sacks of old clothes out on the grass. "Okay," he said. "Next is a relay race. Everyone has to change clothes at each end of the run."

"Dad!" Jill pulled at his sleeve. "I just thought—Dede can't do buttons."

"Oh-oh...um...okay. I need a judge for this race. Dede—how about it? Will you be the judge?"

"Yeh!"

Dad showed her where to stand.

She's having a good time, Jill thought. It's going to be all right.

Dad blew his whistle and everyone shrieked and giggled and clutched. They fell down and got up and struggled forward. As the last two raced for the finish line, they were very close. Ayisha made it just ahead of Inez.

Dede pointed to Ayisha. "She won!"

"She did not!" Inez cried. "It was a tie!"

"She won," Dede insisted. "I kn-know."

"What do you know? You don't know anything!" Inez yelled. "How would a dummy like you know anything!"

"Hey, hey! That's enough of that kind of talk!" Dad spoke quietly, but Inez shut up, her face flushed. "Dede is right. Ayisha's team won."

"You did good, Dede," Jill said in her ear. "Inez's just acting stupid."

"Yeh."

"Now, we're going to play Duck, Duck, Goose," Dad said.

"Duck, Duck, Go-ose! That's for first graders!" Maria groaned. "I'm not playing."

"Me neither," Kyanna said. She always did whatever Maria did.

Dad said, "Too bad! You two will miss the fun."

The rest made a circle under the tree and began to play. Jill was It first, and she tapped Jackie. Karen and Connie tapped each other twice. Even if it was a little kids' game, they kept running and laughing.

Jill looked at Dede—part of the circle with everyone else. Nobody has tapped her yet, Jill thought. Next time I get the chance, I'll tap her and let her chase me. But in the end she didn't. She might fall down and get hurt, Jill told herself. But she'd chickened out and she knew it.

Next was tag.

"I can p-play tag," Dede told Kyanna.

"Yeah?" said Kyanna. "Well, I'm It. Got you!" And she tapped Dede's shoulder.

Dede grinned. She went after Marla, but Marla was too fast. Karen ran past. "G-got you!" yelled Dede.

"Dede! You're It?" Karen groaned.

"Yeh." Dede ran away behind the tree, laughing to beat the band.

During the game, Mom had the boys set up a long table and she put out sandwiches and cake and ice cream.

"Time to eat," she called out. "Your name cards will tell you where to sit."

Jill had printed Dede's name card big and put it next to her own place. Barney helped out. While everyone was looking for her seat, he ambled out of his spot under the bushes and sat down next to Jill. "Hey, Dede!" Jill shouted. "Barney's found your place for you!"

Dede was the last to leave the party. Jill said to her, "I'm going to help Mom clean up. She hasn't been feeling so great. You can get home okay with Barney, can't you?"

"Yeh," Dede nodded and smiled. "J-Jill..." Suddenly she put her arms around Jill and hugged her tight. "Y-you're my friend...I love you..."

Jill could hardly breathe. "Hey...Dede!" She wriggled free. "It's okay. I'm glad you had a good time."

"Yeh! I had a good time!"

"That's great. I'll see you."

Jill watched Dede go down the street. Even from the back you could tell she was smiling. Jill's arms still hurt from being hugged so hard. Nobody had ever said "I love you" to her before—nobody but Mom and Dad anyway. Karen or Marla wouldn't say something like that. Probably they wouldn't feel it.

The weight of it came down on her. When someone loved you as much as that, it was something you couldn't fool around with.

☞   XXIX

CHAPTER TEN

The mellow fall turned nasty. The blue sky changed to gray and a raw wind blew down Maple, bullying Squeak along the sidewalk.

Jill ached with cold. "Come on Squeak, let's run!" she said. They did, for the whole three-blocks home.

As Jill burst into the warm house, she complained, "You wouldn't believe how cold it is out there, Mom. I can't stop sh-shaking. That wind goes right through my so-called windbreaker."

"I know. I nearly froze myself this morning. We've got to get organized and buy winter outfits. But I just don't know how we're going to do it. Warm stuff is so expensive, and we all need it. That's one thing we never worried about in San Diego."

"When can we go for the winter clothes? Saturday?"

"I guess so. You'll have to get by till then. I hope it doesn't get any colder. We'll go over to that discount center." Mother's back had been hurting and she leaned forward in her chair for Jill to rub it.

Jill rubbed near the waist, where the ache seemed to be centered. She was sending a message with her hand to the baby inside. "I'm your big sister. I'm going to take care of you—and rock you—and sing to you—and you're going to love it here."

She felt her mother's taut muscles begin to relax. At almost the same moment, she felt a soft thump against her hand. She drew in her breath. The baby! Thump. Thump. "Message received!" That baby had to be okay!

* * *

All week the cold continued. Jill and Dede walked the dogs together. Shivering in her thin windbreaker, Jill dreamed of Saturday—Jacket Day. "We're getting our winter clothes this weekend," she told Dede.

"Yeh?"

"I'm getting a red ski jacket."

"I l-like red."

"So do I. It's my favorite color."

"I h-have a ski jacket. It has a...h-hood."

"I want one with a hood too."

"Yeh."

As Jill walked to school with Marla the next morning, she told her, "I'm getting a winter jacket tomorrow."

"Don't you have one?"

"We didn't need them in San Diego."

"No kidding."

"I think I'll get a red..."

"Hey, Karen oo-hoo! Wait up, Karen! I have to tell you something..." Marla waved at Karen, walking a block ahead.

Jill shut up. If she doesn't want to listen, she thought, I'm not going to bother talking. Her excitement leaked away as she listened to Marla gab to Karen about going to Boston on Saturday and how it was for a special reason she couldn't talk about. Big deal!

That night, when Dad got home, he was super happy and excited because he'd been given a bonus and told that he was doing well in his new job. Jill realized for the first time how scared and worried her parents had been all along about money and the future of their family.

Saturday they all went to the big discount store. Jill picked her jacket out of three racks full. It was the one—shiny red, puffy with Dacron polyester filling, a hood you could zipper on or off or out of sight into its own hiding place, and plenty of pockets.

It was late afternoon when they finally got home and the lights were on at Marla's.

"She's back from Boston. I want to show her my jacket," Jill said, scrambling from the car.

Mrs. Burns opened the door, "Well, hi there!" she said. "Come on in and join the party!"

"Party? Oh, I'm sorry...I just...I'll come back."

"No-o! Don't be silly, Jilly." She pulled Jill inside. "Silly Jilly—hey, I'm a poet and I don't know it! Isn't that right?" She smiled at a man sitting in a chair by the fire. "Me and my friend were just having a little pick-me-up after the trip from Boston. How 'bout you, Silly Jilly?"

"Laraine!" Marla came into the room. She looked mad. "Laraine—I'll take Jill up to my room."

"O-kay. Have fun, hon." She laughed.

"Come on, Jill," Marla said.

When they were upstairs, Jill said, "Who's that? Al?"

"No. His name's Morton Tanzhandler. He's her agent. He's trying to get her some work around here."

"Oh. Boy, I'd like to see her dance!"

"How about me?" Marla's voice was sharp. "Don't you want to see me dance?"

"Sure I do. I'd love to see you dance, Marla."

"Okay."

Jill twirled around. "Notice anything?"

"You got a winter jacket."

"Yes. Isn't it neat? Look at the pockets and the crest on the shoulder. Don't you love it? It's really warm—I wore it home to test it out."

"It's a very nice jacket, Jill," Marla said. Then her eyes lit up. "Look at what my grandma got me in Boston!"

The bed was covered with clothes. Corduroy gauchos. A long print skirt with a peasant blouse. A white angora sweater. And a ski jacket. Brilliant royal blue. A ski patch already sewn on each shoulder. Pockets everywhere. A hood, framed in soft white fur. And white fur mittens lying beside it.

"Oh!" Jill had never seen anything so beautiful.

"It's goosedown. That's the warmest you can get, you know. Much warmer than an ordinary polyester filling. It'll keep me warm at 60 degrees below."

Jill thought, I'd like to see you somewhere where it's 60 degrees below.

"The mittens and hood are real fur." Marla rubbed a glove against Jill's cheek. "Feel it—isn't that divine! My grandma says furs and jewels should always be the real thing."

"Yes. They…they're really great, Marla. You're the best-dressed kid in fifth grade, that's for sure…Well. I have to be going…"

"Oh. Do you? Can't you stay a while? What did you come over for?"

"Nothing special. I'll see you, Marla."

☞   xxx

Jill let herself out. She didn't want to go home. Mom would ask what Marla had said about the jacket and then she'd drag out some wise old saying….She couldn't stand hearing that right now.

She put her head down against the wind, the red hood drawn around her face, and marched down Maple feeling mad.

"H-hi, Jill." Dede and Barney were crossing Elm, coming toward her.

"Oh. Hi."

Dede pointed toward Jill's house. "We were c-coming to see you."

"You were? We've been to the store buying winter clothes. See? I got my jacket."

"I l-like that!" Dede's smile broadened. "It's red. I like that." She touched the sleeve. "I like it, Jill. Pockets. Th-that's good. P-pockets are g-good."

☞   xxxi

"There's a zillion of them. It's part of why I picked this one. There's a pocket for change. And one for a ski-lift ticket or a bus ticket or something. And side pockets for mittens…even some inside. Look!"

Jill unzipped the jacket. The wind whipped in. "Brrr!" She shivered and did it up again in a hurry. Warmth surrounded her again. It was a great jacket, whether Marla thought so or not.

"Why were you coming over now?" Jill asked. "It's dark. You should be home."

"I want to ask you something. I couldn't wait." Dede smiled. There was a silence.

After a moment Jill said, "Well? What?"

"Oh. Yeh. Uh…w-we're having a Christmas party at school. We can ask a f-friend. So I want to ask you. You asked m-me to your party. You're my f-friend."

☞   XXXII

CHAPTER ELEVEN

"I can't go. I can't." Jill heard her voice rise.

"Nobody's making you, Jilly," Dad said quietly. "What did you tell her?"

"I…I said I'd have to ask and I'd let her know."

"When is it?

"The Saturday before Christmas."

"There'll be a lot going on then," Mom said.

"I know and I'll probably be very busy…"

"We'll talk about this later. Let's eat now. Dinner's getting cold," Dad said.

It was a quiet meal. Everyone concentrated hard on eating and a heavy silence blanketed the table, broken only by the clatter of their forks. Jill was trying to get rid of the picture filling her mind—the faces in the windows of Dede's school bus.

She pushed her plate away. "I don't want any more," she said. "I have some homework. Can I be excused?"

Mom nodded. "Clear your place…And, honey, we'll work something out."

Jill climbed the stairs slowly, hearing conversation break out in relief as soon as she left the room. She stretched out on her bed in the dark. From time to time, a car whooshed by and the headlights made shadows jerk along her wall. Like the shadows of retards, she thought.

Dad came up after a while. "How's it going, baby?"

"I don't know what to do."

"I know."

"Either way, it'll be bad. I mean, if I don't go, I know she'll be disappointed and I'll feel terrible about letting her down. But if I do go…oh, Dad…if you want to know the truth . . I'm scared to go."

"I remember you telling me a while back that Karen was scared of Dede."

"Yes. But I know Dede. And anyway, Dede's much better than most of them. You should see them, Dad. I've seen them on her bus. They're gross. Some are all twisted and some are blind and some have to wear helmets…"

"That's really gross all right."

"Oh, Dad." She was ashamed. "I can't help how I feel."

☞ · XXXIII

"I don't mean to make fun of you, Jilly. But I do think you're letting yourself be spooked by the idea of going because you don't really know what to expect when you get there."

"That's it! I mean...what can a bunch like that do at a party? They can't even talk so you can understand, some of them..." Panic rose again, smothering her words.

"Can you guess how hard it must be for them—trying to say something and having nobody understand? Wouldn't it make you mad?"

"Yes. I guess so. But suppose I do try, and I still don't understand? Then I'll say 'Excuse me?' and then they'll say it over, and it'll sound just the same and I'll say 'Excuse me?' again..."

Dad nodded. He stared at the dark wall. Then he said, "You know, they always say that the worst fear of all is fear of the unknown...Think things over, honey. You'll figure out what's best." He patted her shoulder, sighed, and left her.

All day Sunday, the decision she had to make weighed like something heavy growing inside her. It loomed in her thoughts, putting everything else out of focus. It deadened the day.

Monday, she saw Dede in the distance and ducked down a side street, feeling like a criminal.

Tuesday was worse. Marla did a really funny imitation of somebody and she couldn't even smile. She kept losing track of what she was doing in class and Mr. Lopietro yelled at her.

"What's with you?" Karen asked on the way home.

Jill just shook her head. She didn't want to tell them. Oh, they'd say right off how gross it was and of course she wasn't going and it'd be the same story all over again. Everyone ganging up against old Dede—Jill Harvey, her so-called friend, included.

That night, Jill headed out into the cold. "I'm taking Squeak for a walk," she said, zipping her red jacket.

She climbed the steps to Dede's house and rang the bell. She knew Dede would be out. It was her night to swim at the Y.

"Hi, Jill, come on in." Mrs. Atkins said. "What can I get you? Juice? Milk? Soda?" She was too welcoming.

"Nothing, thanks. Mrs. Atkins..."

"Well, at least sit down here by the fire for a moment. I see Squeak's already found himself a spot." Jill sat down. "So! What's on your mind?"

Jill sat on the edge of the chair. "Mrs. Atkins..." She felt her face getting hot. "I...I wonder if you could tell me what it's like at...at Dede's school?"

"What it's...why, it's real nice. It's a new building and it's light and airy—lots of windows—and everything painted fresh and bright."

"Oh."

"That's not what you meant. Is it?"

"No." Jill stared at her hands and then looked up, feeling almost defiant. Why did she have to feel so guilty about asking. "I need to know, Mrs. Atkins. About the...other kids."

Mrs. Atkins leaned back. "I knew Dede was going to ask you to the party. She was so all fired up about it she couldn't sleep the night before." She spoke urgently, "It's the first time she's had a friend to ask, you know. It means a lot to her."

"I'm sorry, Mrs. Atkins," she said, not looking at her. "I need to know."

"Yes," Mrs. Atkins got up and got herself a cup of coffee. "I can see how the idea of all those children together might make you nervous if you weren't used to them." She settled back in her chair. "There are a whole lot of those kids at Dede's school—it's shocking to see so many, so many...They're disabled in many ways. But the teachers put the classes together according to what they can do rather than by age or handicap, so it works out pretty well."

"But how do they get that way?"

"Oh, honey...it can happen for so many reasons. Sometimes it seems a wonder to me any children are born normal..."

Jill looked down at her lap.

"There's Down's syndrome," Mrs. Atkins was saying, "What Dede has. That's the result of an extra set of chromosomes in each cell in her body—it's like Mother Nature made a mistake in her arithmetic." Mrs. Atkins smiled faintly. "Then there are the kids who have spina bifida. That happens when things don't get together right before the baby's born and there's damage to the spinal chord. Lots of times kids like that are paralyzed, so they're in wheelchairs. Some of the older children at the school are PKU kids, whose brains were damaged as tiny babies because their bodies were missing a certain enzyme. A way to test for that has been discovered and now most babies are checked out as soon as they're born. There's a special diet for PKU kids that'll prevent brain damage, but that discovery came too late for the kids at Dede's school."

The fire was dying down. Mrs. Atkins put another log on. "Have a soda or something to keep me company?" she said.

"Okay."

They went into the kitchen and Mrs. Atkins opened a can of soda. "There're ice cubes in the freezer, honey. Do you want to hear more?"

"Yes."

"Well, some of the kids are retarded because their mothers had German measles before their babies were born. Then sometimes a baby will be fine right up to the moment of birth, when something happens to cut the oxygen supply to its brain. It only takes a little lapse to cause brain damage...Sometimes disabled children have a whole lot of things go wrong at once—blindness and deafness, maybe epilepsy, too—on top of the retardation. Dede's one of the lucky ones, believe it or not."

They went back to the fire. Jill tried to imagine what they looked like, all those kids, all those different things wrong with them all together in one big room.

"I still can't figure out what they do in school. I don't see what they can do!" she said.

"You'd be surprised. I'm going to be straight with you. Some are at a very low level. I mean, they're still learning to go to the bathroom by themselves. And some of them can't even do that and have to be taken every half hour by an aide."

"You mean the little kids."

"Age doesn't have anything to do with it. One of the boys is eighteen, I think. Dede's age."

☞   XXXIV

"Dede's…? You mean Dede's eighteen?" Jill couldn't keep the shock from her face.

Mrs. Atkins said quickly, "But some of the others are learning to read and write and do simple arithmetic, so they can make change, things like that. And they do arts and crafts. Dede wove this little coaster here. And gym and homemaking—you know, ironing, cleaning, simple cooking. And some are beginning to learn a job, so they can go to a sheltered workshop later and earn a little money. There's a lot they can do. More than people give them credit for." She pushed a candy box at Jill. "Have one, honey. You know, the school has put Dede on a diet! Just when I'd told her we'd be baking Christmas cookies!" She laughed nervously and then poked at the fire, "This Christmas party is their big chance to show their families and friends around. They look forward to it very much. They want to demonstrate what they've been learning for the Special Olympics for the handicapped."

"Dede talked about it once. But I thought she meant…well…I just thought…"

"I know. Nobody thinks they can do anything. But they can. It takes them a long time and they have to work real hard at it. But they can do a lot, if people'll just understand and give them a chance."

Jill stared at the fire. Mrs. Atkins leaned forward in her chair, her eyes urgent.

"I'd drive you up there, Jill…and drive you home afterward."

"You'll be there too?"

"Sure. The whole time. I'm taking some of the food. I'll be right there with you…"

"I hadn't thought about that. Of course you'll be there." Jill laughed with relief. "And there'll be the other mothers and other friends…"

"Sure. You won't be alone. And my Dede'll be there. She'll look after you."

CHAPTER TWELVE

Jill threw down the paste pot. "Look at that!" she said. "It's sliding sideways. I pasted it straight and it's sliding sideways!" She stared at her model of a Greek theater, which was subsiding before her eyes on its cardboard base. "I hate projects! I've been working on this for two hours and now it's self-destructing, stupid thing!" She pushed her chair back. "I refuse to do any more to it. I'm going out!"

Mom grinned. "You could use a break. Take Squeak."

Jill put on her jacket and pulled the hood around her face. Squeak came running at the jingle of the leash and they set off down Maple, walking fast. They could make a better pace without Dede, who had a bad cold.

The street was empty. Jill breathed in the cold air and felt exhilarated and alive all over. Suddenly, she felt something, and looked up to realize it was snowing—her very first snow! "I love it!" she sang as she whirled around. Squeak yipped excitedly, joining in the fun. Jill ran back up the street.

"Marla!" she yelled under Marla's window. "Come out! It's snowing!"

Marla stuck her head out. "Hey, great!" She quickly ran out, wearing her fancy blue jacket.

"Let's walk to the schoolyard and back," said Jill.

When they got to the schoolyard, Jill ran for the swings. "I love to swing." She laughed. "I'm too big to use them in school time." She pumped her legs, going higher and higher until she was flying with the snowflakes—so high that the swing chains began to tremble.

"You'd better come down before you fall off," Marla called.

"Uh-uh."

"Come down."

"Why don't you swing?"

"Because I don't want to. There's snow all over the seat. I don't want to get wet." Marla stared up at Jill. "I'll tell you something if you come down. Something I haven't told anyone yet, not even Karen."

"What is it?"

Marla dug her toe in the snow. "Well. Maybe I shouldn't. It's nothing really. I'd better not."

"Marla Burns! You fink!" Jill jumped off the swing.

"I was trying to save your life, dum-dum."

"Don't pull that. I can tell there's something..."

Marla grinned and then her face went serious. "Okay. But I'm swearing you to secrecy!"

"Okay."

"It's the biggest thing that's ever happened to me in my entire life!"

"I believe you! What is it?"

"Well, okay. All that's happened is...I got picked to dance in the *Nutcracker* in Boston!"

"You...I don't believe it!"

"I know. Neither do I! I went to audition a couple of weekends ago. I never would've had the nerve, but my grandma made me. Then I was called back and we heard for sure today."

"Oh, Marla..."

"I have to rehearse every day from now on. Laraine's driving me to Boston in the morning. I have to live at my grandma's until the run is over."

"The run?"

"The run of the ballet. That's what they call it. There're going to be eleven performances."

"What about school?"

"They said I could go. I have to do an extra paper about the ballet—the story and the music and how it is to work onstage and what it's like backstage. And they're going to send me work and I have to send it back by mail. And I have to do extra reading. It's only for four weeks though—two weeks rehearsing, then the show. I guess they figure I won't get too far behind. Anyway, what if I do?" She pirouetted across the playground. "But I've left the best for last!"

"What?" Jill ran after her.

"You're all coming to the opening."

"Who?"

"You. And Karen. And Connie. My grandma's so excited, she said I could ask my best friends to see my debut. She's inviting you to sleep over at her apartment."

"Marla—don't kid around."

"I'm not—she's arranging the whole thing."

Jill's head whirled. "I've never been to a real ballet. You know, professional. And in Boston! I've wanted to go to Boston ever since we moved here."

Marla laughed. "And there I'll be—right up there on the stage! Then you'll come?"

"Will I! Try and stop me! When is it?"

"The Saturday before Christmas."

☞   xxxv

Chapter Thirteen

Jill started taking Squeak on a new route.

"It's boring going the same old way all the time," she said, "so now I go the other way on Maple, then cross Butternut, down Acacia, and back across Elm."

"You mean you're not going by Dede's any more?" Mom asked.

"No."

☞   xxxvi

"Dede'll miss walking with you."

Jill pulled open the closet. "She…doesn't go out so much in this weather." She tugged at her jacket. "This stupid zipper! It's always sticking on this stupid jacket!" she said, her voice shaking. "Anyway…well…well, I don't see why it has to be always me who has to walk with Dede all the time."

"Why, Jilly! You told me you liked walking with her."

"I do! Only…oh, quit bugging me!"

"You don't have to snap."

"I'm not snapping. Just leave me alone."

"Gladly."

Jill stomped up the stairs to her room. She lay on her bed and stared at the ceiling.

☞   XXXVII

She was still staring at the ceiling an hour later when Dad came home. She heard him greet Mom and whistle as he hung his coat up. Why did he have to whistle all the time! That's all he ever did nowadays, whistle, whistle, whistle.

Larry and Tom came slamming into the house. Jill listened as everyone downstairs was talking and laughing. After a while she heard Dad say, "Where's my girl?" and a few moments later he came up the steps two at a time.

"Here you are," he said.

Well! That's pretty obvious, she thought.

"Doing your homework?" He sat on the bed.

"No."

"Oh…What's the matter?"

"Nothing."

"Come off it, Jilly. This is your old dad talking. What's going on in that head of yours? Your mother says you're in a bad mood."

"I'm fine."

"You could've fooled me!"

Why doesn't he go away? she thought. He's always poking around in my mind. It isn't any of his business how I feel.

Dad stood up and wandered around her room. Then he sat down again abruptly.

He broke the heavy silence. "What did Dede say?"

"When?"

"When you told her."

"I haven't."

"Jilly!"

"I know! I just…haven't seen her around, that's all. I'll do it."

Dad looked at her. "Do you want us to do it?" His voice was gentle.

If only you could, she thought. But she said, "No. She wouldn't understand…hearing it from you…" She stared miserably at the wall. "Oh, Dad. Why did it have to turn out this way? Of all the stupid days of the year!"

"It's a darn shame, all right."

"I won't miss the chance to go to Boston. And I can't miss the ballet!"

"I know."

"I'll never get another chance like it!"

"I know."

I know, I know...is that all he could say?

The next day, a postcard came from Marla: *Dear Jill—I'm having a fabulous time. Boston is fabulous and I've got a fabulous costume to wear. Wait till you see it! Love, Marla.*

Late that afternoon, Jill went to Dede's.

"Come on in, honey," Mrs. Atkins said. "Turn the TV off, Dede. Jill's here."

The fire was blazing and the room was warm and cozy. Barney sniffed her hand in welcome, tail waving. Dede came out of the den.

"Hi, Jill. Want to w-watch TV?"

"No. I can't stay today, Dede. I just came because I have to tell you something..."

Dede smiled. Her face was wide open.

Jill thought, I can't. But she knew if she didn't it would still be waiting. Better to get it over.

"Dede—I'm sorry, but I can't come to your Christmas party after all."

The smile stayed on Dede's face.

"You see, I really thought I could come and I know it'll be fun and I'm real sorry about it..."

"Well, we're real sorry too. Aren't we, Dede?" Mrs. Atkins' voice was high and polite.

"What it is, Mrs. Atkins, is that I...I was going to be invited to Boston for the same day...only I didn't know about it when I said..."

"Sure. We quite understand. Don't we, Dede?" Mrs. Atkins was smiling. All except her eyes.

☞ XXXVIII

"It's true, Mrs. Atkins. You can ask my mother."

"Sure. Now, if you'll excuse us, Dede and I were just about to have our supper."

"Dede...I'm sorry..."

Dede nodded. "I know," she said. But now her smile was gone.

Jill walked home.

When she came in, she felt Dad looking at her, a question in his eyes. She nodded and shrugged her shoulders. Question answered.

* * *

"Get all your clothes packed tonight," Mom said on Friday. "Don't leave it till morning. You know how you are in the morning!"

"You already told me that a hundred times!"

"Lay it all out on your bed and I'll come and make sure you haven't forgotten anything."

Jill put out her clothes and put on the *Nutcracker* music so she could listen to it while she packed.

The phone rang. It was Connie. "Are you all packed yet? Don't forget extra money for souvenirs. Are you taking a camera?"

"No, I'm still packing...don't have a camera...See you."

She started putting stuff in her suitcase. The phone rang again. It was Karen. "Should I take my mother's opera glasses? Did Marla say how far we'll be from the stage? Maybe we'll need opera glasses. What do you think?"

"I don't know...she didn't tell me...maybe we should."

Jill stared at the open suitcase. The phone rang a third time. When she picked it up, Jill heard a whispery little voice say, "Hi! This is your friendly neighborhood ballet dancer calling."

"Hi, Marla."

"Are you all set? Laraine's picking you up at eight-thirty tomorrow morning. Oh, you're going to love it! You can't believe how fabulous it is. Wait till you see my costume—it's pink and it has silver spangles and when I'm under the lights I look fabulous! Grandma told me. She's been sneaking into the rehearsals and then working with me afterward to improve my dance. We've even put in a couple of little extras—you know, difficult steps—because she says this is a real showcase for me. The director didn't notice, isn't that a gas!...Jill...Are you there?"

"Yes, I'm here."

"Well, I may not be able to see you after the show because I have to go to a cast party at this fabulous restaurant. But Grandma said she'd get the teenager who lives in the next apartment to take you home after the show. We'll be driven over in this big limousine, can you imagine!...Yes, Grandma, I am hurrying..."

"Marla..."

"And Grandma bought me a new dress for the party which is just..."

Marla's voice chattered on in Jill's ear. But it was Dede's face that filled her mind.

"Marla..."

"What?"

"I'm not coming."

Silence at the other end. Then, "I didn't hear what you said."

"I said I'm not coming. I'm sorry, Marla. You know I want to. But...well, something's happened here, and...well, there's something else I have to do instead."

"What do you mean? It's all set up. You've got to."

"Maybe you could give the ticket to someone else."

"You mean you're serious? You're really not coming? But I've told everyone here you're my best friend...you, not Karen...and that you're just dying to see me in the show. If you don't come, what'll they think? They'll laugh at me. You've got to come, Jill. I need you to come. Jill, it's my first big show..." Marla's voice sounded far off. "Jill? Why aren't you coming? Tell me! What's so important? What is it you have to do?"

"Well...what happened was Dede had asked me to this party at her school..."

"That retard?"

"Yes. They're having a Christmas party and she was counting on me going and I had told her yes before you..."

Marla's voice rose. "What's the matter with you? Are you crazy? You're going to pass up a chance to see me in a professional show, just to go to some dumb party with her? She'll never know the difference. But I will...Please come, Jill. Please. I really am petrified, Jill. I need my friends out there."

"Dede needs a friend, too. You've got Karen and Connie, but she hasn't got anyone else but me. Marla, I can't let her down."

"What about letting me down? And I came to your stupid party for her—you owe me for that, Jill Harvey, and you know it..."

"I'm sorry. It's just that..."

"Okay. Forget it. And you can forget you're my friend from now on, Jill Harvey. I think you're a creep. Just like your creepy friend!"

Far away in Boston, Marla slammed down the phone. Jill listened to the hum of the empty wire. She felt light. Like...bread rising...Very gently she hung up the phone. Laughing and crying, she ran to the kitchen.

"Mom! Hey, Mom! I'm going over to Dede's for a couple of minutes!"

☞   XXXIX

CHAPTER FOURTEEN

Jill settled Mrs. Atkins' chocolate cake more squarely on her lap and stared ahead as the car started climbing the long approach to the Pearson School. "Good Luck, honey," Dad had said. "You'll do fine!"

Easy for him to say. He'd never faced a school full of retarded kids. Come to that, Jill thought, I bet nobody I know has.

As Mrs. Atkins pulled into a parking space, Jill swallowed, trying to moisten her dry throat. Oh, couldn't we wait a minute, she thought. But Mrs. Atkins had already come around to her side of the car.

"I'll take the cake, Jill. You bring that box of sandwiches from the back seat."

She followed Mrs. Atkins toward the low buildings. There were Christmas decorations on the windows. Jill had expected bars.

But it was cold. "That wind's raw," Mrs. Atkins said. "I wish it would warm up—Dede's still got a cold. Ordinarily I'd have made her stay in today, but I didn't have the heart—she's been looking forward to this party so much."

Mrs. Atkins headed for a side door and motioned Jill in front of her.

She was inside. The door closed behind her. Why aren't I in Boston? she thought. She looked carefully around, trying not to catch anyone's eye, trying not to show she was curious. She imagined someone waltzing up to her and saying,

"Do you come here often?" the way they did in the movies. She felt giggles rising crazily inside her.

"We'll take this stuff to the kitchen," Mrs. Atkins said briskly. Jill followed her down a corridor, staying close. "You see, honey, it's not so very different from your school, is it?"

Jill shook her head. What had she expected? Chains—locks—awful noises? What she saw was bulletin boards, classrooms with tables, blackboards, pianos...

They came to an open space, separated by shelving.

"See, this is their kitchen," Mrs. Atkins said. "They've got everything here they'd find in a standard kitchen. This is where they learn to cook, wash dishes, put stuff away properly..."

Jill nodded.

Next to the kitchen was a kind of sitting room, with couches and chairs, a TV and tape player.

"The kids take breaks in here," Mrs. Atkins said, "and the staff uses it to teach them about correct behavior when they're with other people—you know, in a social situation. Also they practice their household skills here—dusting, polishing, vacuuming..."

Jill nodded. She knew she hadn't spoken a word since they'd entered the building. She had to say something. "Uh...Dede must know more than I do about how to do those things," she said.

"Right!" Mrs. Atkins beamed at her. "Now look over here, Jill. This is their supermarket area."

Cans of soup and vegetables, boxes of cereals, tea, and pet food lined the shelves on both sides of an aisle.

"Here the kids learn how to stack the shelves neatly, with everything right side up. Some of them might get jobs in a supermarket later on. And they learn how to shop—pick stuff out—recognize labels even if they can't read. It helps them to be more useful to themselves and their families. They feel good when they can be self-sufficient, and it's even better when they can share in the work of the family.

"Yes," Jill said.

A boy was coming toward them. His head was too big for his body, and his tiny round ears stuck out like cup handles. Jill slipped around to the other side of Mrs. Atkins.

"Hi, Mrs. Atkins," the boy said in a slow, deep voice.

"Hi, Donald. How are you today?"

"I'm f-fine, Mrs. Atkins. How are you today?"

"Just fine, thank you, Donald."

The boy went on by and Jill realized she'd been holding her breath. Supposing he'd talked to me? she thought. It's easy for Mrs. Atkins—she's used to them.

They left the food in the kitchen. "Let's find Dede," Mrs. Atkins said.

The corridor was empty. Mrs. Atkins put her arm around Jill's shoulder. "It's not too bad, is it?"

Jill shook her head. But she couldn't bring herself to come right out and say it. Mrs. Atkins gave her a squeeze. "They'll be waiting in the gym."

Jill could hear voices and laughter as they got closer. A girl who looked sort of like Dede overtook them, pushing a wheelchair with a small boy in it. His body was propped like a rag doll, legs dangling. He was laughing fit to bust. After they'd passed, Jill realized she was smiling. She felt her stomach begin to ease.

The gym was just like hers at York Falls Elementary. They play basketball? she thought, staring at the court laid out in red on the polished wood floor. There were windows high on the walls and equipment stacked neatly at one end of the gym. Students and parents were everywhere. But not many kids like me, Jill thought, looking warily around.

"H-hi, Jill!" Dede touched her arm. "I knew you'd come!"

"Hey, Dede! You have a nice school!"

"Yeh. I l-like it!" Dede said. "Let's s-sit down over here." She led the way and they sat down next to a big blonde girl in a blue dress.

"Hi, Babe!" she greeted Jill. A pretty weird way to say hello! Jill thought.

Dede said, "Jill, th-this is my very good friend, Debbie."

It sounded...funny...formal. She'd never heard Dede talk that way. She didn't know how to answer. She looked at Mrs. Atkins. Mrs. Atkins was nodding encouragement.

"Uh, hi, Debbie. Uh, my name is Jill."

Debbie said, "Sit down."

They already were sitting down, but Jill said, "Thank you." She felt like Alice in Wonderland. Everything was just a bit...off center.

A lot of the students looked like Dede. Quite a few others wore football helmets.

"Is that the boy that goes on your bus, Dede?" Jill looked at someone near them. "I saw a boy in a helmet on your bus."

"Th-that's David. G-George goes on my bus."

"Why does he wear a helmet?"

"He f-falls down sometimes."

"Oh...yeah," Jill said.

☞ XL

"Good afternoon." A woman spoke from the far end of the gym. "I'm Barbara Lanz. I'm pleased to welcome all of you to the Pearson Christmas party. Today, our students are going to show you the school and what we can do. We hope you enjoy yourselves. Thank you for coming."

"C-come on, Jill," Dede said, grabbing her arm. "We go this way w-with Mrs. L-Linner." She pulled Jill toward a tall, dark woman.

"Is she your teacher?"

"Yeh! Sh-she's nice!"

Mrs. Linner led her group of students and parents through some locker rooms to the swimming pool.

"You're lucky!" Jill said. "We don't have a pool at York Falls."

They watched some kids jumping from a low diving board into the water. One after the other, they went off the board like frogs, came bobbing to the surface and swam to the side. At the end of the line, a boy about eight clung to the teacher. "No!" he wailed. He was crying, shaking his head, his tears flying in different directions.

"That's Freddie," Dede said.

"Are they going to make him do it?" Jill said.

"It isn't high."

"But if he doesn't want to..."

"F-Freddie doesn't like water."

"He's so afraid."

"He always does that."

They watched as the other students and teachers crowded around Freddie, trying to talk him into it. After a while, he must have realized there was no way out. He walked to the end of the board. I know how he feels, Jill thought. He jumped off. A teacher was waiting in the water and swam with him to the side.

"You see, Freddie. You can do it!" the teacher said, boosting him out of the water. "That was good!"

"Yeah!" Freddie strutted out to the end of the board again.

☞   XLI

"Let's move on to the workroom," Mrs. Linner said. They followed her along a hallway to an area where different projects were laid out on benches. A couple of students stood by.

"That's Jamal," Dede told Jill, pointing to a thin boy. "H-hi, Jamal! And that's Danielle. Sh-she's my friend. Hi, Danielle!"

Jamal didn't reply, but Danielle said, "Hi, Dede."

Mrs. Linner lined them up so everyone could see the work in progress. "Danielle prints custom-made matchbook covers on this press here," she said. Danielle lifted the printing lever, placed a plain silver cover down on the plate beneath, and then brought the lever down sharply on top of it. She lifted it and picked out the matchbook cover so everyone could see what she had done. The crimson initials stood out on the silver. "Danielle will be glad to fill your orders for Christmas, bar mitzvahs, silver weddings, any festive occasion..." Mrs. Linner smiled. "That's very good, Danielle."

"Jamal here..." Mrs. Linner looked around. Jamal was hiding behind Danielle. "It's okay, Jamal," Mrs. Linner said. She pulled him out gently. "No need to hide— we're all friends today." She looked at her audience. "Jamal has had some unhappy experiences with strangers." The boy stood awkwardly in front of everyone, staring at the floor. He doesn't look retarded, Jill thought. He just looks shy. He must hate everyone staring at him.

"Jamal is a whiz at counting," Mrs. Linner said. "So he counts the matchbook covers for Danielle and packs them into boxes of fifty. He hasn't made a mistake in six months." Jamal smiled at the floor. "Jamal and Danielle will be graduating soon. Then they'll be going to the sheltered workshop every day. They can earn money there doing some of the things they've learned here."

Mrs. Linner led them through the kitchen and supermarket areas and into a classroom where ten little kids were sitting in a circle, singing and clapping their hands. Every time the verse ended, a different child got up, turned around, and said his or her name.

In the middle of the song, a teacher's aide very quietly took one of the kids by the hand and walked out of the room. Bathroom, Jill thought. A while later, they came back. "Hi, Paula," Dede said. The aide led Paula back to her chair and then marked a chart on the wall.

One of the kids began running around. She looked almost like Marla.

Her teacher said, "Sit down, please, Charlene."

Charlene sat down, only in front of one of the others, making faces at him. All the kids started laughing and making faces. The teacher didn't get mad. But she picked Charlene up off the floor like a doll and popped her into a big cardboard box in the corner so tall that she disappeared. Jill gasped. She waited for howls from the box. But there wasn't a sound.

☞ XLII

Mrs. Linner beckoned the group out of the room.

"Charlene hasn't been here very long," she said. "When she came to us, she'd been very spoiled—everyone at her home did everything for her and she's used to being the center of attention. She's learning not to disturb the class but some-times she forgets." She smiled at Jill. "Don't worry. Her teacher will take her out in a minute, as soon as she settles down."

Jill turned. "Dede..."

Mrs. Atkins said, "She's gone to change. We'll catch up with her in the gym."

The gym was full of students dressed in gym suits. The gym teacher blew his whistle. "I want to explain to our visitors that we are training for the Special Olym-pics in the spring, a day of sports events for the handicapped. Everyone can go— the idea is to take part—but we try to do the best we can by training hard. To help us, we're lucky enough to have a group of sixth graders from Kellingford Middle School to work with our students."

Jill stared at the helpers. They were only a year older than she was. Imagine coming to a place like this and working with the kids! They were like...profes-sionals.

The helpers were grinning and fooling around with the students. They didn't look a bit scared of them. I would be, she thought. I'd be scared to death to try to teach them anything. Well...not Dede, of course...but then I know her, so that's different.

The gym teacher spoke again. "The first thing we'll do is run to the wall at the end of the gym and back again." He blew his whistle and the kids began running. Some went fine. Some fell down. Some didn't move.

"Come on, Margaret. You can run!" a helper urged. Margaret stood still, frowning. "I'll hold your hand and we'll run together," the helper said. Margaret shook her head. Another helper said, "I know what she wants. She wants us to swing her, like last time!" Margaret smiled. Holding hands, the three of them began to run along together and, when they got going fast enough, the two helpers swung Margaret up between them, while she laughed and cried, "Again!"

"Now, pay attention!" the gym teacher said. "You're going to start out running. But when I blow my whistle, you're going to stop and crouch. Then when I blow again, you're going to get up and start running again. Okay. Let's try that!" He blew his whistle. Some of the kids ran. But some crouched instead of running. One boy near Jill began to cry. Jill thought, He doesn't know which to do. But his helper said, "It's okay, Carlos. That's hard. We'll practice it together." The boy stopped crying.

"Next, we're going to roll along the floor," the teacher called. He demonstrated by getting down on the floor himself and everyone laughed as he rolled over and over like a log in water. Some of the kids were rolled along by their helpers because they couldn't do it by themselves.

Jill was watching some kids clustered around a girl lying on the floor. "Roll, Dawn!" they said. She shook her head and jammed her thumb into her mouth. The teacher came up. "Hey, Dawn, you sunbathing or something?" In a moment he had her laughing and on her feet. He didn't make her roll and Jill was glad. "Dawn says she'll try for me later," the teacher said. He patted her shoulder and turned to help a girl whose student was stamping his foot and screaming. "Rob, no!" he said, sharply. "You must not do that! Bad!" A sixth grader near Jill whispered, "Rob bites when he gets mad." She sounded matter-of-fact about it.

Her friend said, "I'd be scared to work with him."

"I know. So would I. But Irene really loves him. She visits him at the home. His family never goes to see him."

"It's hard for him," Mrs. Atkins said. "He feels mad inside and he doesn't know how to tell anyone. The teachers understand. But they have to help him manage his feelings."

Jill looked back at Rob. He was crying now. The gym teacher and Irene were both hugging him.

Where is Dede? Jill thought suddenly. She looked from one face to the other and finally found her at the other end of the gym, being guided backward by her helper. When they got to Jill's end, they picked up a ball and Dede started shooting baskets. She made four out of six.

"I never knew she could do that! She's good!"

"Yes. She's not bad. Considering." Mrs. Atkins looked pleased.

"She's not bad, period!"

The boy with the cup-handle ears stood in front of them.

"Hi, Mrs. Atkins," he said. "How are you today?"

"Just fine, thank you, Donald," Mrs. Atkins said, as if she hadn't spoken to him earlier.

He came to Jill. "Hi. How are you today?"

"Er...just fine, thank you, Donald."

☞　XLIII

Jill sat with Dede and Debbie in the lunchroom and realized she wasn't feeling afraid any more. She felt welcome. More than that. She felt...important to them.

"We'll be leaving soon, kids," Mrs. Atkins said.

"I have to sh-show Jill something," Dede said. She coughed harshly.

Mrs. Atkins looked worried. "Don't be long then. I'd like to get you home." She started picking up empty glasses and plates.

"I have to sh-show Jill s-something." Dede pulled Jill out of the room. They went along the corridor and down some stairs to a lower floor.

In a dim storeroom, a row of clay pots stood on a shelf.

"There!" Dede said.

"What are they?"

"Flowers. They're fl-flowers." She sneezed.

"Bless you," Jill said, looking at the pots. They were filled nearly to the top with earth. Poking up out of each one was a rough brown cone, a clumsy dead-looking thing. "Dede...are you sure? I mean, they don't look like flowers to me."

"The fl-flower's inside."

"Dede, is anyone...helping you with them? I...I don't think they're even alive, Dede. Look at them. They're all..."

"I'm growing them. J-just me. And n-nobody knows but you. I p-planted them in October. I'm w-watering them and taking c-care of them. I know there's a flower inside."

CHAPTER FIFTEEN

Jill tramped down the front walk. The New Year's snow squeaked underfoot and the wind tore her breath away. To think there was warm sun shining in California!

Halfway down Dede's block, Jill stopped. An ambulance was standing at the curb, and two men were heading into the Atkins' house carrying a stretcher.

Horrified, Jill began running, her breath coming in painful gasps. "Dede!"

When she got there, Dede was being brought out, wrapped in a cocoon of blankets. Her eyes were glittering and her face shone with perspiration. She was breathing in short, sharp, little breaths.

Mrs. Atkins came down the steps carrying an overnight bag. "Jill! Dede has pneumonia. She's had it before. Once she gets a cold.... She doesn't have any resistance."

"Mrs. Atkins! Oh! Tell her...tell her I'll take care of Barney for her." The ambulance drove away.

Jill walked home, thinking and worrying about Dede. Later, at home, she stared at the fire while her brothers talked about the big football games and her parents tried to rest.

"I want you kids to help your mother all you can. She's pretty uncomfortable at this point and getting ready for the holidays kind of took it out of her. And you know, waiting for this baby is quite a strain on her."

"We'll pitch in, Dad," Tom said.

"I can do all the cleaning," Larry said. "I'm getting my system down pretty good."

"Don't worry," Jill said. "We'll take care of her. Everything's going to turn out okay." She was as sure of that baby as Dede was of her flowers, curled up in the dark and growing toward the light.

Suddenly, she turned to her father. "I want to ask you a favor."

Dad spread his arms wide. "Ask me anything!"

Jill explained about Dede's bulbs. "She's so sure they're going to flower. But they won't, because she won't be there to water them...Dad, I want to go to Pearson tomorrow to get them. I've just figured out how you could do it on your lunch hour. I get out of social studies at eleven-seventeen, and I don't have another class until twelve because of lunch and recess. We can make it. You'll just have to give me a note...Okay?"

* * *

Tuesday morning the air was like crystal. Jill ran down her steps just as Karen came up the street.

"Hey, Karen! Did you have a good time at your cousins'?"

"Fantastic! There were eight of us kids there and we skated every day. I've gotten really good. Look, there's Marla."

"Oh. She must've come home last night."

"She did. She called me. Hi, Marla."

"Hi, Karen," Marla said. Jill smiled. "Hi, Marla."

"Hi."

"I didn't know you were back."

"I called my friends."

☞   XLIV

"Oh. Say, listen, Marla, I really am sorry I had to miss your show...Karen and Connie told me you were...fabulous."

"You don't have to say that. I got the picture. You had more important things to do."

"Marla...I explained all that in my Christmas card."

"Really? Did you send me a Christmas card?"

"You know I did. A ballerina dancing near a Christmas tree."

"I may have seen it. It's hard to remember one particular card. I've been getting such a lot of mail. Karen, didn't we have an absolutely fabulous time?"

"Yes…fabulous." Karen looked uncomfortable.

Jill tried again. "I told you I couldn't help it."

"Sure. As my grandma said at the time, it was your loss, not mine! Come on, Karen."

Jill let them go.

* * *

At eleven-thirty the car headed up the hill to Pearson.

"I'll wait outside for you, Jilly."

"Dad, you have to come in with me," Jill said. "They'll pay more attention to me if you're there. Anyway, I can't carry all the pots by myself. I think there were six."

"Well, okay."

"What's the matter?"

"It's just…I've never been in a place like that before…"

☞   XLV

Jill grinned. "You'll do just fine, Dad. Just fine!"

At the desk, they asked for Mrs. Linner.

"She's on her lunch break. I'll see if I can find her," the receptionist said. They waited by the desk.

"Hi. How are you today?" a deep, slow voice said.

Dad turned. "Oh…er…um…"

Jill said, "Just fine, thank you, Donald. How are you today?"

"Just fine, thank you." Donald walked on down the hall.

"Say, Jill. You seemed right at home with that boy."

"I know him. That's what it takes."

In a moment, Mrs. Linner appeared. "Yes?"

"I'm Jill Harvey and this is my dad. We're friends of Dede Atkins."

"Yes?"

"Well…You know Dede's in the hospital and she's been growing some flowers here at school and…and we came to pick them up. She might miss seeing them bloom if she's out of school for a while."

"I'm afraid you're mistaken, Jill. We're not growing anything at present. We'll be doing that in the spring."

"She is. She showed them to me at the Christmas party. I know where they are."

"My goodness—by herself? How did she…" Mrs. Linner smiled. "Well, you'd better show me their hiding place."

Down in the storeroom, the pots stood in their peaceful twilight.

Mrs. Linner switched on the light.

Jill flinched from the glare and then ran to the bulbs. "She did it! Look at them! Oh, I'm so glad we came, Dad!"

The bulbs had broken open. Pale green tips reached up toward the light from five of the six brown shells.

"I'm amazed she was able to carry out this project on her own. She had no help whatsoever?" asked Mrs. Linner.

"No."

"Wonderful! We have noticed she's gained confidence in the last few months. She has made great strides."

☞   XLVI

They carried the pots upstairs.

"Hi, Babe!" Debbie was standing by the desk.

"Hi, Debbie," Jill said.

"Wh-what you got?"

"Dede's flowers."

"I don't see no flowers."

"The flowers are inside, Debbie."

On the way home, Dad said, "You get along with those kids, don't you?"

"I guess so. I was even thinking...well, maybe next year...when I'm in sixth grade, I might work up there sometimes. They need kids like me to help kids like them."

"That's a nice idea, Jilly."

He speeded up. "I'm due back. We'd better drop these off quickly, then I'll take you on to school."

Jill set down one of the pots and rang Dede's doorbell. No answer. "Mrs. Atkins is out, Dad. Shall I just leave them on the porch?"

"Yes. I'll bring up the others." Dad climbed the porch steps. "She's probably at the hospital. Why don't you leave a note?" He pulled a pencil and an old envelope out of his pocket.

Jill took them and wrote: *Mrs. Atkins, these are some flowers Dede was growing at Pearson. Maybe you could take one to the hospital to make her feel better. She's been waiting for them to bloom. Love, Jill.*

CHAPTER SIXTEEN

Jill jogged all the way home from school. It's a good way to keep warm, she thought. And I won't have to listen to Marla. She let herself in the house quietly, in case Mom was napping.

"Jilly! Thank goodness you're home!" Mom stood at the top of the stairs, looking scared.

"Why? What's the matter?"

"Jill..." Mom came down the stairs carefully. "I called your dad. But he's out of the office. Honey, I...I think the baby's coming."

"The baby? But…it's not February…it can't…it's not time yet!"

"I know. But I woke up all of a sudden with a contraction. And then I had another. I thought…I thought they'd go away, but they haven't, Jilly. They're coming faster…" She clutched Jill's arm. "I'm frightened, Jilly. It's too soon. Oh, I knew something would happen…"

"Momma! What should I do? Do you want to lie down? I'll call Dad again…No, the doctor! Or the hospital? Mom…don't…you…you're not going to right away, are you?"

When the ambulance came, Jill was throwing Mom's toothbrush and night-gown into a suitcase.

"Did you get through to your father?" Mom was looking lost and scared. "I want him. I want Joe. The baby's too early. It's going all wrong…"

"He's still out. They're looking for him. He's in one of the other mills, they think."

"Jilly, I…"

Jill put her arm around her. "It's going to be okay, Mom. I have this feeling…honest…You're going to be fine and the baby's going to be fine…"

"I want to think so. But things aren't the way they should be…Oh, where's Joe? I don't want to be there alone."

"He'll come. And I'll go with you."

The ambulance men brought in a stretcher and carried Mom out of the house. Jill took the suitcase and climbed in the back and they pulled away. She remembered the driver. He had come for Dede.

"Hold on, little momma," the other man said. "We'll get you there in time."

It was the smoothest ride she'd ever had, but at even the tiniest bump, Mom winced. It seemed to take forever—the baby working away to be born and all of them willing it to hold back. But, finally, the ambulance slid up to the emergency entrance and they whisked Mom inside.

"Tell them at the desk we've taken her right up," the man said to Jill.

The nurse at the desk told Jill she had to wait downstairs in the lobby. Jill was watching for Dad. She flipped through a magazine without seeing the pages. She looked at the shiny floor and the shiny chairs and the shiny tables. She had to go to the bathroom, but didn't dare leave her chair in case she missed him. She checked the clock. Two hours had gone by…

"Jill! What are you doing here?" She jumped. Mrs. Atkins sat down beside her. "You know, they won't let you see Dede, honey."

She'd forgotten Dede was upstairs somewhere, too.

"I'm waiting for my dad. Mom's here."

"Not the baby? But I thought…"

"It's early, Mrs. Atkins. That's bad, isn't it?"

Jill could see Mrs. Atkins didn't want to admit it. She patted Jill's arm. "Oh, not dangerously early, honey," she said. "What is it? Three weeks? A month? Of course…it'd be better if it had waited…"

Jill stiffened. "It's six weeks early."

Mrs. Atkins said quickly, "Six weeks? That's nothing. All I meant was...well, the baby would be just a bit bigger and stronger...but I'm sure it'll be okay. Lots of babies come early...they don't read the books!"

Jill tried to smile. "Uh...how's Dede? I left something for her on your porch."

"That's nice of you, honey." She frowned. "This is the third time she's had pneumonia. I try to be careful—keep her wrapped up and all—but she's so delicate..."

That seemed weird, calling Dede delicate.

Mrs. Atkins went on, "You know, kids who have Down's syndrome used to die young, taken off by pneumonia or other diseases—they just couldn't resist infection. Thank heaven for antibiotics! But Dede's lungs have been damaged and this climate is wearing her down." She leaned back and closed her eyes. "I've got to take her away. Somewhere warm, dry."

"A vacation would do her good."

"I don't mean a vacation. I mean—move."

Jill stared. "Leave here for good?"

Mrs. Atkins opened her eyes. "That's right. I've made up my mind. I'm going to pack up and take her to Arizona just as soon as she's well enough to go. We can stay at my mother's place till we find a place of our own. She'll do better in the sun there..."

"But...how can you just go like that?"

"I can. It's only a question of doing it. I've put it off too long already and Dede's health has suffered." She blew her nose. "Well, I always thought it'd be hard on Dede, moving, having to start over again in a new place, new school, trying to find friends. She has a happy life here. Her teachers are fine people and they've taught her so much and then you came along and she loves you so..."

Jill couldn't say anything. It was too sudden. She felt mixed up. Sure, it'd be good for Dede. But Dede would miss her. And she'd miss Dede, too. And old Barney, Squeak's buddy.

* * *

"Jilly!" Dad ran across the lobby. "What happened? Is Mom okay?"

"I don't know. They took her up ages ago."

He hurried over to the desk.

Mrs. Atkins said, "I'll be on my way home now your dad is here. Do you want to come home with me?"

Jill shook her head.

Mrs. Atkins said, "Call me if you need anything, Jill." She touched her shoulder and left.

Jill sat tense in her chair, her eyes fixed on Dad. The nurse had picked up the phone. After a moment, she put it down and he leaned forward. Then his shoulders slumped.

"It can't be! It's not fair!" Jill remembered the sturdy little thumps against her hand long ago. I don't believe it, she thought. She ran to her father.

Dad turned slowly and there were tears running down his cheeks. "Jilly!" He choked and held her tight. "Oh, Jilly."

"But I was so sure!"

He held her away from him. "No, Jilly! No! You were right! Don't they always say faith moves mountains? Your mother and the baby are both okay!"

CHAPTER SEVENTEEN

Barney barked his welcome as Jill stamped snow off her boots.

"Your jacket's really wet, Jill," Mrs. Atkins said. "Can you stay a minute? I'll hang it in the laundry room to dry." She led Jill into the den. "I'll get back to work. The house is on the market, you know, and I think I've got a buyer. I've been packing up the books and the good china. We'll be out in that Arizona sunshine pretty soon, won't we, Dede?"

☞ XLVII

"Yeh." Dede coughed.

"Are you feeling better today, Dede?" Jill asked.

"Yeh." Dede smiled, but she looked very tired.

"What do you want to do?" Jill asked.

"I don't know."

"We could watch TV if you like...or make some cookies..."

"Yeh."

"Hey—how are your bulbs doing?"

Dede's face brightened. "I'll sh-show you." She led the way upstairs.

"Dede!" Jill gasped as they came into Dede's bedroom. The bulbs were ranged along the windowsill, a blaze of pink and white and blue. The whole room was filled with cool fragrance.

"What are they?" Jill asked.

"They're f-flowers."

"I mean...what kind?"

"Hyacinths," Mrs. Atkins answered, coming into the room behind them. "Dede must've found them in the toolshed. I was planning to plant them last fall but I forgot all about them."

"They took such a long time to bloom, though," Jill said. "October to February. I don't know if I could wait that long."

"They're s-slow," Dede said. "The f-flower's inside."

Mrs. Atkins smiled at Dede. "Some things are worth waiting for, aren't they?"

* * *

Jill worked the baby carriage carefully along the sidewalk. The wheels balked in the slush, but the baby slept on, snuggled under her blankets. Jill leaned down to touch little Faith every now and then—make sure she was breathing. She couldn't explain how she felt—people would probably laugh at her if they knew—but it filled her with awe that they'd been given a living, working baby, and that something so small could be so complete, that each tiny finger had a tiny fingernail, that the hair was growing, and the delicate fan of lashes shaded eyes that cried and smiled and turned to watch the world around her.

Squeak trotted beside them, pulling harder as they got closer to Dede's. The moving truck was already parked outside. Jill stopped the baby carriage and watched the procession of things disappearing through the gaping doors at the back. Dede was nowhere around. She still had to stay indoors.

Karen's brother John got off his bike to watch the movers. So did some other kids and neighbors. Jill, refusing to join the watchers, headed home.

As she carried Faith in, she heard Mom singing in the kitchen. Mom just about never stopped singing these days. But Jill didn't feel happy and didn't want to be with someone who was. She put Faith in her crib and then stretched out on her bed and stared at the snow beginning again, driven by the wind that was driving Dede away. In a few hours, Dede's house would be just as empty as Mrs. Lacey's and Dede just as surely gone out of her life. Funny I should feel so bad about it now, she thought. In the beginning, she hadn't even wanted to know Dede and, in lots of ways, things would be easier without her around. So why did she have this empty feeling inside?

She tried to read, but she couldn't. Faith stirred in her crib and began to cry. Jill went in and picked her up, cradling her against her shoulder. She held her long after she'd stopped crying and walked to the window. Mrs. Atkins and Dede could grow a garden full of flowers in Arizona, she thought. But would she find someone to show them to? Or would the kids in Arizona make fun of her and tease her and after a while ignore her so they wouldn't have to be bothered with her? Jill turned from the window and held Faith closer.

☞   XLVIII

She heard the doorbell ring. Mom called up the stairs, "Come down, Jilly. Dede and her mother are here to say good-bye."

Everyone stood around smiling and saying all the same old things, like "Have a good trip!" and "Boy, I wish I was going to Arizona!" They were just things to say to fill the time…Jill and Dede stood in the middle of all the cheerful talk as if they were alone. Dede didn't seem to understand she wouldn't see Jill again, that she was going away for good. She didn't know what lay ahead of her.

Suddenly, Jill was hugging Dede hard. Words wouldn't come. Dede said, "It's okay. It's okay." She knew what Jill was saying. Good-bye. Take care. I love you.

* * *

Jill stood on the sidewalk waving the car out of sight.

Marla came up the block. "Who're you waving at?" she asked.

Jill turned. "Dede. She just left for Arizona."

"Oh, that's right. I heard they were going."

Jill tried to speak lightly around the lump in her throat. "I know it sounds weird…but I'm going to miss her."

"No kidding? You really will? You know, I never could figure why you liked her so much. I mean…like, she's pretty strange. You have to admit that. And she doesn't know anything about anything."

There was a silence.

Jill said slowly, "Dede Atkins may never be a ballerina—but she knows more about being a friend than anyone else I know."

☞   XLIX

CHARLIE'S HOUSE
by Clyde Robert Bulla

STORY SYNOPSIS — Set in the eighteenth century, this story focuses on a poor English boy who is tricked into becoming an indentured servant in America. Finally, he escapes from being the "personal serving boy" of a seven-year-old girl on a plantation in Carolina.

OBJECTIVES — In hearing and discussing Clyde Robert Bulla's *Charlie's House*, children will be afforded the opportunity to stretch and clarify their thinking on such important ethical problems as the limits of individual responsibility. Children will also be given a glimpse of the problems and choices of young people who lived in other times.

TIME — This story is short enough to be read and discussed in about four forty-five-minute sessions.

HOMEWORK — I have grouped possible homework assignments at the end. You can decide whether to use them during the story or after it.

PROCEDURE — This is a story full of surprises and intense involvement for children. Read it as dramatically as possible.

DISCUSSION AND HOMEWORK QUESTIONS

The Way the World Is

 I

Pause for what will be children's shocked reaction. Also, be sure they understand that it was a horse-drawn wagon used in that time which ran over Charlie.

 II

Pause to be sure the children understand what the mother means about silk and owning land.

Master Minton

 III

You might need to explain that Charlie is a poor boy in an England totally ruled by social class. The comparison with our values of individual worth and open opportunity is upsetting and interesting to children. Depending on the group, this highlighting of another society's values is worthwhile.

☞ IV

I think you should not hesitate to "ham it up" here.

Something Better

☞ V

You can mention that this was true. Even children could be hanged or otherwise severely punished in that time.

Captain Beezy

☞ VI

* *Should* Charlie trust Fred?

* In general, if someone asks, "Do you trust me?" should that make you suspicious?

The Bond

☞ VII

Pause for the children's reactions.

☞ VIII

* *Did* Fred really do Charlie a favor? Why or why not?

    After all, Charlie had very few options for himself, and he might very well have chosen to make himself an indentured servant in America.

* What would have made the contract an ethical one?

    Most children are quick to perceive that it would have been ethical if Fred Coker had *told* Charlie about what he was doing.

* But what if this turns out to be the best possible thing for Charlie?

    You will probably get the response, "He still should have told him!"

These are engaging ethical questions for children because they touch on issues of how people with more power or status *should* treat those with less and resonate with their own experience vis-a-vis the adult world. The value of fully respecting another person is clarified.

There is also the important point that intention matters. Fred's *intention* was to use Charlie for his own profit, therefore Fred was unethical regardless of the results for Charlie.

A New Home

 IX

I often reach over and (asking permission) demonstrate on the chin of a nearby child to illustrate in a tiny way the indignities of slavery.

A Game of Cards

 X

* What do you think of Master Greer?

 XI

Pause to allow for the children's shock and outrage.

* Were the Chapmans more or less wrong because they seemed kind and originally treated Charlie well?

Sometimes children may offer that Master Chapman seemed drunk and that perhaps that excused his action. I am emphatic about this: drunkenness is no excuse for such a serious action! Master Chapman would never have "lost" his own son or nephew in a card game!

Willow Bend

 XII

Pause to be sure that the children understand that Charlie is now at Master Greer's plantation.

 XIII

* Why does Charlie feel sick?

 XIV

Pause for the children's reactions.

The Tea Party

 XV

Pause for children's reactions.

 XVI

Give the children a chance to react.

Children, hearing the story, become ever more excited, exclaiming, "She's *spoiled!*" Now the class discussion questions become very difficult:

☀ Whose fault or responsibility is it that Miss Dessa is so obnoxious?

Children will say, "Her father's! He spoiled her!"

☀ Whose responsibility or fault would it be if she were twenty-five instead of seven?

Now they are a little uncertain, but will answer that at that age it's her own fault.

☀ Well then, what if she's twenty? fifteen? ten? (the actual age of most of the class) How do you decide?

These are clearly vexing questions. The teacher should freely acknowledge that such issues of individual responsibility have been solved only arbitrarily or provisionally by any of us, but they are very important to think about.

☞ XVII

☀ Why does Charlie prefer the hard field work to serving Miss Dessa? Would you?

"Thank You, Miss Dessa"

☞ XVIII

Enjoy "hamming it up" as the obnoxious (this is a favorite word of children) Dessa.

☞ XIX

Allow for children's reactions, which will be strong.

Three Men

☞ XX

☀ Why do you think Norrie helps Charlie?

The Whip

☞ XXI

Be sure the children understand the cruelty of Master Greer's friends.

The River

☞ XXII

Be sure the children understand that Charlie was very sick and delirious.

Drogo

☞ XXIII

✳ Why can't Drogo just leave?

☞ XXIV

Be sure that the children understand that Charlie will be able to grow a beard and look quite different in a few years, and because his skin is white, people won't automatically assume he's an escaped slave.

☞ XXV

I think it is important to make the point to the class that for Drogo and the other runaway slaves there at Black Swamp, there was really no escape. It would be a full hundred years after the end of the story before slavery was abolished in America, and another hundred years before the struggle for civil rights and an end to racial segregation began.

Homework Assignments

Here follow some sample homework questions for *Charlie's House*:

✳ In *Charlie's House*, Fred Coker made a deal to get Charlie to America. What made this deal unethical? What made it ethical (if anything)? If you yourself made a deal, for someone's own good, should you always explain it to the person? Why or why not? If Fred's deal had ended up very well for Charlie, would that have made it ethical? Explain.

✳ Most people would say that it's her father's fault that Miss Dessa is a "spoiled brat," but if she were just a few years older, they would say it's her own fault. Why? How do you decide? If she does something unethical, should her father be punished along with her (if he could be)? Why? If she does something wonderfully kind, who should get the credit or praise? Why?

✳ In the story, *Charlie's House*, there are several difficult ethical problems. For instance, there is the problem of whether the Chapmans were good to Charlie, whether it was Miss Dessa's fault (or her father's) that she was so obnoxious, whether Charlie was right to run away. Choose the problem that you think is most interesting and explain its ethics, both good and bad. (You may pick a different ethical problem from the whole story if you wish.) Remember to use complete sentences.

✳ After the end of *Charlie's House*, imagine that Charlie lived a few years in Black Swamp, grew up, and made his fortune as a free man. Which character in the book would you have him go back to? What should he say? Why?

(This is a good assignment as children often react with frustration when the story ends. They want to find out what happens to Charlie.)

CHARLIE'S HOUSE————————————————
by Clyde Robert Bulla*

THE WAY THE WORLD IS

Charlie Brig was born near the town of Durford, England, in the year 1736. He lived on a farm with his mother, father, and ten brothers and sisters. They farmed the land for Master Minton. The farm was stony and poor, and Master Minton took most of what they raised.

When Charlie was eight years old he went to Durford with two of his older brothers. He had never been to town before, and there he saw something that was a great wonder to him. He saw some men building a house.

He had never thought much about houses. They were just there, like rocks or hills or trees. Now he saw how the floors and walls were made to fit together. He saw how the roof went on. After that day he looked at houses to see how they were built. He asked questions about doors and windows.

No one answered him. His brothers and sisters began to jeer when he talked about houses, and his father told him to "sing another tune." Then he knew he had said too much and made himself look foolish.

Charlie's father had never liked him. Neither had his brothers and sisters. He thought it was because of the way he looked. His hair curled and his eyes were blue. All his brothers and sisters had straight hair and gray eyes.

Sometimes he thought his mother liked him, but he was not sure. She worked from morning till night and had little time for him.

One day he wandered off to town. He wanted to see how the house looked now.

It was finished, with people living in it. He remembered it with the walls open and sky showing through the roof. He smiled as if he and the house were friends, as if they had a secret.

As he was starting home, he fell in the muddy street, and a wagon ran over him. He was pressed into the mud. Except for that, he might have been killed. As it was, he was badly hurt.

"So you had to go off to town and get yourself run over," said his father. "Now you'll be just another mouth to feed and never any use again."

☞   I

Charlie could not walk. Day after day he sat in a chair and looked out the window. A little girl named Polly lived down the road, and she came to see him. She brought him things she thought were pretty—a bird's nest and bits of ribbon and small stones.

He asked her if she could find him a knife and some pieces of wood. She brought them to him.

* *Charlie's House* by Clyde Robert Bulla, copyright ©1983 HarperCollins Publishers, reprinted by permission of the publisher.

Then he asked for reeds from the river and some of the tough, dry grass that grew by the roadside. He asked for bark from the dead oak tree across the road.

She brought everything he asked for. She watched him cut the bark and reeds and weave them together with the grass. And one day he had made a little house.

It was so neat, so pretty, with its doors and windows, its roof and tiny chimney, that she could not look at it enough. Charlie liked to look at it, too.

"I could make a better one now," he said.

"We'll have no more of that," said his father.

Because Charlie was getting well. He was able to stand again, and as soon as he could walk, he was put to work.

Before long he could walk and work as well as ever. There was no more time for play, but he thought about the little house—he had given it to Polly—and he wished he might make another one.

He told his mother, "I could build a real house if I had the land to build it on."

"I could make a silk dress if I had the silk," she said, and she looked at him with tired eyes. "Listen to me. You'll never have a piece of land with your own house on it."

☞   II

"Why not?" he asked.

"Because you are poor," she answered. "You were born poor, and poor you'll stay. That's the way the world is."

MASTER MINTON

By the time Charlie was twelve, he had grown strong and tall. He was already the tallest in the family.

This did not seem to please his father. "No doubt you think yourself a man," he said. "You'll find there's more to it than standing tall and having a proud walk."

Charlie asked his mother, "Do I have a proud walk?"

"Yes, you do," she said. "You hold your head too high."

"It isn't because I am proud," said Charlie. "It's the way my head sets on my neck."

"You must learn to keep your head down," she told him.

"Why must I?" he asked.

"Because a poor boy has no right to hold up his head," she said. "You don't watch your tongue, either. Sometimes you talk when you should listen."

☞   III

He tried to remember what she said. He kept his head down. He watched his tongue.

But one day he forgot.

Master Minton had come for the rent.

"I can't pay," said Charlie's father.

"So—you can't pay," said Master Minton. "How do you expect to live on my land if you can't pay?"

He let his eyes wander about the farm. He looked at the pigs in the sty, the chickens and geese in their pens, the horse and the cows in the pasture. "The horse looks the best of the lot," he said. "I'll have him."

Charlie's father looked down at his shoes and said nothing.

Charlie spoke. "If you take our horse, how can we plow? If we can't plow, how can we raise a crop? If we can't raise a crop, how can we *ever* pay the rent?"

Master Minton gave no sign that he had heard. "I'll have the horse," he said, "and one of the cows as well."

He drove away with the horse and the cow tied to the back of his wagon.

Charlie's father turned on Charlie. He began to shout.

Charlie's mother came running. "What has he done?" she asked.

☞ IV

"He spoke up to Master Minton!" shouted Charlie's father. "Master Minton was going to take the horse. Then he took the cow as well, and all because—Charlie—spoke up—to him!"

His breath was short. His face had turned red. He sat down suddenly upon the ground.

Charlie tried to help him up. His father struck at him. "Don't you put a hand on me!" he said.

"Keep away from him—go!" whispered Charlie's mother, and Charlie went off down the road.

He stayed in the field the rest of the day. When evening came, he went home. His mother was out by the gate, as if she had been waiting for him.

"You can't stay," she said. "Your brothers are looking for you. They're going to pay you back for what you did to your father."

"What did I do?" he asked.

"He's in bed—he can't move. When you spoke up the way you did, it was too much for his heart. If your brothers catch you, who knows *what* they might do? Charlie, you have to go."

"Where shall I go?" he asked.

"*I* don't know. Just go."

"And not come back?"

"Maybe—maybe you'll find something better...." She looked away. She said, "Why did you have to do it?"

"I didn't—" he began, and she gave him a hard little push.

He went down the road. He walked quietly so that his brothers would not hear him if they were waiting in the dark.

SOMETHING BETTER

Charlie walked toward Durford. Except for home, it was the only place he knew.

But what was there for him in Durford? And wouldn't his brothers look for him there?

When he came to the town, he went on through its dark streets without stopping. He had a new plan. He would go to London.

The great city was a long way off—a hundred miles, he had heard people say. But once he was there, wonderful things might happen.

"Something better," his mother had said. In London there *must* be something better.

He was four days getting there. He walked more than half the way. A man in a cart gave him a ride into London, gave him half a loaf of bread and three turnips, besides.

The sun had set when they came into the city. The man let Charlie down and drove away.

Charlie looked up and down. There were people everywhere. Where had they come from? Where did they live, and how?

There were the rich, on horseback or in coaches. There were the poor in their poor clothes. Some were begging. He saw that there were many more poor than rich.

He walked about until he was tired. He found a dark doorway, and there he slept that night.

In the morning he was back on the streets. By daylight he could see how dirty and ugly they were. He came to houses where food was sold. Women and men were calling, "Pies, pies—beef and pork! Get your hot pies here!"

Charlie was so hungry, the smell of food brought tears to his eyes. He thought of seizing a pie and running with it. But a boy could be hanged for less.

☞   v

He went into a house where a woman was taking pies out of an oven.

"Will you give me one of those?" he asked. "I'll work for it."

"Better go wash yourself," said the woman.

A man came out of the back room.

"What's this?" he said, and threw Charlie into the street.

Charlie almost fell. He caught hold of a lamp post and leaned against it.

A man walked past. He stopped and came back. He was fairly young, with a round, smooth face, and he wore good clothes.

"What's the matter?" he asked. "Are you sick?"

"I—I—" Charlie looked toward the food house.

"Hungry?" asked the man.

Charlie nodded.

"Just come from the country?"

Again Charlie nodded.

"Are you alone here?"

"Yes," said Charlie.

"Where are you staying?"

"Nowhere."

"What is your name?"

"Charlie Brig."

"Mine is Fred Coker," said the man. "Come along, Charlie."

CAPTAIN BEEZY

They went into another food house. This one had tables and chairs. They sat at a table.

"I've got no money," said Charlie.

"I'll pay," said Fred.

Charlie ate two pies and washed them down with tea. He was still hungry, but he was ashamed to say so.

Fred asked him, "What do you think of the city?"

"Not much," answered Charlie. "It isn't the way I thought it would be."

Fred laughed. "You sound like a wise young man. Tell me, what happened to send you off to London?"

Charlie told him.

Afterward they went to Fred's home. It was two rooms in an inn near the London docks. Charlie had a wash. He put on the clean clothes Fred brought him. Then there was more to eat.

All the time, Fred seemed to be thinking.

"So you can't go home," he said.

"No," said Charlie.

"And there's not much for you in London. Boys like you come here by the hundreds. They have nowhere to turn and nothing to do. They get into trouble and they're thrown into jail. You can see that, can't you?"

"Yes," said Charlie.

"You're not like the most of them. I'd say you're a good boy, and you look strong and able to work. Charlie, did you ever hear of America?"

"Yes," said Charlie.

"Ever think of going?"

"To America? No."

"Why not?"

"It's so far."

"No place is far these days," said Fred. "You get on a ship and you go." He began telling Charlie about America. "They need people there. They need them to work the land. You could make a fortune."

"A boy like me could go?"

"They need boys, too. Charlie, I have this friend. He's captain of a ship, and he's off to America any day now. I couldn't promise anything, but—"

"Would he take me, do you think?"

"I don't know. We could go see him. Have you ever been on a ship?"

"No," said Charlie.

"Come along then," said Fred. "Let me do the talking. Just put yourself in my hands. And Charlie—?"

"What?"

"Can you read and write?"

Charlie shook his head.

"That doesn't matter. If there are papers to sign, I'll sign them for you. You trust me, don't you?"

☞ VI

"Yes," said Charlie.

* * *

The ship was in dock, only a few steps from the inn. They went aboard, and the captain greeted them. Captain Beezy was his name. He was a short, wide man with a bald head that shone and a gold tooth that twinkled.

He took them to his cabin. They sat at a tiny table, and the men drank rum and told stories. Charlie did not understand much of the stories, but he liked hearing their voices, and he liked the smoky cabin with its dark wood walls.

After a while he heard Fred laughing and telling him to open his eyes.

Charlie sat up. He was ashamed to think he had fallen asleep.

Captain Beezy said, "Didn't you hear me young man? You and I are shipping out together."

Charlie looked from him to Fred. Fred gave him a wink and nodded. Then Charlie knew. The captain liked him. The captain was going to take him to America!

"The adventures you'll have!" said Captain Beezy.

"A boy like you will make his fortune," said Fred.

Charlie knew he should feel excited and happy. He *was* excited, but he was a little afraid as he thought how quickly all his life was changing.

THE BOND

The name of Captain Beezy's ship was *Four-and-Twenty Blackbirds.* On a fine summer morning she sailed out of London. Fred had not come to say good-bye, and Charlie was sad, since Fred was his only friend.

But the ship was crowded with young men and boys. He was sure he would make friends among them.

Some of them were loud and rough. They laughed at Charlie and called him "country."

One of the boys was a redhead named Flitters. He was near Charlie's age and size. He kept dancing about Charlie and trying to box with him.

"Leave me alone," said Charlie.

"Come on, come on," said Flitters. "Fight like a man."

On deck one day some of the others made a circle around Charlie. They pushed Flitters into the circle.

"Fight!" they said.

There was no way out of it. The two boys fought. While Flitters was dancing and boxing, Charlie knocked him down.

After that, he had an easier time of it. He and Flitters even came to be friends.

Flitters asked him, "How did you get on this ship?"

Charlie told him about Fred.

"I know who he is," said Flitters. "He works for the captain."

"He does?"

"Yes. He gets men and boys to go to America," said Flitters, "and the captain pays him."

☞ VII

Charlie was puzzled. "What does he pay him for?"

"The captain gets a price for everyone he brings to America," Flitters told him. "People in America buy our bonds from the captain."

"What are bonds?" asked Charlie.

"You don't know much, do you? Didn't Fred Coker and the captain sign a paper for you?"

Charlie tried to remember. "I think they did."

"That was your bond. Maybe Fred Coker pretended he was your father or uncle or something, and he signed you over to the captain."

Charlie was more puzzled than ever. "Signed me over—how? What does that mean?"

"It means somebody in America will buy your bond, and then you work for him. You work for seven years."

"Seven years!"

"It's not so bad," said Flitters. "Look at it this way. You'll still be young when it's over, and then the good times start. You get fifty acres of land. Anyway, that's what I get, and I should think you'd get the same. Fifty acres is enough to make a man rich. And there's more besides. You get a new suit of clothes and a shirt and shoes and stockings and a cap. Then you get two hoes and an ax. It's all there in the bond."

"But seven years! It's like—" Charlie stopped.

"Like being a slave? Is that what you mean?"

"Yes," said Charlie.

"There's a difference. We're free in seven years, but a slave goes on being a slave."

Charlie was thinking of Fred. "I thought he was my friend."

"Who? Fred Coker? Maybe he was your friend, after all. Maybe he did you a good turn without knowing it."

☞   VIII

A NEW HOME

In late summer *Four-and-Twenty Blackbirds* sailed into Philadelphia harbor. The voyage to America had taken six weeks. Charlie looked out on the city with its rows of neat houses, both brick and wood, and he longed to set foot on land. He had had his fill of the sea.

As soon as the ship docked, Captain Beezy lined the men and boys up on deck. "Look sharp," he said. "Here come the gentlemen."

Men had been waiting to come aboard. When the plank was down, they came running. Some pushed their way ahead of the others.

"They're going to choose," Flitters told Charlie. "Everybody wants the best."

A man chose Flitters and drew him aside.

Another man stopped in front of Charlie. "What about this one?" he asked Captain Beezy. "Can he put out a good day's work?"

"That he can," said the captain. "You'll make no mistake if you choose him. All muscle he is. And look." He caught Charlie by the chin and pulled his mouth open. "A full set of teeth."

☞   IX

That was how Charlie met George Chapman, the man who bought his bond. He was a quiet man with gray in his hair. He had a slow way of talking that put Charlie at ease. From the first he felt *right* with Master Chapman.

For three days they rode together in Master Chapman's wagon. They rode through the most beautiful country Charlie had ever seen. There were woods and fields and swift little rivers. All across the land, people were going about their work. Everyone looked happy. No one looked poor.

Master Chapman talked as they rode along. Once he showed Charlie a piece of paper with writing on it. It was the bond he had bought from Captain Beezy. "Have you read this?" he asked.

"No, sir," answered Charlie.

"But you know what it means?"

"Some of it."

"You owe me seven years' work. Do you understand that?"

"Yes, sir."

"You're to give me seven years' work, unless you run away. For every time you run away, you must work two years more."

"Yes, sir," said Charlie.

"But you'll not be running away, will you?"

"I shouldn't think so, sir."

"I'll try not to give you cause," said Master Chapman, and he smiled at Charlie.

* * *

They came to the Chapman house. It was a log house set among old elm trees.

A woman came out. She looked at Charlie, and he saw the disappointment on her face.

"This is our boy," said Master Chapman. "Charlie, this is my wife, Mistress Chapman."

"I thought you were going to bring home a man," she said.

"I was slow getting on the ship, and all the men were taken," said Master Chapman. "But I'd have had to pay more for a man. Besides, I liked the look of this boy. I don't think we'll be sorry."

She came closer to the wagon. She was looking into Charlie's face.

"No," she said, "I don't think we *will* be sorry," and she took his hand in hers.

They gave him a long, low room high under the roof. They set a place for him at the table. They gave him new clothes bought in Philadelphia.

That night he lay awake in his room and looked out the window by his bed. He saw the sheds and the road and the trees in the moonlight that was almost as bright as day. And for a little while he thought of his mother and father, his brothers and sisters. He wished they might look in on him now. He wished they might see the home that was his.

A GAME OF CARDS

Most of the Chapman farm was covered with woods. Charlie helped clear the land, to make it ready for the plow. He and Master Chapman cut trees and pulled out stumps. The work was hard and slow, but Charlie was strong and he grew stronger.

He wondered which fifty acres would be his and where he would build his house. He thought often of his house. On a scrap of paper he had drawn a picture of it, and he carried the paper in his pocket.

When he had his own farm, he would still be near the Chapmans, he thought. He would always help them if they needed him.

Charlie came to know the neighbors. He went to barn dances with other young people. He listened to the fiddle music and watched the dancers and pretended he was dancing, too.

When the rivers and ponds froze over, he went to moonlight skating parties. But almost every night he was at home with the Chapmans. Mistress Chapman was teaching him to read and write.

* * *

A visitor came—a man named Oliver Greer. He was Master Chapman's cousin from Carolina. He had come north on business.

He was slim and dark, with a neat, black mustache. He dressed like a gentleman, and he seemed proud of the way he looked.

He thought the Chapmans were much too good to Charlie.

"That boy thinks he's one of the family," he said.

While Master Greer was there, Charlie never ate at the table with the others.

Master Greer gave him work to do, and he never called him by name. "Boy," he would say, "shine my boots. Boy, light my pipe."

☞　x

"Do as he says, Charlie," said Mistress Chapman. "It won't be for long."

But Master Greer stayed on and on. Every night he and Master Chapman sat up, drinking and playing cards.

"I do wish he would go," said Mistress Chapman. "Sometimes I'm so afraid—"

There was a change in Master Chapman. He took to staying in his room all morning. He looked ill. He often stumbled when he walked.

Master Greer had been there almost a month when Mistress Chapman called Charlie into the kitchen. She said, "Master Greer is leaving today."

He thought she would be glad. Instead she began to cry.

Master Chapman came in. His face was gray, and his hands shook. "Charlie, I must talk to you."

"Yes, sir," said Charlie.

"My cousin is going home," said Master Chapman, "and you—you are going with him."

Charlie heard the words, but he did not believe them. He waited.

"You are going with him," Master Chapman said again. "I lost you. I lost you in a game of cards."

☞　XI

"But you—" began Charlie.

Master Chapman turned away from him. "I'm sorry."

"I came to work for *you*," said Charlie. "*You* bought my bond."

"That's true, but Cousin Oliver won it from me. The bond will be the same. You'll still have your land when you've worked for it—only you'll work for him instead." Master Chapman said, "Now go. Cousin Oliver is waiting."

Charlie looked out the window. Master Greer's carriage was in front of the house. Master Greer was standing beside it.

WILLOW BEND

They were two weeks on the road. It was night when Charlie first saw Willow Bend. That was the name of Master Greer's home in Carolina. Charlie had been asleep inside the carriage. Now he woke and saw lights shining behind a row of tall, white pillars.

☞   XII

A girl came running across the porch. She looked no more than seven or eight. "Father!" she cried.

Master Greer jumped down from the driver's seat. He picked the little girl up in his arms. "Dessa, baby! You don't know how I've missed you!"

A man came out of the house. Master Greer spoke to him. "Take the horses."

"Yes, Master," said the man.

The girl was patting her father's pockets. "You brought me something—I know you did!"

"Yes, but not in my pocket. Come here, boy," called Master Greer.

Charlie got out of the carriage. He climbed the steps and stood on the porch.

"Who is he?" asked Dessa.

"You told me you wanted your own serving boy," said her father.

"Is he mine?" she asked.

"Yes, baby," he said.

She looked Charlie up and down. She was frowning, with her lips pushed out.

"Don't you like him?" asked Master Greer.

"I...don't...know," she said.

"You don't need to make up your mind tonight. You can look at him again tomorrow." Master Greer picked her up and carried her into the house.

Charlie stood there. He did not know where to go or what to do. After a while a woman came out. She was old and black, and she had a purple cloth tied about her head.

"Come along," she said.

He followed her inside and up a stairway. She showed him a small, bare bedroom.

"You can sleep there."

She gave him a lighted candle and went away.

Charlie blew out the candle and lay down. The smell of flowers came through the window. It was heavy and sweet. He breathed it and felt sick.

☞   XIII

* * *

In the morning the woman woke him and led him out back. Behind the big house were rows of little houses. One was a bathhouse. She left him there with two young black men.

They washed Charlie's hair. They gave him a bath in a tub of hot water.

Afterward they had clean clothes ready for him to put on. The clothes were some that he had brought from Master Chapman's.

The woman came again and led him into the big house.

"You go in there," she said.

He went into a sunny room where Master Greer and Dessa were having breakfast.

The little girl clapped her hands. "I like him better now," she cried. "I like him *ever* so much better!"

"I hoped you would," said her father.

"I like the way his hair shines." Dessa got up from her chair to look at Charlie. "But his clothes are ugly. I'll have to have something made for him. I'll need a name for him, too."

"He has a name," said her father.

"Has he? What is it? *You* tell me," she said to Charlie. "Speak. What is your name?"

"Charlie Brig," he told her.

"Charlie Brig—Charlie Brig. That's funny." She did a little dance, hopping from one foot to the other. "Oh, it's going to be such fun having someone all my own!"

☞   XIV

THE TEA PARTY

Dessa had clothes made for Charlie—a jacket and short breeches. They were of green silk. She found white stockings for him, and black slippers with silver buckles.

He put on his new clothes. She made him walk up and down for her. She called the other servants to look.

"Isn't he beautiful!" she said. "Now he needs something to wear on Sunday—a white suit, maybe. But isn't he beautiful in the green!"

Charlie was Dessa's own servant. When she went riding, he helped her up on her pony. When she had her meals, he stood behind her chair. Sometimes he carried her dolls from one room to another.

☞   XV

He saw the other servants laughing at him.

Dessa gave a tea party for her dolls. She had a little tea set, with real tea in the pot.

"Pour the tea, Charlie," she said, and he filled the cups.

She took a sip of her tea and made a face. "This is *cold*!" She picked up her riding whip and gave him a cut across the legs with it.

He jumped and dropped the teapot. It broke on the floor.

"You broke it. My best teapot, and you broke it!" She began to scream.

Her father came into the room. "Baby what *is* it?"

"See what he did." She was kicking Charlie and striking at him with her whip.

"I thought you wanted him," said her father. "I thought you liked him."

"Well, I don't," she said. "I hate him!"

☞   XVI

* * *

Again Charlie's life had changed. He was no longer a house servant. He was a field hand.

He lived in one of the tiny houses behind the big house. He hoed in the tobacco fields with the other workers. Most of them were men, but some were women and children, and all were black.

He asked a girl, "Are you a slave?"

She looked frightened, and all she said was, "I don't know."

At first the others left Charlie to himself, but after a few days they seemed to grow used to him. One of the boys began to talk with him as they worked side by side. The boy's name was Norrie. He had bright, black eyes, and he could talk without moving his mouth.

"I know who you are," he said, "and I know why they put you in the field. My mama works in the big house, and she told me."

"I'd rather be here," said Charlie.

☞   XVII

"You don't say!" said Norrie.

"In the field I know what I'm supposed to do. I don't want to go back to the big house."

But field work was hard. The rows were long. The sun beat down on the workers' heads and backs.

Charlie said one day, "I wish I had a drink of water."

"So do I," said Norrie, "but we have to wait till they tell us."

"I'm not going to wait," said Charlie. "When I get to the end of this row I'm going to get myself a drink."

"Where?" asked Norrie.

"Out of the river."

"You don't dare," said Norrie.

"You'll see," said Charlie.

At the end of the row, he slipped under the fence. The river was there, at the edge of the field. He slid down the bank, put his face into the water, and drank. Then he slipped back into the field. He was gone hardly a minute.

Norrie looked scared. "You'll catch it now," he said.

"Are you going to tell?" asked Charlie.

"No, but somebody will," said Norrie, "and you'll wish you'd never been born."

"Why?" asked Charlie.

"When Master comes home, you'll find out."

"Where is Master?" asked Charlie.

"He and Miss Dessa, they went to the city. They went to find a boy to take your place."

* * *

That evening Charlie was sitting in front of his small house.

Norrie came by. "They just got home," he said. "Master and Miss Dessa."

"Did they find another boy?" asked Charlie.

"They looked," said Norrie, "but they couldn't find one to please Miss Dessa. Charlie—"

"What?"

"Master found out about your drink of water."

"Did you tell him?"

"No, but somebody did." Norrie shook his head. "I wouldn't want to be you."

"THANK YOU, MISS DESSA"

Early in the morning there was a meeting in front of the big house. All the field workers and house servants were there.

Master Greer came down the steps. His eyes found Charlie. "You," he said. "Come here."

Charlie stepped forward.

"You left your work yesterday," said Master Greer.

"Not for long, sir." Charlie's throat had gone dry. "I wanted a drink—"

"You left your work!" Master Greer spoke to one of the field workers. "Get him ready."

The man pulled off Charlie's shirt and tied him to a tree.

Master Greer made a speech. "I hope you will all learn something today. This boy has had an easy life. He thinks he can do as he pleases here. Yesterday he broke the rules. This is what happens when you break the rules."

The front door opened. Dessa ran down the steps.

"What are you doing?" she asked.

"Go back inside," said her father.

"Are you going to whip Charlie?"

"This is not for you to see," said Master Greer. "Go back inside."

"I won't! You can't whip Charlie. I won't let you."

"But baby," said her father, "he has to be punished."

"Not unless I say so. He's mine."

"Not any longer. You said you didn't want him."

"I never said it."

"Baby, you *did*."

"If I did, I changed my mind. Let him go."

"I can't—" He stooped as she began to scream. He tried to pick her up in his arms. She beat at him with her fists.

Charlie heard him say something in a low voice. One of the field hands came over to the tree. He untied Charlie and let him go.

* * *

Charlie was back in the big house. He was there with Dessa in the sun room, among the potted plants. She was sitting on the window seat. She was smiling now.

☞   XVIII

"Aren't you glad I took you back?" she asked. "Well, aren't you?…Speak up, Charlie."

"Yes, Miss Dessa," he said.

"Because if I hadn't, you know what would have happened to you."

"Yes, Miss Dessa."

"So you'd better be good. If you're not, I'll give you back to my father." She got up off the window seat. "Come here."

He went to her.

"Kneel down," she said.

He knelt before her.

"Kiss my hand."

He kissed her hand.

"Say, 'Thank you, Miss Dessa.'"

"Thank you, Miss Dessa."

"Say, 'Thank you, Miss Dessa, for saving me.'"

"Thank you, Miss Dessa, for saving me."

"Now you can go to the stable and clean my pony's stall. I don't want you in the house anymore today. Not in those dirty clothes. Have a bath and be sure to wash your hair. In the morning you come in and put on your suit and—Charlie!"

"Yes, Miss Dessa."

Her eyes had grown narrow. "Was that an ugly look I saw on your face?"

"No, Miss Dessa."

"I won't stand for any ugly looks. You'd better remember that. And from now on, you belong to me. You'd better remember that, too."

"Yes, Miss Dessa," he said.

☞   XIX

THREE MEN

Charlie sat on his bed that night. He had opened the door, and coolness came into the little house. It was his last night at Master Greer's. That much he knew. His thoughts had taken him no further.

He had asked himself where he could go. He had thought of Master and Mistress Chapman's. Would they make a place for him, or would they give him back to Master Greer?

He knew the answer. They had given him to Master Greer once, and they would again.

In the Chapman woods there were hiding places. But how could he find his way there? He never could.

Someone came to the doorway and looked in.

"You there?"

It was Norrie.

"Yes," answered Charlie.

Norrie sat down in the doorway. "You going to the big house tomorrow?"

Charlie said nothing.

"My mama says you're going back to the big house. Everybody says so."

"Leave me alone," said Charlie.

"They take you out of the fields and put you back in the big house. You don't like that?"

"Just leave me alone," said Charlie.

Norrie was still for a while. Then he slid a little way into the house. "I saw you at supper," he whispered. "I saw you put the bread in your pocket. Why did you put the bread in your pocket?"

Charlie did not answer.

"You better not do it," said Norrie.

"Do what?"

"What you been thinking about."

"How do you know what I've been thinking?"

"I know. If you run away—"

"I never said I was running away."

"You don't have to *say* it. You listen to me. If you do run away, you don't want to go north."

"Why not?"

"Because they'll catch you. And you don't want to go south or west. They got traps there, too. Charlie—"

"What?"

"The best way to go is east. If you think you have to go, go east to Black Swamp. Nobody can find you there."

☞   xx

* * *

Norrie had gone. Charlie had been waiting. Now the big house was dark and quiet, and he left the little house and closed the door softly.

He went to the stables. He knew Cato, the groom who slept there at night. He called his name.

A sleepy voice answered. "Who is it?"

"It's Charlie."

"Who?"

"Charlie. You know me, Cato. I used to come for Miss Dessa's pony. I'm back in the big house now."

"I know. What you want?"

"Master sent me to fetch the black mare."

"This time of night?"

Charlie had the answer ready. "Master's going night fishing."

Cato made grumbling sounds, but he lighted a lantern and put a saddle and bridle on the black mare. He was beginning to look doubtful.

"Are you sure—?" he began.

"I'll take her," said Charlie.

He led the mare past the big house and into the road. He turned her head to the east. Almost before he was in the saddle, she was off.

He had seen people ride. A few times he had ridden an old mule in from the fields. That was all he knew about riding. He held to the saddle, and the mare took him along.

He could see the road a little way ahead, and he could see a patch of stars low in the sky. He watched the stars.

After a while the mare slowed to a trot, then to a walk. Just before sunrise, he turned off the road and tied her in a thicket. He lay down under a tree to rest and eat a piece of bread he had carried in his pocket.

He thought how far he had come, and he wished he might keep on riding. But the word must be out already—"Watch for a runaway boy on a black mare." Better if he turned her loose and went ahead on foot.

He lay back and looked at the sky. It seemed to swim before his eyes. He was tired, and he could feel himself dropping off to sleep.

He woke with the sun in his eyes. Three men stood before him. He knew who they were. They had often come to the big house to go hunting with Master Greer.

One of them said, "This boy runs away in style."

"Yes," said another. "On Master Greer's mare."

They were laughing. They sounded almost friendly. But when Charlie looked at their faces, he was afraid.

THE WHIP

They played a game with him. They were giving him a chance to go free, they said. They told him to run, and he ran.

One of the men had a long, leather whip. When he snapped it, it reached out like a snake and caught Charlie about the legs. When the man jerked the whip, Charlie fell.

They played the game again and again. Each time Charlie ran a little more slowly. At last he fell and lay still.

☞ XXI

"Run!" the men said, and Charlie felt the whip sting his shoulder, but he did not move.

He heard the men talking.

"Shall we take him in now?"

"No hurry. He won't be going anywhere for a while."

"Is Oliver coming this way?"

"He said he might. We'd better wait."

"Why don't we get the guns? Maybe another flock will come, and then—"

The voices moved away. Charlie heard the sound of guns. The men were firing at something. At birds flying over?

Charlie lifted his head. There were bushes in front of him. He began to crawl toward them.

He reached the bushes. He was hidden in them. He bent low and tried to run, but he was slow. In another moment he would be missed. The men would be after him, and he could not outrun them.

He looked for a place to hide.

Just ahead was a stream with a tangle of roots along its bank. He slid down into the water. It was not deep.

He crouched in the shadow of the bank. He pulled some floating sticks and leaves over his face. He bent backward until only his nose and mouth were above the water. He could breathe through the sticks and leaves.

Once the bank shook, as if someone were running almost above his head.

Then all was quiet.

He tried to be as still as a rock or the trunk of a tree. He began to feel cramped and cold, and he moved his arms and legs a little. Slowly he lifted his head. He saw no one, yet for all he knew, the men might be near.

Not until night did he climb out of the stream. All the time he was watching, listening.

From now on, he would make no mistakes. He would be swift as a deer and cunning as a fox, and he would never be caught again.

THE RIVER

By night he followed the roads, except where they led past houses. Houses meant people and barking dogs.

By day he disappeared into the woods and became part of their stillness and shadows. He found water there when he was thirsty. He found berries and bitter acorns to eat.

Once he heard voices, and he hid in the berry bushes just before men came walking by.

Another time he thought he was caught. It was in the daylight. He had come out of hiding to look for food, and he came face to face with a man leading a cow.

The man stared at him. Charlie stared back. Neither spoke, and the man went on.

Charlie ran from the place. He walked through a stream to hide his trail.

When he took to the roads again, he started at every strange sound. He had been seen. How long would it be before Master Greer and the hunters closed in about him?

He lost count of the days and nights. Sometimes he was ready to believe Black Swamp was only a dream.

Then it was there before him. He had been sleeping in a thicket on a hilltop. When he looked out in the noon brightness, he saw the dark woods ahead. They stretched as far as he could see. A mist hung over them like a long, low cloud.

Black Swamp, he thought. It *must* be Black Swamp.

Without waiting for night, he started toward it. He would need light for finding his way.

He saw no farms or roads near the swamp. He found himself in a sea of tall grass. While he was fighting his way through it, night fell, and he lay down to sleep.

In the morning he came out into a clearing. A shed was there, the kind a hunter or fisherman might use. The front was open, and he could see into it. No one was there.

A path led from the shed to a river. On the bank was a boat with a pole beside it.

Charlie saw no one, heard no one. He went quickly down the path and pushed the boat into the water. He held it there while he picked up the pole. He stepped into the boat and poled himself out into the river.

There was a current that tugged at the boat, dragging it toward the swamp.

He put the pole down, leaned over the side, and drank. The water was brown. It had an odd, sharp taste.

Now he was among trees that shut out the sunlight. The boat began to tip to one side. It was taking on water. It was sinking.

He poled it out of the current. There were vines overhead, and he caught hold of one and swung himself to shore. He rested on the roots of a tree before he tried to go any farther.

* * *

Time after time he fell, and the soft earth pulled him down. Each time he dragged himself out he felt weaker.

He was ill. It was the water, he thought. He had drunk too much.

There was night, then day, then night again. He dreamed of faces looking down through leaves and branches. In the dream a voice was speaking strange words, and the voice sounded like his own. Once a great, white flower seemed to burst open before his eyes.

He thought he was being carried. He thought he was rocking in a boat. He heard someone laughing—or was it the cry of a bird?

☞   XXII

DROGO

He lay in a nest of leaves. Overhead he saw the sky, deep blue, with a few white clouds. There was wood smoke in the air.

He tried to sit up, and a man bent over him. The man's hair was white, his skin was dark. His face was bright and gentle and smiling.

"Lie back," he said. "You are still weak." He asked, "Do you know me now?"

"No," said Charlie, yet it seemed the face was one he *should* know.

"I am Drogo," said the man. "I found you, remember? I saw the big bird over the swamp. He was following you, and I followed him until I found you. It was good for you that I did."

"Where are we?" asked Charlie.

"This is our island."

From where he lay, Charlie could see woods and a few huts. He thought he saw a man among the trees, and he cried out.

"Do not fear," said Drogo. "You are safe. Master Greer will not find you here."

Charlie felt a chill when he heard the name. "Do you know him?"

"Only from what you said. You talked to me. All the days you were ill, you talked. You do not remember?"

"No."

"Your story is much like mine. I, too, ran away. I was lost, and I found this island in the swamp. I was the first ever to find it, I think. Now it is home for me and for others."

"What others?"

"Others who ran away. I helped them. I brought them here."

* * *

Charlie met the others. There were nine men, five women, a boy, and a girl. Some of them talked to him. Some kept away, almost as if they were afraid of him.

He learned their names. He saw how they hunted, fished, and tended their gardens. They had hoes, knives, and axes.

"Where did you get these?" he asked.

"I brought them from outside," answered Drogo. "I can go back and forth without being seen. There are ways I know."

Charlie lived in Drogo's hut. As he grew stronger, he found work to do. He made fishhooks out of bones. He wove a hammock of reeds and grasses.

The day came when he said to Drogo, "I am well now."

They were sitting on the floor of the hut, mending a fishnet. Drogo stopped working and gave Charlie a long look. "So. You are well."

"Yes. I am well enough to go."

"Where?"

"Outside. Into the world."

"You have good hands, and a good head, I think. We are glad of your help. Why not stay?"

"*Live* here, you mean?"

"Do you know a better hiding place?"

"No, but..." Charlie said slowly, "I don't always want to be hiding."

"You want to go where Master Greer will find you and take you back?"

"No, but in all this land there must be places where I can go—where Master Greer could never find me."

"You are not happy here?"

"Sometimes, but sometimes I feel the swamp around me like a prison!"

"Ah, yes..." Drogo looked away. His eyes had grown sad.

"Don't *you* ever think of going away and finding a place out in the world?" asked Charlie.

"You forget."

"What?"

☞   XXIII

"The color of my skin. Whoever saw me would know what I am—a slave who ran away. But if this is a prison to you, then you must go."

"Will you help me?" asked Charlie.

"Yes, when it is time."

"Tomorrow?"

"You are young, Charlie. As you grow older, you will change. You may change so much that Master Greer would not know you on the road. Then you will be safe out in the world."

☞   XXIV

"That would take years!"

"Perhaps not so many. Think on it. Sleep tonight and think again—and tell me what you are thinking."

That night Charlie slept and woke and slept again. He was awake at daylight. He went outside and stood there, looking.

Near the hut was a little hill. He walked slowly around it, seeing it from every side. He climbed to the top of it.

A breeze blew in from across the swamp, and branches moved over his head. The sky was red where the sun would soon be rising.

Drogo came outside.

"This may be the place," said Charlie.

"The place?"

"To build my house," said Charlie.

Drogo did not seem to understand, and Charlie told him, "If I stay, I'll need a house."

"Then Drogo began to smile. "Ah," he said. "Ah, yes."

The house was there in Charlie's mind, with walls of smooth logs and a roof of leaves and grass. It was straight and strong, but a little rough, because he had only an ax for smoothing the wood. His next house would be better.

☞   XXV

LAST LOOK

by Clyde Robert Bulla

STORY SYNOPSIS — In the story, a girl, desperate for friends and acceptance, behaves awkwardly and then very badly toward the popular girls, especially their leader, Monica. The story is simple, but has the "hook" of a mystery, and is quite effective in getting children to think afresh about the feelings of a pariah.

OBJECTIVES — Through involvement in Clyde Robert Bulla's *Last Look*, children will be stimulated to see peer relationships from new perspectives.

TIME — This is not a lengthy story, and children will get so caught up and excited by it that it requires only two or three forty-five-minute sessions, including discussion.

HOMEWORK — Children's excitement in the story will be so strong that I think homework is best saved until after the story is finished and discussed.

PROCEDURE — This book's message is most effectively conveyed if there is little discussion as you go along. Children need to be "caught unawares," sharing in the disregard for or rejection of "the new girl" along with the protagonist and her friends. Then, when the story is done, they and you can go back and find the incidents which were so hurtful.

These points are indicated in the text by 🐾. Save these points until you discuss "shutting the door" at the end of the book.

Other points, indicated ☞ , deserve attention as they arise. The questions and comments in the next section apply to them.

DISCUSSION AND HOMEWORK QUESTIONS

Rhoda

☞ I

* What do you think about the way Rhoda's acting? about the way Monica and the other girls are treating her?

    Children are likely to feel that Rhoda is "too pushy" but also to remember strongly how hard it was to be "the new one" in any social situation.

* Have you ever been in a situation when you were the new person? How did it feel?

The Four

  II

   ✳ How do these three girls feel? Have they got a point? What could you say
      to them?

Beauty and the Beast

☞ III

   ✳ Has Rhoda got a point? Should parts in a play be given just on the basis
      of popularity?

"Tell No One"

☞ IV

   Give the grandmother a kind of witch's voice. Ham it up!

The Sheriff

☞ V

   Pause to be sure the children get this.

At Mrs. Gorman's

☞ VI

   Remember, Mrs. Gorman is a little weird and creepy.

☞ VII

   Pause for children's reactions.

☞ VIII

   Pause for children's reactions.

Midnight

☞ IX

   Use a spooky voice.

The Old Garden

☞ X

Pause for children's reactions.

✳ Can you think of reasons why Rhoda was so upset?

☞ XI

Pause for children's reactions.

The New Girl

☞ XII

Let Monica shout here.

☞ XIII

Give this time to sink in. It usually has a powerful effect.

✳ What does "close the door" mean?

Some children may not understand that "closing the door" is a metaphor.

✳ How did Monica and her friends shut the door on Rhoda?

Illustrative incidents are indicated 🐾.

Homework Assignment

1. Using complete sentences, write about what "closing the door" on someone can mean.

2. Give specific examples of ways Monica and her friends could have been more accepting of Rhoda.

   Some children may argue that Monica did nothing whatever wrong, that she and her friends should not have to accept as a new friend, "give a chance" even, to a person who doesn't appeal to them. And they have a point in that pity can hardly be the start of an ethical friendship. In such cases, I have argued that "not closing the door" means having an open mind as well as an open heart.

   I remark that I know I've behaved badly, not "like my real self" at times when I felt awkward or new, and hasn't everybody? We all agree that what Rhoda did was terrible, but we still need to think about how excluded she was made to feel. And we need to be more sensitive to people we scarcely realize we're excluding every day.

LAST LOOK
by Clyde Robert Bulla*

RHODA

Monica was walking to school with her two best friends, Fran and Audrey. She was telling them about the surprising thing that had happened over the weekend. When she finished, they stopped in the middle of the road and stared at her.

Fran said, "I don't believe it!"

Audrey said, "Are you *sure*?"

"Diane told me herself," said Monica.

"But she was at school on Friday," said Fran. "Why didn't she tell us then?"

"She didn't know," said Monica. "She probably didn't find out till Saturday. She called Madame Vere first, and then she called me."

"Why didn't she call the rest of us?" asked Fran.

"There wasn't time," said Monica. "Her father's company said, You have to go *now*, and that's the way it was."

"Life is so weird," said Audrey. "Friday she was at school. Now she's on her way to Switzerland, and we may never see her again."

"Ah, Switzerland!" said Fran. "All those lakes and mountains! I'd like to go there."

"I'd like it if it could be an adventure—maybe something like a secret mission," said Monica. "But just to take a trip, no. I'd rather be here."

They started walking again. Fran said suddenly, "I wonder who the new girl will be."

"There *will* be a new girl, won't there?" said Audrey.

"There always is," said Monica.

They were in their last year at Madame Vere's School. It was a summer school for girls from six to twelve. Madame's schoolhouse was her home, and she had room for no more than thirty pupils at a time. There was always a waiting list. When a girl dropped out or moved away, another was always waiting to take her place.

"It could be somebody little," said Fran. "Somebody in the first grade."

"I hope it's somebody older—about our age," said Audrey. "That would be more interesting."

They turned down a side road. They could see Madame's house ahead, with the tall white pillars that made it look like a Greek temple. Behind it was the lake, silver-blue and dazzling in the morning light.

* *Last Look* by Clyde Robert Bulla, copyright ©1979 HarperCollins Publishers, reprinted by permission of the publisher.

They were almost late. They slipped into the study hall that was really Madame's living room. They took their places.

"Look!" whispered Fran. "She's here already!"

And there she was, in Diane's old place by the window—the new girl.

Madame was at her desk. Tiny Madame with her dyed black hair and a dab of rouge on each cheekbone.

"Good morning," she said. "As some of you know, one of our girls has left us. Diane and her family have gone to live in Switzerland. She asked me to tell you she enjoyed being in school with you, and she wished there'd been time to say good-bye."

Madame's shrewd, kindly eyes looked out at them all. "And now I'd like you to meet a new pupil. Will you stand please, Rhoda?"

The new girl stood. She was thin and fairly tall. Her short hair was blonde, but her eyebrows were dark. They almost met above the bridge of her nose. Her face was long and rather bony. She stood there, looking perfectly calm.

"Rhoda has come to spend the summer with her grandmother, Mrs. Gorman," said Madame Vere. "We hope you'll be happy here."

The new girl said, "Thank you." She glanced coolly about the room before she sat down.

* * *

At noon Monica, Fran, and Audrey took their lunch boxes to the shady side of the house.

"What do you think?" asked Audrey.

"She looks older than any of us," said Fran. "Don't you think so, Monica?"

"It may be her hair," Monica said. "That haircut makes her look sophisticated."

"Imagine spending the summer with *Mrs. Gorman*," said Fran.

"Quiet!" Monica warned her.

Rhoda was coming toward them.

"Hello," she said. Her voice was a little louder than it needed to be. She sat down on the grass with them and opened her lunch box. It seemed to be empty except for an apple.

"What are your names?" she asked.

They told her.

"Are you summer people, or do you live here all year?" she asked.

"We're summer people," Monica answered. "Our families have cottages here on the lake."

"I guess not many people live here the year round. My grandmother is one of the few." Rhoda was watching their faces. "Do you know my grandmother?"

"We know who she is," said Fran.

"And where she lives," said Audrey. "Just up from the haunted house."

"You mean the empty house down by the lake?" Rhoda was still watching them. "Why do you call it a *haunted* house?"

Monica, Fran, and Audrey looked at one another. They began to laugh. "It's an old joke," said Audrey.

"It *looks* like a haunted house, don't you think?" said Fran.

"I don't know. I don't know how a haunted house is supposed to look." Rhoda bit into her apple with her long white teeth. Monica thought of a horse—she couldn't help it.

"I think you'll like our school," said Audrey. "Madame is a wonderful teacher. She goes all over the world, and she—well—she kind of brings the world to us."

Rhoda took another bite out of her apple. She said, "I'd like to join your club."

"What club?" asked Monica.

"The one you belong to."

"I don't belong to any."

"You mean you don't have a club—the three of you?"

"No. What made you think we did?"

"You keep together," said Rhoda. "When you came in this morning, I heard somebody say, 'There's the club.'"

 I

"Somebody was being funny," said Monica. "We're friends and we're together a lot, that's all. We live close together."

"Where?" asked Rhoda.

"Well—Fran and Audrey live side by side, just beyond Lake Drive. I live a little farther on. It's the white cottage with the blue tent in the yard."

"I saw that tent," said Rhoda. "What is it for?"

"I sleep in it," Monica told her.

"Why?"

"I just like to. It's nice out there under the trees."

"We all live in a row. That's good," said Rhoda. "We can all walk together."

For a little while no one spoke. Then Monica said slowly, "Yes—I suppose we can."

THE FOUR

So the three became four. On the way to school, on the way home, they walked together.

Toward the middle of the week, Madame Vere took Monica aside and said, "I was afraid the new girl might be lonely, but everyone has made her welcome. That's partly because of you. You've always been one of our leaders, and for you and Rhoda to be friends—well—I know what it means to her."

"I'm not so sure we *are* friends," Monica started to say, but Madame gave her a pat and sent her away.

On the Friday of Rhoda's first week at school, the four were walking home together.

"You hear about Lake Chester," Rhoda was saying, "and you think it's a city or at least a town. But it's just some houses strung along a lake. I don't think this place will ever get to be a town."

"I hope not," said Fran. "We like it the way it is."

"There's nothing much here," said Rhoda. "There's not even a theater."

"There's a movie theater over on The Point," said Audrey.

"I don't mean that. I mean a real one where they have plays." Rhoda sighed. "I miss the theater."

"I like the theater, too," said Monica. "When we're in New York, we go to some of the Broadway plays."

"Then you must have seen my mother," said Rhoda. "She's Elaine Boston."

"No, I don't think I have," said Monica. "I've heard her name though."

"I should hope so. After her next play, she just may be the best-known actress in the country. We were in a play together once."

"You're an actress, too?" asked Audrey.

"I only had three lines." Rhoda laughed. "But I learned a lot. There's such excitement in the theater. I just may go on to be an actress."

"We have a school play every year," said Monica. "We make our own sets and costumes—"

"Not like Broadway, of course," said Fran.

She and Audrey stopped off at their houses. Monica and Rhoda went on together.

Rhoda said, "Why don't we plan something for the weekend? Let's have a picnic. We could ask Fran and Audrey if you wanted to, but I thought it might be fun for just the two of us."

"I can't," said Monica. "My father works in New Jersey, and he comes up every weekend. He and Mother and I always do something together when he's here."

❧

"It doesn't matter," said Rhoda. "My mother may be coming from New York anyway."

They had stopped in front of Monica's house. Monica's mother called from the doorway, "Telephone!"

Rhoda went on. Monica ran into the house.

Fran was on the telephone. "Can you come back here?" she asked. "We want to talk to you."

Monica walked back to Fran's. Fran and Audrey were waiting at the gate.

"How much longer is this going to go on?" asked Fran.

"What?" asked Monica.

"You know what," said Fran. "Every time we turn around, *she's* there."

"We used to have fun together," said Audrey. "Now we don't."

"Today was the worst." Fran held her nose and spoke in a loud singsong, "'I miss the theater...I just may be an actress.'"

"There *is* an Elaine Boston," said Monica. "I've heard of her."

"Do you think Rhoda was really in a Broadway play?" asked Fran.

"I suppose she could have been."

"If she was or if she wasn't, it's not important," Audrey spoke up. "The thing is, does she have to be with us every minute?"

"I'm not enjoying it any more than you are," said Monica, "but Madame is proud of the way we're being nice to the new girl. She told me so. Are we going to let her down?"

Fran said, after a moment, "We don't want to let Madame down. You know that. But do we have to let Rhoda push herself in wherever we go?"

☞   II

"*I* don't know what to do," said Monica, "but things have a way of changing. Let's give it another week and see what happens."

LAST LOOK

It was Monday again. The four were on their way to school.

Fran said to Monica, "I saw you go by with your father Saturday. He has a new car, hasn't he?"

"No, it's the same one. We went past The Point and there was a carnival. We came back and picked up Mother, and we all went to it."

"We sailed over to the island," said Audrey. "You know the pretty beach with the big red rock? We had it all to ourselves."

"Mother and Daddy and I went riding yesterday," said Fran, "and if any of you go to the stables, don't let them give you a horse named Lightning. He won't move!"

Rhoda had been quiet. Monica asked her, "Did your mother come up from New York?"

"She phoned me instead," said Rhoda. "We talked an hour and a half. Listen, I've been thinking. Why don't we have a club? There could be just us at first. Later, if we wanted to, we could take in some others."

Monica felt Fran and Audrey looking at her. "What kind of club?" she asked.

"Just for getting together and—and having talks," said Rhoda.

"That's not much of a reason," said Monica.

"We could *think* of a reason."

No one answered, and they left it there.

After school Madame asked Rhoda to wait.

The other three went out on the front steps.

"Are we supposed to wait, too?" asked Audrey.

"Nobody told us to," said Fran. "She and Madame are in there talking. Let's go."

They started toward the highway.

"This is the way it used to be," said Audrey.

"And isn't it nice!" Fran was in the middle. She linked arms with Monica and Audrey.

"It *is* nice," said Monica, "but you can almost feel sorry for her sometimes."

"I don't feel sorry for her," said Fran. "Why is she always pushing herself in where she's not wanted? Why is she always giving herself airs? The tales she tells—you *know* they aren't true. Like her mother calling and talking an hour and a half—*that* never happened."

"How do you know?" asked Monica.

"Because her grandmother doesn't have a telephone. We know Elmo, the telephone serviceman, and he says old Mrs. Gorman won't have one."

"I thought everybody had a telephone," said Audrey.

"Not Mrs. Gorman. She won't have one. She won't fix up her house either. It looks worse than the haunted house."

Audrey gave a moan. "Don't look now, but—"

Rhoda was running after them. "Wait!"

She caught up with them. She was waving a magazine. "Madame wanted to give me this. There's a picture of my mother on page twenty-four."

They looked at it. It wasn't much of a picture—a small, dim face among other faces—but the name was below for all to see: Elaine Boston.

"You can't tell much from this," said Rhoda. "I have some really good pictures I'll show you."

No one answered.

They came to Audrey's, then to Fran's.

As Fran started up the walk, Monica called after her, "Watch out for the bears!"

Fran looked toward her. "What—?"

"Last look!" said Monica and turned her head.

"Monica!" called Fran. "I forgot to tell you something. Monica—!"

Without stopping or looking back, Monica hurried on down the road.

"What was *that* all about?" asked Rhoda in a bewildered voice. She was running along beside Monica.

Monica was laughing. "It's a game. Didn't you ever play it?"

"Never!"

"When Fran left us just now, I made her look back, and I said, 'Last look.' Then she tried to make me look at her so *she* could say it. But I wouldn't look, so I won the game."

"It sounds like something little children would play."

"It is. We played it all the time when we were little. We're too old for it now, but sometimes something comes over us—"

"I suppose you always win," said Rhoda.

"Oh, no. I took her by surprise that time. Next time she'll probably surprise me."

BEAUTY AND THE BEAST

It was time to talk about the school play. Madame Vere had called a meeting in the study hall.

"We're doing *Beauty and the Beast*," she said. "We'll need actors, stagehands, and people to make sets and costumes. Let me know what you'd like to do. There's work for everyone."

"Who will the actors be?" someone asked.

"That's what we always think of first, isn't it?" said Madame Vere. "We'll need a Beauty and a Beast, of course. Then we'll need Beauty's sisters. Let's take Beauty first. Do you have any ideas?"

"Monica," said one of the smaller girls, "because she's the prettiest."

Others took it up. There was a chorus of "Monica!"

Madame looked pleased. "A good choice. Monica, will you take the part?"

Monica's cheeks were pink. "If—if you want me," she said.

"Now," said Madame Vere, "the next part—"

Someone broke in. "May I say something?"

It was Rhoda.

"Beauty is the only part worth having," she said. "Do you think it's fair just to hand it out without giving anyone else a chance?"

The room grew still.

"The part wasn't just handed out," said Madame Vere. "It seems to me that Monica was chosen by the school."

"Excuse me for saying so," said Rhoda, "but that's not a very good way to cast a part. The best way is to try out for it."

☞   III

Madame Vere looked thoughtful. "Very well," she said. "Who wants to try out?"

Rhoda's hand went up.

"Who else?" asked Madame. There were no other hands. "Of course, you're trying out, Monica."

"I'd rather not," said Monica.

"I understand how you feel," said Madame Vere, "but others in the school would like to see you in the part. Don't you think you owe it to them to try out for it?"

Monica didn't answer.

"Shall we have the tryouts now," asked Madame Vere, "or do you want time to study the part?"

"I'm ready now," said Rhoda.

"And you, Monica?"

"Yes," said Monica.

She went up to the desk and stood beside Rhoda.

Madame Vere opened a book. "Here's something from Act Two. Who wants to read first?"

Rhoda took the book. She read in a loud, clear voice: "This castle is lovely to the sight, yet how I wish myself at home! Each night I weep, not knowing what may come tomorrow. All is strange here, even the bird calls...Hark! What was that?"

"Thank you," said Madame Vere. "Monica, please."

Monica read the lines. She read them badly, she thought. Twice she stumbled over words.

Madame thanked her. "How many feel that Rhoda should play the part? Raise your hands."

No hands were raised.

"How many feel that Monica should play it?"

There was a burst of applause. Hands went up all over the room.

Madame Vere said to Rhoda and Monica, "Thank you. You may take your seats."

As they sat down, Monica heard a whisper, "Rhoda could be the Beast!"

If Rhoda heard, she gave no sign. She looked calm. She was even smiling.

"Since this *is* a girl's school," some of you will be playing boys' parts. Would anyone like to try out for the Beast? It's a good part, too...No? Then we'll talk about it and try to make a choice."

The meeting went on.

"We'd like you to have a part, Rhoda," said Madame Vere.

"Couldn't I work on the sets?" asked Rhoda.

"Of course, if you'd rather. I'll put you down for that."

After school the four started home together.

Rhoda said to Monica, "Congratulations, Beauty."

"Thank you," said Monica. "You read better than I did. You should have got the part."

Rhoda's mouth curled. "You don't think I *wanted* it?"

"You mean you *didn't* want it?" asked Fran.

"Certainly not."

"Then why did you pretend you did? You made things awkward for everyone."

"I was teaching Madame a lesson," said Rhoda. "She was going to hand the part to Monica on a silver platter. I was letting her know things aren't done that way."

"Things *are* done that way. In our school they are," said Fran. "We talk about the parts and who might be best for them. Then we sort of vote on it. This isn't a Broadway theater. It's a little play in a little school."

They walked along without saying anything, without looking at one another. Audrey turned off at her house. Fran turned off at hers. Monica and Rhoda went on together.

Monica tried to start a conversation. Rhoda hardly answered. She seemed to be deep in her own thoughts.

Monica stopped at her gate. "Good-bye," she said.

"What?" said Rhoda.

"I live here, remember? I said good-bye."

"Oh. Good-bye." Rhoda went on.

There was something sad about her. She looked lost as she walked up the road with the dark pines on either side.

Monica wanted to say something more.

"Rhoda—" she called.

Rhoda stopped and looked back.

And then Monica could think of nothing to say—nothing except, "Last look!"

It was ridiculous, but she said it and turned quickly toward the house.

"Monica—wait!" called Rhoda. "Monica!" Her voice rose. "Help me! *Help*!"

Monica let herself into the house.

Her mother came out of the kitchen. "Who was that screaming?"

"Rhoda," said Monica. "She was trying to make me look back."

"She was certainly trying hard," said her mother.

"She was, wasn't she?" said Monica. "She's really good at the game. She nearly made me look."

"TELL NO ONE"

The next day was Saturday, and Monica slept late. She was barely awake when a car pulled up beside her tent.

She opened the flap. "Father!"

He slid out of the car—a long-legged man in jacket and jeans.

"You must have left New Jersey in the middle of the night," she said.

"Just about." He grinned at her. "Still sleeping in that tent, I see, when you have a perfectly good bedroom."

"You don't know how nice it is out here," she said.

"And I may never find out, as long as I have a roof to sleep under. Come on. Get dressed. We're going out for breakfast."

They had breakfast at a pancake house on The Cove—Father, Mother, and Monica. They drove all the way around the lake.

It was noon when they came back to the cottage. There was a woman at the gate. She wore an odd-looking brown dress—long in front, short in the back—and her hair was gray and wild. She half waved as they drove in.

"It's Rhoda's grandmother!" said Monica. "I'll go see what she wants."

She ran out the gate. "Hello, Mrs. Gorman," she said.

The woman looked ill. Her skin was blotchy. She put a hand to her face as if the light hurt her eyes.

☞ IV

"Are you Monica?" she asked in a hoarse, deep voice.

"Yes, I am."

"Is she—is my granddaughter here?"

"Rhoda? No, she isn't."

"She didn't come home with you yesterday?"

"No."

"Well, then—" Mrs. Gorman smiled. It was a ghastly smile. "It's all right, dear. I understand now. Thank you so much."

She was on her way up the road.

Monica ran after her. "Do you mean Rhoda didn't come home from school yesterday?"

"Well, yes—I suppose she did. But I never saw her. Sometimes I'm in the back of the house, and I don't always—" The woman smiled again. "It's all right."

"If you haven't seen her, how can you say it's all right?"

"Oh, she went to her mother's. She went to New York."

"Without telling you?"

"She *did* tell me, in a way. She's not very nice to me, you know. Sometimes she's not nice at all. She's been saying she was going home to her mother's. She said she had her own money and she could take the bus, and that's what she's done."

"Are you sure?"

"Oh, yes. I'm sure now."

"And you're not worried?"

"No, no, and don't you be worried either. Good-bye, dear, and thank you."

Monica told her mother and father afterward, "She hasn't seen Rhoda since yesterday morning, and she doesn't see why anyone should worry. Do you think I should have told her about yesterday?"

"What about yesterday?" asked Mother.

"Don't you remember? About playing Last Look. Maybe Rhoda wasn't playing. Maybe she really saw something—"

"What could she have seen in the road in the middle of the afternoon?"

"You heard how she screamed. Maybe she was in danger."

"What kind of danger?" asked Father.

"I don't know."

"You don't know, but you're building up things in your mind. Here's how it looks to me," he said. "This Rhoda and her grandmother don't get on too well. The girl walked out and took a bus to her mother's. The grandmother thought she *might* have spent the night with you. When she found out Rhoda wasn't here, she knew the girl must be with her mother, so she stopped worrying. And you should stop, too."

* * *

Father left on Sunday night. The next morning Monica was walking to school with Fran and Audrey.

"This is like the old days," said Fran. "Just the three of us again."

"I think we've seen the last of Rhoda," said Audrey.

"Aren't you worried at all?" asked Monica.

"Why?" asked Fran. "She can take care of herself."

At school Monica told Madame what had happened.

"It may be nothing serious," said Madame. "I think Rhoda will soon be back with us. I know how much her mother wanted her to come to our school."

On the way home that afternoon, Monica asked Fran and Audrey, "If you hear anything about Rhoda, will you let me know?"

"What is there to hear?" asked Fran.

"I thought she might give one of us a call from New York," said Monica.

"She wouldn't call me," said Fran.

"Or me," said Audrey. "She might give you a call, although I doubt it."

"I wish she would. Then I'd feel better," said Monica.

But there was no call from New York. She really hadn't expected one.

It was a quiet evening. She did her homework. At half past nine she said good night to her mother and went out to the tent. The night was dark, and she found her way with a flashlight.

She lay in her sleeping bag. She listened to the wind for a long time before she went to sleep.

Something wakened her. It was a rustling sound. Not the wind. The wind had died, and the night was still.

She saw the clock on the ground beside her, its face glowing in the dark. Two o'clock.

She found her flashlight and turned it on. In its beam she saw something stuck in the tent flap. A piece of paper.

She took out the paper. There were words on it—words made up of letters cut from a newspaper.

> *Monica. Tell no one. Rhoda in danger. Go to haunted house Tuesday at midnight. Receive message. Go alone. Tell no one.*

THE SHERIFF

Monica felt her way through the dark house. She couldn't remember how she had gotten there. She found the door of her mother's bedroom.

"Mother—"

The light came on. Mother sat up in bed.

"What is it?"

The paper shook in Monica's hand. "This was in my tent."

Mother took the note. "What on earth—!"

"I heard a sound," said Monica. "I think it was someone slipping the paper into the tent."

Mother read it aloud, "'Rhoda in danger.'"

"We have to call the police."

"Monica, I don't understand this. Could it be a joke?"

"A *joke?*"

"Maybe one of your friends—"

"No!"

Mother got out of bed. "I suppose I'd better call Hal."

Hal Ericson was the sheriff. He lived a mile down the road.

Mother called him. He was there in half an hour. He was a big man with thick white hair and pale blue eyes. He looked sleepy, and he looked bored.

He read the note. "Who is Rhoda?"

"Mrs. Gorman's granddaughter," Monica told him.

"Oh, yes. And her mother is an actress in New York. I used to know her name. Elaine—"

"Elaine Boston," said Monica.

"What about the girl?" asked the sheriff. "When did you last see her?"

"Friday, after school. She walked home with me. We were playing Last Look—"

"What's that?"

"A game. It's like playing tag with your eyes. Rhoda looked at me, and I said, 'Last look.' Then she tried to make me look at her so *she* could say it. I wouldn't look, and she started screaming. I thought she was just playing the game, so I didn't turn around. And then—"

"Yes?"

"Her grandmother came over the next day. She wanted to know if Rhoda had stayed all night with me."

"Was she upset?"

Monica tried to remember. "She didn't seem to be. She said Rhoda must have taken the bus and gone back to her mother's."

"And you think that didn't happen?" asked the sheriff. "You think she disappeared while you were playing your game?"

"She could have, couldn't she?"

He was reading the note again. "'Go to haunted house.' Is that the old Fenwick place where nobody lives?"

"It must be," said Mother.

Hal Ericson frowned. "I don't like empty houses. They make mischief. Stories grow up around them. Mystery stories." He looked at Monica. "You like mystery stories, don't you?"

She looked at him without answering.

"Some of your friends like them, too, don't they?" He sat back in his chair. "I remember some little girls here on the lake. They thought it would be fun to play ghost and maybe start a few ghost stories. One night they went to the old Fenwick place. They had candles. They might have burned the place down, but that didn't bother them. They went through the house and played they were haunting it. Somebody saw the lights and called me. The little girls didn't get away fast enough, and I caught them. They looked pretty foolish, I can tell you. They said they were just having fun, and I told them the police had better things to do than go out in the middle of the night for nothing. I guess you don't remember those girls. Their names were Fran, Audrey, and Monica."

☞ v

Her face had grown warm. "That was a long time ago."

"Right. A long time ago. I should hope you wouldn't do anything like that now." The sheriff got up. "Good night. Try to get some sleep."

Mother went with him to the door. She came back.

Monica flung herself into a chair. "He didn't believe me. He didn't believe a word I was saying!"

"You'll have to admit the story does sound strange," said Mother.

"What's strange about it?"

"If Rhoda is in danger, why did the note come to you? Why didn't it go to her grandmother?"

"How should I know? All I know is you don't believe me either."

"I never said that."

"You don't have to say it. Just because of what happened years ago, you think it's some game I'm playing. I'm sorry I told the sheriff, and I wish I hadn't told you."

"Monica—"

"I should have gone to the haunted house without telling anybody. Maybe I'd have found out something."

"Monica, I'll be honest with you. The sheriff does think it looks like some kind of joke. But he took the note with him. He's going to look into it. He's going to see Mrs. Gorman. He even said he'd go around to check the old house."

"He's doing me a big favor, isn't he?" Monica's voice was bitter. "It may be a matter of life and death, and he thinks it's a joke."

"You're tired, and so am I," said Mother. "Go to bed."

"Out there?"

"No, in your bedroom. Good night."

AT MRS. GORMAN'S

Mother said the next morning, "You won't talk about this at school, will you?"

Monica shook her head.

"The sheriff wouldn't want you to. It's easy to say too much about a think like this."

"I know." Monica added to herself, I said too much last night. I shouldn't have told anyone.

But it was hard to be quiet. She wanted to say to Fran and Audrey, Rhoda is missing. I think she's being held for ransom.

When Madame asked about Rhoda, Monica could hardly keep from saying, She won't be in school today. She may be kidnapped.

Fran asked on the way home, "What's the *matter* with you?"

"Nothing," said Monica.

"You're a million miles away," said Audrey.

Fran said, "It's something about Rhoda, isn't it?"

"You had a fight," said Audrey, "and that's why she didn't come to school."

"We didn't have a fight, and I don't know why she didn't come to school."

"But it's *something* about Rhoda, isn't it?" said Fran.

"You may as well tell us," said Audrey, "because we'll find out."

They left her. She walked on.

She didn't stop at home. She walked up the road past the place where she had last seen Rhoda. The pine woods on either side looked dark and strange.

A little way beyond the woods was Mrs. Gorman's house. It was big and old and falling apart. With the broken windows in the attic, and the sagging porches and balconies, it looked more haunted than the haunted house.

Monica went to the front door and knocked.

There were dragging footsteps inside. There was a crash, as if a chair had been knocked over. The door opened, and Mrs. Gorman peered out.

☞ VI

"Who are you?" she asked. "What do you want?"

"Don't you know me?" asked Monica. "You came to see me. You came to ask about Rhoda."

"Oh—yes—" Mrs. Gorman rubbed her eyes. "You'll have to excuse me. When you knocked, I thought it was that man again, the one who came and asked me all the questions. What was your name, dear?"

"Monica."

"Yes, that's it. Monica. Did you come to see Rhoda? She's not here. She's with her mother."

"Have you—have you heard from her?"

"Heard from her? Oh, no. That child never writes."

"But do you *know* she's at her mother's?"

"Oh, yes. She kept saying that was where she was going, and I said, 'Go if you want to. Nothing's stopping you.'"

☞ VII

"When did she go?"

"Yesterday—or it might have been the day before. I can't stand this light. Why don't you come in, child?"

Monica followed the old woman into a room that was littered with books and papers. Every window was closed. The air was stale and sickening. Monica began to cough.

"Would you like a drink of water?" asked Mrs. Gorman.

"No, thank you." Monica was looking at a picture on the mantel, the picture of a pretty, smiling woman with a flower in her hair.

"That's Rhoda's mother," said Mrs. Gorman. "That's Elaine. I can show you some better pictures." She dusted off an album and put it into Monica's hands.

Monica turned the pages. There were pictures of Rhoda's mother in a dozen different poses, then pictures of a dark-haired young man. He had a thin moustache and a cruel smile.

"That's Rhoda's father," said Mrs. Gorman. "He left when Rhoda was born. Just disappeared, and nobody ever saw him again."

She brought out another album. "This has pictures of Rhoda. You wouldn't think it, but she was a pretty baby. If you'd like to see—"

"I can't stay. I'll come back when Rhoda is here."

Monica escaped into the sunlight and the clean fresh air. She went home.

Mother told her, "The sheriff stopped by. He's been to see Mrs. Gorman, and he found out about Rhoda. She's in New York with her mother."

"How does he know that?"

"Mrs. Gorman told him."

☞ VIII

"I've been to see Mrs. Gorman, too," said Monica. "She's in a fog. I don't know how the sheriff can believe what she says."

"I think we can trust him," said Mother.

* * *

The evening was long. They went to bed early, but Monica was still awake at midnight when the telephone rang.

She went to Mother's room. "Who was it?"

"The sheriff," answered Mother. "He just came from the haunted house. Everything was all right. He didn't see anyone."

"Why did he go over there?"

"Because of the note. It said to go there tonight, remember?"

"It said for *me* to go."

"Well, nobody was there, and Rhoda is safe in New York, so we can all stop worrying, can't we?...Can't we, Monica?"

"What about the note?"

"The note?"

"Yes. Who wrote it?"

"We *don't* know that yet, do we?" said Mother. "But I think the sheriff will find out if we just give him time."

* * *

In the morning Monica started to school. She went down the walk, past the tent, nearly to the gate. There she stopped. There'd been something about the tent—something that hadn't quite belonged there....

She went back. This time she saw clearly what was different—a small patch of brown against the blue of the tent. It was a piece of paper tucked into the flap. Another note.

These words were not made of cutout letters. These were printed on the paper.

> *Monica. You have betrayed me. This is your last chance. Come to haunted house tonight. You can still save your friend. Come at midnight. Tell no one. Tell no one.*

MIDNIGHT

That day there were two Monicas. One was Monica-as-usual, going from class to class, playing volleyball, having lunch on the grass with Fran and Audrey. The other was Monica-with-a-secret, scared and excited, hot and cold, asking herself over and over, What will happen? What will happen now?

"You're awfully jumpy," said Fran on the way home.

"Jumpy?" said Monica.

"When anyone speaks to you, you sort of jump."

"You're keeping something from us," said Audrey.

They wanted to walk home with her. They wanted her to go over to the lake with them. She had a hard time getting away from them, but at last she was alone. She was at home in her room where she could think.

She took the note out of her lunch box and read it again for what clues she could find. It was printed on a scrap from a torn paper bag. The printing had been done with a pencil. The letters were neat and large, the kind of printing almost anyone might have done.

You have betrayed me. She knew what that meant, of course. She hadn't gone to the haunted house last night. The sheriff had gone instead.

This is your last chance...Come to haunted house tonight...You can still save your friend...Come at midnight...Tell no one...

She tried to picture whoever it was who had written the note, walked across the yard last night, and slipped it into the tent. Someone small and quick, who moved softly? A man? A woman? Someone she knew? Someone who knew her?

"Monica—?" Mother was at the door.

Monica put the note out of sight under her pillow.

But Mother didn't come in. "Dinner," she said, and went away.

They sat down to dinner. Chicken salad with white grapes. Sliced tomatoes. Iced tea. The kind of dinner Monica liked, but she couldn't eat.

"Not hungry?" asked Mother.

"Not yet."

"Maybe later. Everything will keep."

"Excuse me," said Monica. "I need to study my part in the play."

She studied her part. At ten o'clock she went out to say good night.

"Would you like your dinner now?" asked Mother.

"Thank you, I'm still not hungry."

Back in her room, she turned out the light and lay down. Her little clock ticked away on the table beside her. Its face glowed in the dark. She watched the time.

She didn't *have* to go to the haunted house. She could tell Mother about the note, and Mother could call the sheriff.

But he hadn't believed her before. Why should he believe her now? She wasn't even sure Mother would believe her.

You have betrayed me. This is your last chance...You can still save your friend...Tell no one...

She did have to go. She did. Somehow she had become the key. Everything depended on her.

It was 10:30. It was 11:00.

At a little past 11:30 she quietly left her room. Without turning on a light, she went down the hall to the back door. She let herself out of the house.

The night was clear, and there was a half-moon. No cars passed as she walked along the road. There was no light at Mrs. Gorman's. She turned down the lane that led to the haunted house.

She could see the house. Its roof and chimney were dark above the trees ahead.

She pushed through the grass that had grown high in the lane. She came to the house. The door was open. Moonlight shone in and made a path across the floor.

It was midnight—she was here. What now?

Beside the house something moved.

☞ IX

A voice spoke. "This way."

THE OLD GARDEN

The voice was hollow and low. It could have been a man's or a woman's. It said again, "This way."

A figure seemed to float from the shadow of the house. It moved away, and she followed.

She went down three steps into the old garden. She knew the garden. Here was the path with the well on one side and rosebushes on the other. She waded through weeds and vines.

The figure had stopped. It was wrapped in something dark, and it wore a mask.

"Stay there," it said. "Are you alone?"

"Yes," said Monica.

"Did you tell?"

"No."

"Turn your back."

Monica turned. The voice was disguised. She tried to think where she had heard it before.

Steps came toward her. A piece of cloth—a blindfold—was pulled roughly over her eyes.

"No!" She ducked from under the cloth.

"Hold still!"

And now she knew where she had heard the voice before. She faced the figure. She caught at the mask—a paper bag with torn holes for eyes.

The paper ripped, and a face looked out at her. Rhoda's face.

They stood without moving. Rhoda was pale, her mouth drawn thin.

"You had to find out, didn't you?" she said.

"You weren't kidnapped," said Monica.

"Who said I was?"

"*You* wrote the notes. You've been hiding."

"Yes. Under your noses. Do you know where? Most of the time in my grandmother's attic."

"She said you were gone."

"She didn't know. She doesn't know anything. When the sheriff's car came and he flashed his light around last night, I was right over there." Rhoda pointed to the garden wall. "I thought if I tried one more note, I'd get you here, and I *did* get you here."

"Why?" asked Monica.

"Remember the game?"

"What game?"

"You know. On the way home from school. I tried to make you look at me, and you wouldn't. That's when I hid. I thought I'd make you worry, and I did, didn't I?"

"You mean this whole thing is just part of that silly game?"

"That's how it started. But while I was hiding, I thought what I *really* wanted to do—where I *really* wanted to see you." Rhoda's mouth jerked. "If you only knew how much I hate you!"

☞ x

Monica felt as if she had been struck. Rhoda moved closer. "The very first day you shut the door in my face. I wasn't good enough for you. Not when you had Mother and Daddy and all your friends. You were Beauty and I was the Beast."

"Rhoda—"

"You could have anything you wanted without lifting a finger. You even won all the games, but you won't win this one!"

She had hold of Monica's arms. She was pushing her. It was like a slow, crazy dance.

Monica's ankle struck something. She looked back. She had come up against a round wooden circle—the cover of the old well. Just behind her was the well itself, a dark hole with a low stone curb. Rhoda was pushing her toward it.

Monica fought. She twisted almost free. Rhoda seized her again.

They wrestled on the edge of the well. Monica tripped on the well curb. She was falling. Her hand was wound in Rhoda's hair, and Rhoda was falling with her.

They landed in a heap at the bottom of the well. A shower of dirt and small stones fell from above. Then there was silence.

Monica tried to catch her breath. Rhoda was lying across her.

"Get off," she said.

Rhoda moved a little.

Monica straightened her arms and legs. She wasn't hurt. The well was not deep, and the bottom was soft with mud.

Overhead she could see a circle of sky with a few stars in it.

Rhoda was sobbing.

"You're not hurt," said Monica. "You fell mostly on me."

She stood up. Her shoes stuck in the mud. She felt the sides of the well, the damp earth and slippery stones. There were no footholds that she could find.

She thought of asking Rhoda, Do you have any matches? Do you have a flashlight?

It was all completely mad, something not to be believed. One minute they'd been fighting tooth and nail. The next, they were at the bottom of the well, with no one to turn to but each other!

Rhoda whimpered something. It sounded a little as if she had said, "I'm sorry."

"Are you sorry?" asked Monica.

"Yes!" said Rhoda.

"So am I," said Monica. "I'm sorry you thought you had to go through all this."

Rhoda hiccupped.

"And don't be sick!" Monica was still feeling the damp rough sides of the well. "I have an idea...Are you listening?"

"Yes," said Rhoda.

"If I could get on your shoulders—" said Monica. "Stand up."

Rhoda stood up.

"Bend over," said Monica. "Are you bending over? I'll get on your back and—"

"Stop," said Rhoda. "It hurts."

"Can you get on my back?" Monica knelt. "Here—see if you can. Stand on my shoulders...put your hands against the sides. Don't fall off."

Slowly she rose, wobbling under Rhoda's weight. Then the weight was gone. She could hear Rhoda scrambling out of the well.

Monica waited. "Pull me up," she shouted. "Reach down with a stick or a vine or something. Can you hear me?"

There was the sound of laughter. Rhoda's voice came faintly down to her, "Last look!"

The circle of sky was gone. The cover had been dragged over the well.

☞ XI

THE NEW GIRL

Monica stood there, trying to think, trying to understand. She could believe that Rhoda hated her, had plotted to bring her here and push her into the well. But then they'd been in the well together. Rhoda had said she was sorry. They'd had to depend on each other.

Surely Rhoda wouldn't go away and leave her. Not now.

But Rhoda *had* gone. She'd dragged the cover over the well and left her...

Monica wondered how soon she would be missed at home. Probably not until breakfast time. And how long would it be until someone found her? It might be hours—or days.

She shouted a few times, but the well seemed to swallow the sound of her voice. It wasn't far to the top. If she could dig steps up the side of the well—

She found a flat stone and began to dig and scrape with it. She could make hardly a dent in the rocky wall, but she worked at it until she was tired. Her knees bent. She knelt like a frog in the mud at the bottom of the well.

She tried to count the seconds and minutes. It was something to do.

Then she was listening. A sound had come from overhead. There was a light. It shone into the well, blinding her. She heard a voice.

"Rhoda," she said.

But it wasn't Rhoda. It was the sheriff.

He had taken off his jacket and was holding it down to her. She caught hold of the sleeve, and he pulled her out.

Mother was there with a flashlight in her hand. She dropped it and reached for Monica.

"Are you all right?"

"No," said Monica. "I'm all muddy."

Mother began to laugh, and Monica laughed, too. They couldn't stop.

"That's enough," said the sheriff. "You can stop the hysterics."

They stopped.

He picked up the flashlight. He was leading them out of the garden.

Monica asked, "How did you find me?"

"You hadn't been yourself all evening," Mother said. "I went to your room to see how you were, and you were gone. I found the note in your bed, so I called the sheriff. We came here, and he caught Rhoda running out of the garden."

"And she told you where I was?"

"Not at first. She said she didn't know."

"We took her to the station," said the sheriff. "Her mother was there—"

"Her *mother?*" said Monica.

"Yes. I kept thinking maybe the girl hadn't gone to New York after all. I tried to get her mother on the telephone, and finally I got through to her. She didn't have any idea where the girl was. She came right up from New York."

"When Rhoda saw her, she broke down and told everything," said Mother. "It was the strangest story I ever heard."

"Why did she hate me so?" asked Monica.

"She probably didn't hate you as much as she hated herself," said Mother. "And she didn't mean to leave you in the well forever. She was going to let you out after a while. But she had some twisted idea of getting revenge."

"Revenge for what?" asked Monica.

"It's hard to put it all together," said Mother. "She talked about how life had always been against her. She came here to get a new start, and she thought you'd kept her from it."

"Is that—is that what she said?" asked Monica.

"It was something like that," said Mother. "I tried to tell her that you'd gone out of your way to be good to her and make her welcome—"

"Mother," said Monica.

"What?"

"I didn't know she needed help. If I'd known, I wouldn't have shut her out."

"But you didn't shut her out. From the first you were good to her. You made her welcome—"

"I wasn't good to her."

"Of course you were," said Mother.

☞   XII

"I wasn't!" Monica heard her own voice rising higher. "I never was *really* good to her. I—I shut the door!"

The sheriff was saying, "It's been a bad shock for her. Let's get her home."

He picked her up and carried her. With her face against his shoulder, she closed her eyes and grew quiet.

* * *

All the next day she stayed at home. There were telephone calls from Madame Vere, from Fran and Audrey, from some of the other girls at school. They missed her, they said. They hoped she would soon be back.

"Do they know?" asked Monica.

"They know part of it," said Mother. "Not all."

"I don't want to talk about it."

"You don't have to. Not till you're ready."

Monica said, "Maybe I'll go back to school tomorrow."

"Are you sure you're ready?"

"I have to go back sometime," said Monica. "There's no use waiting."

She went to school the next morning. She walked with Fran and Audrey. They asked no questions. She was sure they had been told not to. They were watching her, and she felt strange with them. She almost wished she were alone.

They went into study hall. Madame was at her desk.

"Since we're all a bit early," she said, "I'll tell you the news now. One of our girls has left us. Rhoda has gone back to New York to live with her mother. And"— Madame smiled—"we have a new girl."

Monica looked toward Rhoda's old place. The new girl was there.

"She lives on South Beach, and she is here for the summer," said Madame. "Will you please stand, Martha?"

The girl stood. Her face was small and serious. She made a quick little bow. Just before she sat down, her eyes met Monica's.

She may be my best friend, thought Monica. She may be my worst enemy. She may not be anything much to me, or she may be more than I can imagine. What-ever she is, I don't know now. I'll have to wait to know. And while I wait, I won't close the door. This time I'll try to keep it open.

☞ XIII

THANK YOU, M'AM

by Langston Hughes

STORY SYNOPSIS — In Harlem, New York, in about 1950, a boy tries to snatch a woman's purse. Her response is to take him into her own home for long enough to share her dinner with him and to show him care and respect.

OBJECTIVE — Through appreciation of a classic American short story, children will grow in their understanding of respectful human interaction, even under extreme circumstances.

TIME — This story must be read in one sitting. Reading and discussion can both be accomplished in one forty-five-minute period, but extending the discussion into a second class session is probably best.

HOMEWORK — Most children need some discussion of this story before they can do a good job with homework about it.

PROCEDURE — Explain to your class that they must listen especially carefully, because the story was really written for adults, not children. Tell them they will hear unusual examples of ethical as well as unethical behavior. You could add that the author is a famous African-American writer, that the setting is Harlem, in New York, in the 1950s (to explain the different value of money).

You might practice ahead of time reading the story aloud, so that your expression is dramatic and seamless. Try to postpone all questions until you're through.

Listen and allow for all sorts of strong and interesting responses from the children as soon as the story is done. Then begin leading the discussion. Your questions should be less open than usual, though, in order to help children fully appreciate the ethical concepts involved.

DISCUSSION QUESTIONS

* Why do you think Roger *didn't* thank Mrs. Lucella Bates Washington Jones?

* How did Roger show her his respect and appreciation?

   He offered to go to the store for her; he sat where she could see him easily; he washed his face; he told her the truth.

* Did he need to thank her? Why or why not?

* Why do you think she just closed the door?

For the next question, list children's responses on the chalkboard.

✳ The story is titled *Thank You, M'am.* What are some of the reasons Roger could have thanked Mrs. Lucella Bates Washington Jones?

Here follow some examples:

* She gave him dinner, shared her food with him.

* She showed him she had expectations of him by making him wash his face and comb his hair.

* She trusted him, by just leaving her purse on the bed and not watching him.

* She told him stealing was wrong.

* She wouldn't allow him to lie to her.

* She gave him ten dollars.

* She didn't ask him any questions that would embarrass him.

* She told him she had made bad mistakes herself, "Everybody's got something in common."

* She told him to behave himself.

Ask which are most important. Most children see readily that her respect for his dignity (not asking embarrassing questions) and her lesson about their common humanity are the essential ethical acts, coupled with high standards of behavior. *She helped Roger without ever putting herself above him.*

Once you've gotten started on this list and the children have had a chance to listen to one another's responses to the story, you can assign the list of ways she helped him for homework or for class writing. Then you can discuss all together the concepts, with the benefit of each child's independent, private efforts with the story.

Children usually are moved by *Thank You, M'am,* and there's much else to discuss in it. For example, children may bring up her use of physical force against Roger—the kick and the "half nelson" in the early part of the story. Was this justified by the emergency of his crime against her? by her later sensitivity and generosity towards him? Also, you might need to help children understand that Mrs. Lucella Bates Washington Jones rents and lives in a single room and works hard. It's not as though she has food and money to spare.

THANK YOU, M'AM ————————————————————

by Langston Hughes*

She was a large woman with a large purse that had everything in it but a hammer and nails. It had a long strap, and she carried it slung across her shoulder. It was about eleven o'clock at night, dark, and she was walking alone, when a boy ran up behind her and tried to snatch her purse. The strap broke with the sudden single tug the boy gave it from behind. But the boy's weight and the weight of the purse combined caused him to lose his balance. Instead of taking off full blast as he had hoped, the boy fell on his back on the sidewalk and his legs flew up. The large woman simply turned around and kicked him right square in his blue-jeaned sitter. Then she reached down, picked the boy up by his shirt front, and shook him until his teeth rattled.

After that the woman said, "Pick up my pocketbook, boy, and give it here."

She still held him tightly. But she bent down enough to permit him to stoop and pick up her purse. Then she said, "Now ain't you ashamed of yourself?"

Firmly gripped by his shirt front, the boy said, "Yes'm."

The woman said, "What did you want to do it for?"

The boy said, "I didn't aim to."

She said, "You a lie!"

By that time two or three people passed, stopped, turned to look, and some stood watching.

"If I turn you loose, will you run?" asked the woman.

"Yes'm," said the boy.

"Then I won't turn you loose," said the woman. She did not release him.

"Lady, I'm sorry," whispered the boy.

"Um-hum! Your face is dirty. I got a great mind to wash your face for you. Ain't you got nobody home to tell you to wash your face?"

"No'm," said the boy.

"Then it will get washed this evening," said the large woman, starting up the street, dragging the frightened boy behind her.

He looked as if he were fourteen or fifteen, frail and willow-wild, in tennis shoes and blue jeans.

The woman said, "You ought to be my son, I would teach you right from wrong. Least I can do right now is to wash your face. Are you hungry?"

"No'm," said the being-dragged boy. "I just want you to turn me loose."

"Was I bothering you when I turned that corner?" asked the woman.

"No'm."

"But you put yourself in contact with me," said the woman. "If you think that

* Reprinted by permission of Harold Ober Associates Incorporated. Copyright ©1958 by Langston Hughes. Copyright renewed 1986 by George Houston Bass.

contact is not going to last awhile, you got another thought coming. When I get through with you, sir, you are going to remember Mrs. Lucella Bates Washington Jones."

Sweat popped out on the boy's face and he began to struggle. Mrs. Jones stopped, jerked him around in front of her, put a half nelson about his neck, and continued to drag him up the street. When she got to her door, she dragged the boy inside, down a hall, and into a large kitchenette-furnished room at the rear of the house. She switched on the light and left the door open. The boy could hear other roomers laughing and talking in the large house. Some of their doors were open, too, so he knew he and the woman were not alone. The woman still had him by the neck in the middle of her room.

She said, "What is your name?"

"Roger," answered the boy.

"Then, Roger, you go to that sink and wash your face," said the woman, where-upon she turned him loose—at last. Roger looked at the door—looked at the woman—looked at the door—and went to the sink.

"Let the water run until it gets warm," she said. "Here's a clean towel."

"You gonna take me to jail?" asked the boy, bending over the sink.

"Not with that face, I would not take you nowhere," said the woman. "Here I am trying to get home to cook me a bite to eat, and you snatch my pocketbook! Maybe you ain't been to your supper either, late as it be. Have you?"

"There's nobody home at my house," said the boy.

"Then we'll eat," said the woman. "I believe you're hungry—or been hungry—to try to snatch my pocketbook!"

"I want a pair of blue suede shoes," said the boy.

"Well, you didn't have to snatch my pocketbook to get some suede shoes," said Mrs. Lucella Bates Washington Jones. "You could of asked me."

"M'am?"

The water dripping from his face, the boy looked at her. There was a long pause. A very long pause. After he had dried his face and not knowing what else to do, dried it again, the boy turned around, wondering what next. The door was open. He could make a dash for it down the hall. He could run, run, run, run!

The woman was sitting on the daybed. After a while she said, "I were young once and I wanted things I could not get."

There was another long pause. The boy's mouth opened. Then he frowned, not knowing he frowned.

The woman said, "Um-hum! You thought I was going to say but, didn't you? You thought I was going to say, but I didn't snatch people's pocketbooks. Well, I wasn't going to say that." Pause. Silence. "I have done things, too, which I wouldn't tell you, son—neither tell God, if He didn't already know. Everybody's got something in common. So you set down while I fix us something to eat. You might run that comb through your hair so you will look presentable."

In another corner of the room behind a screen was a gas plate and an icebox. Mrs. Jones got up and went behind the screen. The woman did not watch the boy to see if he was going to run now, nor did she watch her purse, which she left behind her on the daybed. But the boy took care to sit on the far side of the room, away from the purse, where he thought she could easily see him out of the corner of her eye if she wanted to. He did not trust the woman not to trust him. And he did not want to be mistrusted now.

"Do you need somebody to go to the store," asked the boy, "maybe to get some milk or something?"

"Don't believe I do," said the woman, "unless you just want sweet milk yourself. I was going to make cocoa out of this canned milk I got here."

"That will be fine," said the boy.

She heated some lima beans and ham she had in the icebox, made the cocoa, and set the table. The woman did not ask the boy anything about where he lived, or his folks, or anything else that would embarrass him. Instead, as they ate, she told him about her job in a hotel beauty shop that stayed open late, what the work was like, and how all kinds of women came in and out, blondes, redheads, and Spanish. Then she cut him half of her ten-cent cake.

"Eat some more, son," she said.

When they were finished eating, she got up and said, "Now here, take this ten dollars and buy yourself some blue suede shoes. And next time, do not make the mistake of latching onto my pocketbook nor nobody else's—because shoes got by devilish ways will burn your feet. I got to get my rest now. But from here on in, son, I hope you will behave yourself."

She led him down the hall to the front door and opened it. "Good night! Behave yourself, boy!" she said, looking out into the street as he went down the steps.

The boy wanted to say something other than, "Thank you, M'am," to Mrs. Lucella Bates Washington Jones, but although his lips moved, he couldn't even say that as he turned at the foot of the barren stoop and looked up at the large woman in the door. Then she shut the door.

ON MY HONOR

by Marion Dane Bauer

(The book, *On My Honor*, is not included here. It is available through your school or public library in paperback, as a Dell Honor Book [Bantam Doubleday, New York, 1987], or in hardback [Houghton Mifflin Company, Boston, 1986].)

STORY SYNOPSIS — Cautious Joel gets involved, against his better judgment and despite his solemn promise to his father, in the dangerous adventures of his best friend Tony. Tony drowns and Joel must face telling his own and Tony's parents.

OBJECTIVE — Through involvement in a powerful, realistic story of tragedy resulting from a boy's reluctance to be true to his best self with his friend, children will confront issues of trust, autonomy, guilt, and responsibility in discussion with their peers.

TIME — Reading aloud and good discussion of *On My Honor* should require about six forty-five-minute sessions.

HOMEWORK — Most of the discussion questions can and probably should be re-used as homework questions, after each discussion. But it's also effective to have children bring in and share this written work in discussion.

PROCEDURE — There are more questions listed for discussion and for homework than you will need. Use the ones you wish or develop your own. Don't try to use them all.

Note: The writing is especially fine in this book, making it the more memorable and effective for children, but children who have experienced the death or serious injury of a friend may be too "raw" even for the sensitive portrayal in *On My Honor*.

The hand pointer indicates the paragraph in the book just preceding the point for discussion.

DISCUSSION AND HOMEWORK QUESTIONS

Chapter 1

page 9

☞ End of Chapter 1.

Pause to be sure everyone understands everything so far.

＊ Have you ever been in such a situation, where you wanted your parents (or some authority) to "get you off the hook" from the consequences of tough decision making, especially in front of a peer?

You could ask children to answer in writing, just to liberate the true response in that anonymity, but this probably isn't necessary. Almost all children of upper-elementary age will readily admit that they often have had to resort to such tactics. They can identify with Joel's fear and frustration, as well as with the attraction of Tony and his "wild ideas."

✳ What are ways to handle such situations both ethically and effectively?

Nobody wants to look like a "wimp" or "baby" in front of friends. Actual risk rarely seems as bad as humiliation to children. (As a practical solution, some might suggest, for example, that the child could ask the parent to speak privately with her or him so that things can be explained.)

Chapter 2

Just read this chapter without discussion to establish the two boys' personalities and their relationship.

Chapter 3

page 24

☞ End of Chapter 3

Homework Assignment (or Class Discussion)

The following activity can be assigned for homework, or done in class using discussion and writing on the chalkboard

✳ List the unethical actions by each boy so far and compare them.

A sample is listed below.

Joel

- He didn't stand up for his own opinions or fears with his friend.

- He wasn't honest with his father.

- He tried to use his father instead of just talking to him.

- He broke his solemn promise to his father.

- He was first to use violence, shoving Tony hard in the river.

- He said that Tony's father hit kids with a belt.

- He urged Tony to stay in the river.

- He challenged Tony to swim to the sandbar.

Tony

- He pushed his best friend into doing what Tony wanted rather than what the friend wanted.

- He lied to Joel's father about having permission to go.

- He said he had "dibs" on Joel's bike.

- He left Joel's bike carelessly against the bridge.

- He mocked Joel's father.

- He pushed Joel back in the river and took a swing at Joel's head.

- He told Joel he was scared—"chicken."

Most children are irritated with Tony by now, and are surprised to realize that it was Joel who did the more serious unethical actions. In particular, you could ask them to compare what each boy said about the other's father and say which was worse, who was more hurtful. When they all say "Joel!" ask them to explain *why*. Some will be able to articulate the points that Joel's father was only acting to take care of his son, but that what Tony's father *might* have done was nothing like that and surely deeply embarrassing to Tony. All children are sensitive to these points and understand the ethics involved for their peers, even if they can't explain them.

Also Joel's breach of trust with his own father was more serious than Tony's false assurance to Joel's father that he had permission. Children feel strongly about this.

Chapter 4

page 26

☞ Tony says that Rundle and Schmitt might notice them practicing and want to try out for the swim team too.

✳ What can you say about Tony? What is he worried about?

✳ What should Joel do, as his best friend?

Chapter 5

As you read aloud through the terrible events that follow, children are deeply affected. Many children won't believe or accept that Tony has really drowned. Be sure they understand how much Joel risked in his attempts to save his friend.

page 33

☞ "When the river bottom came up to meet his feet, he stood."

✳ Do you understand how dangerous it was for Joel to keep looking for Tony in the river?

Chapter 6

page 45

☞ Save the discussion questions for the end of the chapter. This episode with the teenager and his girlfriend rings true for children.

✳ What do you think of the teenager's efforts? Was he right to keep trying? Was he right to quit when he did?

✳ Was he right to say what he said to Joel?

✳ What is Joel most worried about? Why?

✳ What do you think of the teenager's girlfriend?

✳ Was the teenager right about going to the police station?

Chapter 7

page 48

☞ Joel decides to ride to Starved Rock State Park.

✳ Why does Joel start to go to the park instead of to the police station and home? Why is this wrong of him (although understandable)?

☞ Joel thinks of running away to the woods, then in the next paragraph he thinks of letting himself fall under a huge truck.

✳ Do you understand how Joel feels?

page 49

☞ "*Home*, the narrow tires sang against the pavement. *Home*."

✳ Why does Joel decide to head back toward home after all? What would you do in his place?

page 50

☞ Joel assembles an explanation in his mind and continues to pedal for home.

✳ What is very wrong about the explanation Joel thinks of? Why would it be an especially bad lie?

Joel would be telling a partial truth in order to mislead the people who trust him most about something extremely important.

page 52

☞ Joel musses Tony's shirt that he had just folded.

✳ Why did Joel muss Tony's shirt? Why is this an important kind of lie, even though not a word was spoken?

Children understand this, although it is not especially easy for them to explain. Joel arranged Tony's shirt to make it seem as though Joel *hadn't* been there and seen it, to make it look as if Tony had left it and Joel had never come back and folded it. Joel wanted to create a false impression, partly to protect himself.

Chapter 8

page 53

☞ "the shadow had been a small blob right next to the light."

✳ What does the shadow of the light fixture tell you?

Be sure the children understand that the whole afternoon has gone by, that Joel is at home in his own room.

page 56

☞ "Was that what he'd planned to say? He wasn't sure."

✳ Why won't Joel look at his father or really answer him? Why does Joel try to provoke his father into punishing him?

page 57

☞ Joel's father says he feels responsible.

✳ *Is* Joel's father responsible?

page 59

☞ Bobby runs out of the room and back down the stairs.

✳ What's good and what's bad about the way Joel's treating his little brother Bobby?

page 61

☞ Joel slams the screen door.

✳ Is Joel right to be so angry at both his parents?

* Is this anger at them understandable?

* Do you think there really is a stink from the river that anyone other than Joel can smell?

* Why does Joel want his parents to figure out for themselves what has happened? Have you ever felt that way?

* Realistically, would they be able to figure out what happened if Joel doesn't tell them?

* Is it Joel's responsibility to explain the situation as early as possible? Why?

Chapter 9

page 64

☞ Bobby bags the rolled newspapers.

* Why is Joel so hard on Bobby?

* From the way Bobby reacts, what can you say about the way Joel usually treats him?

> Students will be able to explain that Joel has displaced his rage onto his parents and his little brother.

page 66

☞ "Tony wouldn't have blamed himself. Would he?"

* Does Joel have a right to feel angry at Tony? Why?

Chapter 10

page 71

☞ "—but he never told me he couldn't swim."

* Were there things about Tony, Joel's best friend, that Joel had never even thought about?

* Are there always important "secrets" about people you think you know? Does anyone know everything about anybody? Should anyone know everything about anybody?

Chapter 11

This chapter is so powerful and dramatic that any discussion would probably spoil it.

Chapter 12

page 85

☞ Joel tells his father that he thinks Tony's death is his, Joel's, fault.

* *Is* it Joel's fault that Tony died?

  You may need to clarify that Joel's sense of guilt was probably exaggerated, that Tony was ultimately responsible for his own actions. But the important point that there may be consequences for seemingly innocent or understandable "going along" should not be lost.

page 86

☞ Joel's father asks Joel if he wants to be punished.

* Does Joel *want* punishment? Why?

  Children strongly identify with Joel's desire for punishment, in my experience. To the extent that Joel is responsible for what happened, he aches for some specific, tangible punishment to somehow restore the balance, give relief.

☞ Joel wails that he can smell the river, that it won't go away.

* Why is Joel the only one who's conscious of the smell?

  You might ask some class members to explain (for the benefit of those who might need it) about Joel's sense of the smell from the river (his own guilt, pain, shame).

page 90

☞ End of Chapter 12

* Joel's father feels the most important thing is for him to be absolutely honest with Joel rather than trying to offer insincere words of comfort. Do you agree? Why or why not?

  The resolution of the story is satisfying, though painful. It is so skillfully accomplished by the author that the teacher should be careful not to "overkill" it.

ALAN AND NAOMI

by Myron Levoy

(The book *Alan and Naomi* is not included here but is available through school and public libraries and bookstores. The hardback edition was published by Harper & Row, New York, 1977, and the paperback as a Harper Trophy paper-back, HarperCollins Publishers, 1987.)

STORY SYNOPSIS — The setting is 1944 in Brooklyn, New York. Twelve-year-old Alan is socially insecure as it is, but his parents ask him to befriend a refugee girl who appears to be "crazy." As he helps her and becomes friends with her, Alan is afraid to confide any of this to his one good friend in the neighborhood, Shaun. Finally, Shaun does find out about Alan's helping the girl (Naomi), and is angry at Alan for not confiding in him. Eventually, Naomi recovers enough to attend school, but when she witnesses a bloody fight, she severely regresses.

Despite its skillful humor throughout, this is a mature and serious book, *without* a happy ending. Children become deeply involved in it and may be quite upset by it. The teacher is well advised to read this story ahead of time and plan ahead with particular care. I feel strongly that this book is inappropriate for children younger than sixth grade.

OBJECTIVES — Through sharing the experience of the novel, *Alan and Naomi*, sixth graders will have to think hard about the conflicts of peer pressure versus ethical principles, the problems of helping another person, the nature of commitment, problems of trust and friendship, and issues of free will in ethical choice.

TIME — This book could take many weeks, so rich is it in ethical topics for discussion.

HOMEWORK — I feel that homework is particularly effective for *Alan and Naomi* because the strong feelings it evokes need the discipline of clear written expression. After discussion, try repeating some of the same questions for homework.

PROCEDURE — Reading this book aloud, it is especially effective to affect different voices for different characters. Naomi's French accent for herself and the doll and Alan's nasal Charlie McCarthy voice certainly do add to children's understanding and enjoyment of the book. "Ham it up!"

You may want to do some "ethical editing." For example, several of the adults are depicted in rather broad and stereotypical ways. You may wish to tone this down as you read. Also, the building superintendent is not treated with what I consider to be appropriate ethical respect by the author, and you may want to alter those parts too, as you go. (At least, you can make his name *Mr.* Finch.)

You might want to warn the class that the story begins with a scene in which language inappropriate for the classroom is used, and apologize in advance.

Note: ☞ indicates the paragraph just preceding the location for discussion. Remember, too many questions can be exasperating for the students: pick and choose.

DISCUSSION QUESTIONS

Chapter 1

page 10

☞ "Alan stepped back from Shaun to turn his anger into distance."

* Was Shaun right to keep Alan from fighting Joe Condello?

* Has someone ever "protected" you when you didn't want the help?

* Have you ever tried to help someone and then been surprised when the person resented it?

* Which way would Shaun have shown the most respect for Alan, by helping him as he did, or by standing back and letting him handle it?

* How do you decide when to help a friend in this way?

In relating to their own experience, sixth-grade boys are more likely to think of physical fights, girls to think of verbal hurts, but all will readily see that the principle is the same.

page 11

☞ "It made Alan want to take three steps at a time."

* Why do you think they've never talked about the "Jewish-Catholic stuff" before? Should they have? Why or why not?

page 14

☞ End of Chapter 1

Pause for children's reactions.

* Did Alan do the right thing?

Chapter 2

page 18

I edit out the reference to "mixed neighborhood." It is used here in a pejorative way, and my personal view is that "mixed" or diverse is good.

page 21

☞ End of Chapter 2

Write two headings on the chalkboard: Reasons Alan *should* help Naomi, and Reasons he *should not* help her.

Children might offer such "for" reasons as

- She needs his help.

- He could get her as a new friend.

- It would be an interesting challenge for him.

- He wants to please his parents.

- There's no one else to do it.

- He might learn to speak French better.

"Against" reasons might be

- He would lose his friends in the neighborhood.

- His friend Shaun could be really hurt.

- She might not want his help.

- He wouldn't get to play stickball.

- He shouldn't do it if he doesn't want to.

- In trying to help, he might make things worse for Naomi. He could say or do the wrong thing by mistake.

Now have the class decide which are the most *ethical* reasons and why. The idea that the most ethical reasons are those which embody the most respect for Naomi and also for Alan himself (as distinguished from Alan's mere wishes—obviously a very difficult distinction) could be suggested and discussed.

For example, "Alan might do the wrong thing in trying to help her, and end up making her worse" is an *ethical* reason not to help, as is, "She might really not want his help." "He would miss stickball games," while a perfectly good reason not to help, is not an *ethical* reason. Similarly, "She needs the help" is an *ethical* reason for him to help her, but, "She could be a new friend" is probably just a fine reason but not an *ethical* one. He loves and respects his parents and they have asked (as opposed to insisted) that Alan do this: this is another ethical reason to try to help. That Alan's French might improve if he decides to help is another good reason, neither ethical nor unethical. But be clear that not helping her *could* be just as ethical as helping, and there are ethical reasons on both sides of the issue.

Children in my class have stressed how hurt and confused Shaun would be, how likely that Alan's parents would not have considered Shaun at all. This example of consideration for Shaun is poignant for me, because I *hadn't* thought of it. My class taught me the limitations of my own understanding of ethical reasons and ethical choices. Many a "should" can indeed be challenged by a different "should."

This whole topic of Alan's decision should extend over at least one full class session, with homework to follow. This written assignment would vary according to the progress of the class discussion.

Homework Assignment

1. List three good reasons why Alan should help Naomi and three good reasons why he should not help her, then indicate which of these reasons are *ethical* and which are merely good reasons.

2. Using complete sentences, answer the following questions: If you were Alan, what would you do? What is the *best* reason for your choice? What would change it? Why?

Chapter 3

This chapter, as is, is very effective with children. It does not require much discussion.

page 27

☞ End of Chapter 3

   ✳ *Is* Alan committed to helping Naomi now? Why?

Chapter 4

page 30

References to "yellow" to mean cowardly are confusing to many children, because the word is not generally used that way today. You can explain that it was a common term in 1944; or, you could substitute "chicken." (It is possible that "yellow" had its origins in racist notions.)

page 33

☞ End of Chapter 4

Note: Depending on the group, you may need to explain that this story is set in a different time, when social relations seem immature compared to the present. For example, the stigma attached to boy-girl friendships seems more fitting to eight-year-olds than twelve-year-olds of today. I find this explanation helps remove a barrier of confusion that would otherwise be there.

Alan doesn't have the courage or trust to explain his new commitment to his best friend Shaun. Instead, they have a tentative discussion about prejudice, Alan "testing the waters" with Shaun. Shaun, misunderstanding, "fails" the test.

* Did Alan really give Shaun a chance?

* Were they both right, according to how each understood/misunderstood the situation?

* What is right or wrong about "testing" a friend in this way?

  Such testing may be understandable, but it is a form of lying, because Alan withheld the purpose of his words from Shaun. Shaun was Alan's best friend, and he might have responded differently if Alan had simply "been straight" with him.

(If your group is interested in this topic, pursue it. If not, this issue arises later in the story, and so can be postponed.)

Chapter 5

page 37

☞ Alan says, "No, thanks. I'm really not—you know—hungry."

Pause for children's reactions. The class is likely to respond to this, the idea of kids being "paid" by adults for their good deeds, with some emotion.

The rewards of good ethical acts are intrinsic, and such extrinsic rewards are demeaning to the person as well as corrupting to the act. You can pause to acknowledge this, but it's probably best not to interrupt the strong narrative of the story too much at this point. (This topic also arises later in the story.)

Chapter 6

page 44

☞ Alan says, "I know. You don't have to tell me."

Alan's mother's prejudice against Shaun is made obvious, as is her idealization of Alan. Both make Alan furious.

* Why does Alan's mother's prejudice against Shaun and for Alan seem unethical?

  A related topic of possible interest would be children's use of such perceived prejudices to transfer blame or to seek shelter.

Chapter 7

This whole chapter is very enjoyable. Read the different voices humorously as well as dramatically.

page 54

☞ "Can't. Got an errand."--"Again?"--"Again."

  * What's good about Alan as a friend? What's bad about Alan as a friend? Why?

  * What's good about Shaun as a friend? What's bad about Shaun as a friend? Why?

Homework Assignment

  * Was Alan right to be so angry at Shaun? Why or why not?

Chapter 8

page 60

☞ "I have to be tough sometimes, Alan, or else you'll never become…yourself."

Homework Assignment (or Discussion Questions)

For homework assignment or group consideration, the class might be asked to answer the following questions.

  * What does Alan's father mean?

  * Do you think Alan's father is right?

  * Should someone else have a sense of what another person can or should become?

  * Does anyone, even a parent, have such a right? Or does a parent have the responsibility to have respect in the form of such high expectations?

Chapter 9

page 67

☞ Alan reflects that he had to force himself not to reveal to Shaun how much he knew about Naomi, but that it "felt just like outright lying."

  * *Was* Alan lying to Shaun?

    Alan was telling the technical truth (that he had "heard" her name was Naomi, that "maybe" she could speak English) but of course he was lying to Shaun, because he was deliberately misleading him.

    The discussion here will be very heated! Children will protest in outrage that he wasn't lying, because "How could he be lying if he was telling the truth?"

  * Was Alan's intention to mislead Shaun?

Alan's intention was to mislead Shaun, but even your emphasis on the idea of intention will not daunt most children, according to my own experience. Wait for further discussion by the children themselves, or the homework, to bring this out more fully.

page 68

☞ End of Chapter 9

Alan "tests" Shaun again by asking him loaded questions about Naomi. The class may now want to consider whether it is ethical to "test" a friend in this way. This is a familiar experience for sixth graders, and they will defend the ethics on both sides of this issue.

✳ Is it ethical to "test" a friend in this way?

✳ Is testing a friend in this way like lying to him?

✳ Can such a test be truly fair?

✳ If you were Shaun and you found out about this test later, how do you think you would feel?

✳ What are the most ethical reasons for Alan's testing Shaun in this way?

Homework Assignment

You might assign a homework paper which proceeds step by step:

1. Give your own definition of lying.

2. What is wrong about lying?

3. Give examples of situations when lying *could* be the ethical choice.

   (Possible situations include lying to save someone's life or to spare someone from serious hurt [including hurt feelings], or lying when the lie is temporary and for the purpose of fun—like planning a surprise party).

4. What is the reason Alan answered Shaun's questions about Naomi the way he did?

   (This is critical. Alan's motive was to protect *himself.*)

5. If Shaun had known about Naomi, would *he* have felt Alan was lying to him?

After completing such an assignment in reflective privacy, even the most vehement protestors from class discussion will probably be convinced that a partial truth, intended to mislead, is indeed a lie.

Chapters 10 and 11

These chapters are enjoyable and emotional. They should probably be read with little discussion.

Chapter 12

page 82–83

☞ "Charlie? Are you there?" or "Please, Charlie, visit me, today, *oui?* Charlie, please?"

Ask these questions at either or both of the points indicated above.

✳ What should Alan do? Why?

✳ If Alan acknowledges Naomi as his friend in front of Shaun, is it an act of moral courage? Why?

✳ Is it possible for Alan to pretend he doesn't know Naomi, yet still be an ethical person? Why?

> Alan does what most children fear they would actually do: he pretends to Shaun that he doesn't really know this "crazy girl," Naomi.

Feelings in the class are likely to be very intense! Nearly all of them will have had painful experiences on all sides of this problem. It's very scary to risk ostracism by the most popular or desirable peers for the sake of one's commitment to an uncertain relationship with a peer who is not generally accepted.

The ethical problem should be explored honestly and realistically with the group and followed up with a writing assignment.

Homework Assignment

Using complete sentences, answer the following question.

✳ What is the most ethical and realistic thing for Alan to have said or done when he and Shaun encountered Naomi in the apartment lobby? Explain why.

Chapter 13

page 85

☞ Alan, very upset, thinks maybe he and Naomi could be "secret friends."

✳ What is unethical about the secret friends idea?

✳ How do you think someone would feel if asked to be your "secret friend"?

> Any person wants the dignity of acknowledgment.

Chapter 14

This is a highly dramatic chapter.

page 94

☞ "*MERDE!*" Naomi screamed.

You might need to explain that the French bad word *merde* would have seemed much worse in 1944, and coming from Naomi, than it does now.

Chapter 15

page 98

☞ "The sewing class has arrived. Oink, oink, oink, oink."

✴ Do you think this comment reflects that time or the author's sexism?

Today tasks for boys and girls seem less rigid. (At my school, for example, both boys and girls all learn to sew.)

page 99

☞ "Naomi get better now, quick, he thought. Get better."

✴ Is Alan right about Naomi's needing to cope with these "normal kids"?

✴ How do you think they would treat her?

Chapter 16

page 104

☞ "It's not funny!"

Alan's parents make plans for him and Naomi without consulting him, and Alan is, appropriately, offended.

✴ Is Alan right to be upset? Why?

The rest of the chapter is very effective. (And of course, even "heroes" do cry sometimes. Sixth graders like having that acknowledged.)

Chapter 17

Alan visits relatives and the park, thinking about how lonely Naomi seems.

page 111

☞ "It was strange. He felt older when he was alone."

✴ Why does Alan feel older, less ready to do things just for fun, when he's alone?

Chapter 18

page 115

☞ End of Chapter 18

Alan has a "breakthrough" with Naomi, and, in the flush of his success, also realizes that he really enjoys being with her, that he really likes her. This presents a perplexing topic for ethics class discussion and writing:

✳ Was it more ethical before, when his helping her was more pure duty and less fun?

✳ Does getting some enjoyment from a good deed make it any less of a good deed? any more of a good deed?

✳ Is it usually harder to do the more ethical thing? Should it be?

✳ Is it more respectful of Naomi if Alan likes her when he's helping her?

Chapter 19

This is a very satisfying chapter for children.

page 121

☞ End of Chapter 19

✳ What do you think about Mrs. Landley? about Shaun? about Alan?

Chapter 20

This is a lot of fun, especially if you ham it up!

page 126

☞ End of Chapter 20

✳ *Would* the Puritans have kicked Alan out? Naomi?

Chapter 21

page 129

☞ "He took a breath, but the words wouldn't come. Coward!"

✳ *Is* Alan a coward?

☞ "Could somebody actually be afraid of him?"

✳ Did Alan handle the situation with the catcher well? Was he ethical? Was he realistic?

Chapter 22

This chapter is probably best just read, as dramatically as it deserves, but with minimal discussion.

Chapter 23

Again, just read the chapter.

Chapter 24

As you read this chapter, pause from time to time to allow for any reactions the children may have.

Chapter 25

page 154

I edit out the reference to cigarettes. Others may disagree, of course.

page 158

☞ End of Chapter 25

* Is Shaun right? Can you understand how he feels?

* How do you think Alan and Shaun could become friends again?

* Why do you think Alan expected so little of Shaun?

Children, especially boys, will be deeply moved. Be careful not to "overkill" with too much discussion. The author's words are effective enough.

Chapter 26

page 165

☞ End of Chapter 26

Alan explodes against the insensitivity of the adults. Again, too much discussion might be deadly at this point.

* Do you agree or disagree with Alan? Was his anger justified?

* What was wrong about the adults thanking Alan for his efforts to help Naomi?

Chapter 27

Just let the children enjoy this chapter as Naomi adjusts to regular school.

Chapter 28

This is by far the favorite chapter in the whole book for children. I feel strongly that they should be allowed to savor it, in the privacy of their own thoughts, without intrusive discussion.

Chapter 29

page 177

☞ "Shaun turned and came back."

* ✳ Was Alan right to fight Joe Condello?

* ✳ Was Shaun right to intervene?

page 179

☞ "Everything was where he'd left it."

* ✳ What do you think of the way Shaun and Alan made up their friendship? Why is this (with humor and without explicit words of apology or forgiveness) such an effective way for friends to make up?

Chapter 30

page 185

☞ "'Of both of us,' said Shaun."

* ✳ Why does Shaun tell the police officer that Naomi is *his* friend, too? Is she?

page 186

☞ "Than like you, Alan finished the sentence in his mind."

* ✳ Do you think Alan is right? Which is better, to be "crazy" or to be a person who says "stay away from 'crazy people'"? Why?

page 187

I usually edit out the *hideous* or the *witch doctor* or both, because of what could be seen as white ethnocentric bias. Naomi's face had become a mask, and an entirely strange-seeming one—that's enough.

Chapter 31

page 192

Read through to the very end. Children will be stunned. Emphasize that there *is* hope for Naomi, although Alan is too upset to see it. His father may well be right—with time and care, she *will* get well. Some children will appreciate the realism of the non-happy ending. Others will be very upset.

Homework or In-class Assignment

Use the following questions either for discussion, if the children wish to talk then, or for homework.

✳   If Alan could have known ahead of time how his efforts would end, should he still have tried to help Naomi?

The class could also be invited to write letters to the author of *Alan and Naomi* or to write their own endings for the story and justify them. Careful writing affords an especially worthy outlet here!

The book will have been a rich ethical and aesthetic experience for a sixth-grade group.

THE SAME SUN

by Adrienne Su

STORY SYNOPSIS — A Chinese-American girl is traveling in the Peoples' Republic of China. Chinese people expect too much from her, Caucasian Americans can't even "see" her, and she feels torn about her ethical responsibilities.

OBJECTIVE — Through hearing and discussing Adrienne Su's short story, children will grow in sensitivity about ethical issues of race, culture, and identity.

TIME — This story can be read and discussed in one forty-five-minute class.

HOMEWORK — Some of the discussion questions could be used for homework, either before or after the discussion.

PROCEDURE — Read the story aloud, carefully. You may prefer to save all questions and discussion until the story is done.

You should explain that this story takes place around 1985, when many young Americans were visiting the Peoples' Republic of China. The author herself went to China before going to college. The government was indeed repressive (as it still is), but the experience for visiting Americans, especially Americans of Chinese descent, was mixed and confusing. Native Chinese could suffer imprisonment for their contact with foreigners, Americans could be told to leave China immediately. In such an atmosphere, most ethical questions remain open.

DISCUSSION QUESTIONS

☞ I

Pause to be sure children understand. Later in discussion, help children to see that there are ethical reasons for both sides: helping and not helping.

☞ II

Pause to give the children a chance to react.

✳ Do you think she should have been offended by the comment about stir fry? Why or why not?

☞ III

Pause to be sure children understand and to give them a chance to react.

After the story is completed, listen for children's responses, which will be strong. The following questions could be posed:

✳ The narrator describes in some detail her three encounters with people (the boy at the station, the American couple on the train, the boy at the beach). In what way was each unethical to her? ethical?

✳ Was she right to refuse to do the money exchange? Why or why not?

✳ Was he right to persist?

✳ Was he right to say, "*Your* family made it to America"? Why did she feel especially bad, finally, about this boy?

✳ Why did the American Caucasian couple "look right through" her? Was that unethical? Why or why not?

✳ What about this couple's clothes for traveling in China and their joke about Chinese food? Why could such behavior be considered unethical?

✳ Was the narrator right to lie to the last boy? Why or why not?

✳ He thought she was a local person and "therefore useless." What is the ethical issue there?

✳ Why does she feel so very far from home at the end? Do you agree with her?

THE SAME SUN

by Adrienne Su*

I don't know how I got here, but it isn't bad. It's close to dusk and I'm sitting on a Chinese beach and watching the sun disappear. I'm thousands of miles from home.

I think I came to China for this moment. Most of my stay here has been stinky, dirty, inconvenient, or difficult in some other way. It seems like there are two thousand people on every bus, the streets are full of honking cars and garbage, and I'm always being mistaken for what I'm not. The Chinese think I'm from Japan, and other foreigners think I'm from China. No one seems to get it when I say I'm from New York.

Last night while I was waiting to board my train, a boy in drab blue clothes followed me all over the station. The station was full of smoke and vinyl suitcases and more Chinese people than I'd ever seen in one place.

The boy was short and greasy, and he leaned too close when he talked. But I was feeling patient, so I talked to him. He asked me lots of questions about me and my life in America.

"How old are you?"

"Seventeen," I said in my bad Chinese.

"Where were your parents born?"

"My mother was born here and my father was born in America," I said. "But his parents are from here too."

He didn't stop. Some of his questions were rude, like, how much money does your father make, and how many cars does your family have? He wanted to know how much it costs to go to college in America, and whether you can get good Chinese food in every town.

The more I thought about my family, the foggier they became. It was hard to remember what everything felt like from day to day. All I could recall was that a lot of arguing had been going on and I had decided to go somewhere far, far away for the summer—and that was how I'd ended up here.

"Tuition is different at every college," I told him. I didn't mention that my mother works, too, or that there are parts of America I don't know much about. I wouldn't be able to tell him whether you can get a good Peking duck in Bonner Springs, Kansas.

* * *

He told me he had a friend who needed a medicine from America. "You can only buy it with Foreign Exchange Currency," he said breathlessly. "And you have Foreign Exchange, right?"

Foreign Exchange was what the bank gave me for my U.S. dollars, and for the Chinese, it was hard to get. You could use it to buy things that you couldn't buy with local money. "Well, I don't have much on me," I said.

---

* *The Same Sun* by Adrienne Su, copyright ©1991, reprinted by permission of the author.

"How much do you have?" he asked. "I'll give you 160 in local money for every 100 in Foreign Exchange."

I didn't say anything. I couldn't change money with this guy in the middle of a train station. Besides being illegal, it was close to impossible. There were always a few people looking at me curiously. Even if I'd wanted to duck into a shadowy corner and quickly change the dollars, I wouldn't have been able to find a shadowy corner.

"Please," he said.

I stood up. "I've got to catch my train," I said.

"Please? 170?" he said.

I shook my head and walked toward the boarding gate. People swarmed around it, shoving each other with their bags and shouting. A station attendant stood next to the turnstile, ripping tickets in half.

He ran after me, right into the crowd. Somebody's bag jabbed me in the side.

"Wait, please!" he said.

I turned around, and an old woman scowled at me.

He pressed a wad of local bills into my hand. "Here's 170," he whispered, leaning close.

"No!" I said, and I pushed it back at him.

He wouldn't take it. "Please!" he said. "I can't stay here. My family can't stay here. There's no life for us in China. *Your* family made it to America."

Made it to America? I guess that's what my grandparents did, but as far as I was concerned, we'd always been there. There wasn't anything special about that.

In any case, I wasn't going to make the trade. Probably no one would care if they saw us, but if someone did care, he could be put in jail for it.

"I'm sorry," I said. "Good-bye."

He looked devastated.

I held out my hand. "I'm really sorry," I said.

He took my hand and shook it. "It's all right," he said, smiling like a child who's just been given the wrong birthday present. "Have a safe trip."

I held his hand a second longer than necessary. Something very sad came over me then, so I turned around quickly and let the crowd carry me away.

* * *

☞ I

All night on the train, the clacking of the wheels on the tracks kept me awake. I curled in the sleeper and stared at the ceiling. I was sharing this section with five other people—three on each side of the open cabin—and they were all asleep.

I thought about the boy in the train station. He was just like the dozen or so other people who had approached me during my stay in China. Everyone wanted me to help them get to America, and everyone wanted to learn English. I gave a few English lessons, but people always ended up asking for a lot more than that.

They wanted a room in my house, enrollment in an American school, a dishwashing job in an American restaurant—anything for a new life.

People in China seemed to think there was no such thing as a hungry or homeless American. They thought we lived on huge green estates with private swimming pools and ate expensive steaks every day. After a while, I stopped telling them they were wrong. They wanted to believe in a land where everything was perfect, and I figured I might as well let them imagine that a land like that existed.

* * *

At 5 in the morning, the train made one of its stops in a small town. Some of the people around me gathered up their things and shuffled off the train. Then I heard two American voices, those of a man and a woman.

"It's just a couple of hours away," the man said. "We should try to get some sleep in those two hours."

"Yes," the woman said. "I'm going to dream that I'm at home, with a mushroom-and-pepperoni pizza."

I leaned over the edge of my bunk. The woman was wearing a sweatsuit and sneakers, and the man was in jeans and a ratty T-shirt. They were Caucasian and they seemed big, although the woman wasn't any bigger than me. I looked at her and she looked right through me.

"Craving pizza?" the man said to her. "Don't tell me you've had too much stir-fry." They started to laugh.

I wanted to say something, but I don't know what. Maybe I wanted to tell them that the joke had offended me, or maybe I wanted to tell them I was an American and I thought it was funny. Whatever it was, I never figured it out, and I never said a word, even though I was dying to talk to somebody in English. Instead, I tuned them out and lay there in the semi-darkness, listening to the train humming along on its bumpy tracks.

* * *

☞   II

Sitting here on the sand, I think this could be any beach, maybe one back in the States—in Florida or Massachusetts or California. It's strange that halfway around the world it is the same sun that keeps everything alive. The light is gleaming over the water that seems never to end. The trees are turning into silhouettes against the sky, and the sunlight has almost disappeared when someone walks up behind me and starts talking.

It's a Chinese boy. He's talking in Chinese. "You…are from Japan?" he says.

I turn around to look at him. He isn't like the boy in the train station. This one is taller and thinner, and he's wearing glasses. But he has the same earnest expression on his face.

I'm annoyed. If I tell him I'm from New York, he'll want to change money, practice English, hear all about America. If I tell him I'm from Japan, he'll want to change even more money. And I'm thinking about the train station boy's family and how they will never get out of China. I'm thinking about the Americans who can't tell I'm one of them. I'm thinking about my family and how easily we could be Chinese and not American. I don't know what to say.

So I lie.

"No," I say, in the best Chinese accent I can produce. "No, I live here."

"Oh." He looks disappointed. Now he thinks I am one of them, dressed like a foreigner, but basically just another local person—and therefore useless. "Sorry to bother you," he says.

☞   III

Then he vanishes, and when I turn back around to look over the water, everything has changed. The water doesn't glow, and the sky is heavy and gray. It can't be the same sky I look at from my rooftop in New York, it just can't. Something is wrong with it. I feel there's a storm coming on, even though I know there isn't.

My grandfathers were born in this town, and so was my mother. But I'm about as far from home as I will ever get. Even the shadows of the trees have disappeared, and the sun is completely gone.

THE WHITE CIRCLE

by John Bell Clayton

(*The White Circle* is not included here, but it is widely available in school and public libraries, anthologized in O. Henry Awards, *First Prize Stories 1919–1960*, Hanover House, Garden City, and in *Junior Great Books, Series Six*, The Great Books Foundation, Chicago, 1984. It may also be found in several secondary school textbooks. I think it is quite appropriate for the end of sixth grade.)

STORY SYNOPSIS — Tucker is a wealthy boy who has had pity for Anvil, the poor boy who lives nearby, but cannot recognize his humanity. Anvil is a bully. When Anvil steals some apples from Tucker and otherwise insults him, Tucker is so enraged that he tries to kill Anvil.

OBJECTIVES — Through involvement with this powerful short story, children will appreciate our common humanity against social class prejudice and other issues.

TIME — This story can be read and discussed in one forty-five-minute period, to be followed by a homework assignment.

HOMEWORK — Extensive discussion will be needed before any homework is assigned.

PROCEDURE — Explain that the story is serious and hard. Offer copies for some children who wish to follow silently while you read aloud. Try to read the whole story without pausing but with the drama it deserves. Reject interruptions or questions which break the flow of the story.

DISCUSSION AND HOMEWORK QUESTIONS

When the story is done, ask for general reaction. Sixth graders will be shocked and befuddled.

You might begin by asking these questions:

* Describe Tucker and explain how you know what you do about him (that he is wealthy, for example).

* Describe what you know about Anvil.

    They will mention his poverty, his being a bully.

* What is Tucker's attitude towards Anvil?

    They should point out the animal references in Tucker's descriptions from the beginning.

The answers to these first three questions form the basis for the ensuing discussion.

Choose additional discussion questions from those which follow or develop your own. I try to avoid questions about *why* Anvil became a bully, because I consider such questions the kind of *psychological* probing that is not the proper province of ethics class. All we really need to know about Anvil is that he wants respect, just as Tucker and everyone else does. Anvil's bad deeds are *not* excused by his miserable home life.

You may want to save some questions for a writing assignment.

* For most of the story, we sympathize with Tucker more than with Anvil. At the end, we "change sides" or at least we question our original attitudes. Did the story surprise you or "catch you off guard"?

* What was Anvil trying to teach Tucker and the world?

* What, if anything, did Tucker learn at the end?

* What was Tucker trying to teach Anvil?

* Why were the "dried-up apples" so important to Tucker?

* What was sacred to Tucker and why?

* What was sacred to Anvil and why?

* Which boy seemed better at the end of the story and why?

* Why did Tucker try to give Anvil the apples, and why did Anvil not even answer?

* If someone else had taken the apples, perhaps someone who was also rich, would Tucker have been just as enraged?

* How do you think Anvil felt about Tucker's efforts to be "nice" to him?

* Why did Anvil insult Tucker's father? Why did he want Tucker to say "Old Man"?

* Why do you think the author chose *Anvil* (something you hit) for that character's name?

* Does the name *Tucker* seem to mean anything? What about his family name, *English*?

* Was Tucker secure in his wealth?

* Was Anvil made free by his lack of wealth?

* Which boy was more likable?

* Which was more ethical? Why?

There will be strong disagreement about this story and its ethics message. My own view is that Anvil was trying to teach Tucker (the author is trying to teach *us*) that we are all just human, fundamentally the same. You and your children may have quite different interpretations. Some children hate the story, but most find it very stimulating. Students have come back to me years later to say: "Never stop reading that Tucker and Anvil story in sixth grade!"

OTHER ACTIVITIES

WRITING IN CLASS

Ask children to take a few moments in class to write their opinion, and the reasons for it, on a particular ethical issue. Use index cards, then read the cards aloud without revealing who wrote what. (When I do this, I insist on not revealing *any* identities, even if the children are willing. In this way, as I explain, the shy writers are protected from others' figuring them out by process of elimination.) Besides the obvious advantages of building skills in written expression, this technique brings out ideas that might otherwise be missed (especially from very shy students), allows for more objective examination of ideas, and gives a basis for class discussion.

An effective variation of this is for you to copy each child's written response (e.g., examples of unethical behavior by a particular character in a story), without names, onto separate index cards. Then pass out these cards at random to the children on a different day, and ask them to read the cards aloud, comment on them, or add to what's written on the card. In this way, very good discussion is often engendered by the children's own writing, perhaps because no one knows who wrote what. And the power of clear writing, even just a sentence, is demonstrated for all.

ETHICS JOURNALS

For grades four through six, the children might be urged to keep their own private "ethics-in-action" journals. Fourth graders could make their own out of construction paper and lined paper; fifth and sixth graders may want to use separate notebooks. The journals should be used to record ethical dilemmas the children face or ethical actions they have done and are proud of. Occasionally, they may also include requests for advice about ethics.

Journals should be offered for your scrutiny or comments only according to the child's wishes. It is of utmost importance that the child's privacy be respected and protected, but for some children, writing about ethical issues in such journals is very helpful. I suggested that children fold over and mark "private" the pages they didn't want me to read. They did so, and of course, I never looked at those pages. In any event, such ethical journals can't be included in work that is graded.

DEBATE

Sometimes important ethical issues fill the news and upper-grade children are eager to debate them. These issues change from year to year, and in my experience, are hard for children to debate because they are so complex and so enmeshed in divergent data. However, there are some perennial ethics issues which sixth graders can grasp and use for a class debate.

These topics include capital punishment and animal rights. Year after year, my sixth-grade students have done a serious, fine job on these hard topics and, I think, learned a great deal. It is, of course, essential to make the exact subject of the debate very clear and defined. Which side "for" is, and which side is "against" should be repeated, written on the chalkboard, and repeated again. This is vital, because children can easily get confused. (For example, children may think the animal rights issue involves protecting endangered species, which it does not.)

Three groups of students participate in these ethics debates: "for," "against," and judges, with a roughly equal number of children in each group. Everyone should get a chance to be both judge and debater at some time during the year.

Insofar as possible, children should be allowed to choose their own group in each debate. But they must understand that this is not always possible—people may have to be assigned to a side by choosing a number or flipping a coin. I always tell them that they are much more valuable to the side they believe in once they thoroughly understand the other side. But it has occasionally happened that children will proclaim with wonderment after a debate is over that they have *changed* opinion!

On the day of the debate, each side needs a few moments together to discuss their arguments and who will make which points. The judges need to agree upon their criteria (clarity of argument, number of different reasons, courtesy toward opposite side, originality of argument, for instance) and their method for deciding (perhaps one to five points for strength of each argument made, two points off for any interruption, whatever system the judges decide is fair). They should also clearly explain these rules to the debaters *before* the debate.

Emphasis should be upon ethical arguments, although certainly others will be included. (Some unethical arguments should not be allowed, in my opinion. For example, children often try to say that capital punishment serves to relieve overcrowding in prisons. Whether or not this is true, it can hardly be an ethical argument in favor of the death penalty, as I explain in class. Also, I never allow children to make jokes about "frying" a person in the electric chair.)

The best procedure is for the judges to alternate calling on one person from each side while all remain seated throughout, except perhaps for children who may wish to stand up to make their arguments. There is no need for terms like rebuttal or presentation at this level, just children taking turns to raise their hands and express arguments is sufficient.

This rather informal sort of ethics debate should require about twenty minutes of preparation with the children in class and perhaps thirty or forty minutes for the debate itself on a different day from the original preparation day.

I feel strongly that, once the topic is agreed upon and the roles chosen, but before the day of the debate, *all* children should complete a homework assignment listing good ethical reasons for *both* sides. It is important to understand that good argument requires good preparation, that it isn't just "spouting off." And of course it is vital to begin to understand an opinion you disagree with. As mentioned, some children even change their views. And others don't have opinions on these topics, but soon develop them.

In any event, most older children thoroughly enjoy debate. Amidst the competitive excitement, they are thinking very hard and working to express themselves as clearly as possible.

After the debate is done, take time, best on a different day, to elicit and write on the chalkboard the arguments for both sides. This serves to complete and clarify the whole experience.

Both of the topics provided here as examples are now grounded in the laws of particular states in the United States. Familiarize yourself with its status in your state. The "for" side in the debate is always the side that seeks to change the existing situation.

Here follow some arguments made in my classes on two topics: the death penalty and animal rights.

THE DEATH PENALTY

The *for* position is in favor of using the death penalty as a punishment for people convicted of extremely serious crimes.

REASONS FOR

- Knowing about it might scare potential criminals out of committing terrible acts.

- Some crimes are so terrible that they deserve the most serious punishment.

- The most dangerous criminals would be removed from society, permanently.

- Many polls have shown that the majority of people in America support the death penalty, and in our democratic system, the majority rules.

REASONS AGAINST

- The death penalty teaches violence as a solution to problems.

- There is always the chance that the executed person was innocent.

- The criminal justice system reflects the racist and unfair aspects of our society and therefore can't use such a final act as execution.

- Saying "we'll kill you to show that killing is wrong" doesn't make sense.

- A term of life imprisonment is worse than execution.

ANIMAL RIGHTS

The *for* position is in favor of strict protection against use of small mammals in medical research or consumer product testing.

REASONS FOR

- Innocent animals should not have to die for the benefit of human animals.

- Most research and testing can be accomplished by using computer models and other non-lethal means.

- The results of many animal tests don't apply to humans anyway, so the animals' lives were wasted.

REASONS AGAINST

- Use of animals is the only way to accomplish essential medical research that we all need, and to assure the safety of products many people use.

- Animals can't have "rights" because they can't be part of a moral community, respecting the rights of others.

- Respect for animals is not practiced consistently. What about animals that aren't cute and appealing? or what about non-mammals or non-vertebrates? what about the use of leather or the slapping of a mosquito?

(*Animal Rights,* Opposing Viewpoints Series, 1989, Greenhaven Press, St. Paul, Minnesota is helpful for background on this topic and others for debate.)

None of these lists is exhaustive, but all should give an idea of clear reasons in terms children can understand. In my experience, the most difficult topic is the one about animals. Children's emotions are strong on this, and the concepts involved are hard to articulate.

There is the question of whether you should reveal your personal views on such topics after the debate is done or even before it begins. Most teachers prefer not to, but I disagree. I feel that bias is safest if it's explicit, "out in the light" for general scrutiny. When it's hidden, its influence is more subtle and more suspect, especially in the teacher-child relationship. My favorite times with children are when they proclaim to me, "I realize how you feel about this, and I completely disagree with you!" Also, a teacher's being involved and concerned about important topics of our society is an important model.

MOVEMENT ACTIVITIES

Children need breaks from reading and discussion. In addition to providing such breaks, the following activities have proven effective and enjoyable in upper-elementary ethics classes for the purpose of developing better cooperation and concentration. It is important that this objective be explicitly stated before the activities are begun, so the children are aware of the effort of developing their own skills in this area. Not only does such explicitness model respectful treatment of others, it also makes it easier for children to attain the objective.

All the activities have been and should continue to be adapted according to the capacities of particular groups and teachers. Some activities may already be familiar from other sources or in slightly different forms.

FREEZE GAME

One child volunteers to begin, in the middle of the circle, by showing some distinctive action. This may be shooting for basketball baskets, or planting seeds in a garden, or painting a picture, or almost anything. A few words may be used for clarity and fun. (This is not "Charades." No one is trying to *guess* what the person is doing.) Someone in the circle says, "freeze!" That person must *use* the position the first person was frozen in to make a new activity that the two cooperate to perform together (the first person is "unfrozen" as soon as they begin together). For example, the first was shooting a basket with one arm extended, and now the two together are trying to hang a picture on the wall.

Now a third person says "freeze" and uses some part of the picture-hanging action to make a *new* (third) action for all three (now perhaps a dance class), and so on until five or six people are cooperating for one action. Finally, they "peel off" in reverse order, each explaining in a few words why his/her action now is ending ("Oops, time for lunch. I'll finish these pictures later.") as the group goes through each action again, remembering them in reverse order. There is one person left, doing his/her original action that started the game. Then he/she peels off, sits down, and all are ready for a new round.

Upper-elementary children (some third graders too) pick this up quickly and enjoy it. Also the skills it calls forth are those which are often hard to anticipate: certain children get a rare chance to "shine" before their peers, while all get better at cooperation and concentration. Detail and cooperation of each group action should be stressed.

THE PEOPLE MACHINE

This activity also begins with one person in the center of the circle. That person is making some abstract or semi-abstract motion repetitively. The second person raises his/her hand and is called on by the first person (or the teacher) to join the "machine." The action of the second must fit into the action of the first in a creative, cooperative way so that the two are one "people machine" together. Now a third joins, now a fourth, and so on until five or six of the group are moving as part of one big "machine." This cooperative effort which the children have created functions for a little while, and all participants share the fun. Then everyone is tired as well as satisfied, so all just stop and collapse back into their chairs.

IMPROVISATIONS

Some groups of older children gain a great deal from working in groups of three to five to devise quick "plays" to show ethical or unethical actions (or both, in one play) for all to discuss together.

The rules must be strict and clear:

- Situations must be realistic about kids their own age.
- The characters must be kids, rather than adults, performing the ethical or unethical actions.
- The issues or actions of ethics must be clear.
- The play should not get too "wild."

Also, the improvisations *must* be followed by "debriefing," i.e., good discussion of what they were showing, how well they showed it, and what possible alternatives might be. (Children of this age sometimes like to use television "sitcom" plots. This should be strongly discouraged, in my opinion, because nobody is really learning anything, and the plots have so little to do with real experience.)

"Judges" are a fine device for organizing and clarifying this debriefing discussion, as well as for providing a good role for shy or otherwise reluctant class members. (Often, the children who are prone to be "wild" are the ones who make excellent judges.)

The three or four judges should have index cards, clipboards (if possible), and pencils. They are instructed to work together to agree upon their criteria and scoring system. "Clarity" (help them learn this word if they do not know it), "acting," "ethics," and "realism" are typical criteria, with "humor" a favorite as an "optional." Typical scale would be ten points for each criterion.

It is essential that, once the judges have decided upon their system, there be time for them to explain it to the group before any plays are performed. People deserve to know ahead of time how their efforts will be judged!

The judges prepare (they take this very seriously, in my experience) while each group of players is also preparing. First, judges explain their system. Then the plays are performed for the whole group in turn, followed by the judges-led discussion.

Especially at the fourth-grade level, children have little trouble coming up with good ideas to show in this way. Respecting differences, blaming, lying, repeating rumors, doing favors, eavesdropping, excluding, telling secrets, helping, forgiving, cheating at games, and managing conflicting loyalties are some of the topics for good plays and discussion. If players have trouble getting started, you can have ready a few possible situation cards of realistic ethics situations.

One frequent and painful problem for this age level is that of kindness/ acceptance for someone who is poor at sports. Focus on this has brought nice surprises too. One boy spoke movingly about his recent experience outside school when children were teasing someone: "I felt really bad because they were insulting him for something he couldn't help!" But a "star athlete" confessed that it's also not so good to be the best, because "it puts so much pressure on you all the time" (thereby astounding the poor athletes in the group).

Sometimes fourth or even fifth graders enact their ethical problems directly, and sometimes they are able to reverse roles in the play to powerful effect. For example, the most popular child will take the role of the excluded one, or the shy child will be the "group leader." The ensuing discussions are particularly illuminating when this happens.

ETHICS-IN-ACTION PROJECTS

Children should be assisted to arrange "helping projects" within the school. Teachers can work together to arrange for fourth graders to help kindergarten children in all sorts of activities, from playing with blocks to learning letters, or for sixth graders to play mathematics games with second graders or help in the lunchroom or whatever is appropriate and practical at an individual school—possibilities are various and wonderful, as are results.

Ethics-in-action jobs should be set up to be accomplished on a regular basis over weeks or months, on the "free time" of those doing the helping. Such external rewards as gold stars or "brownie points" are to be avoided, since the intrinsic rewards of helping others are what is being learned and stressed. One-to-one connections across ages are particularly special and valuable to the whole school community. It's great to see a first grader rushing happily to "his" sixth grader before school, just to say hello.

All need to be advised about their role. Helpers are *not* there to do the younger kids' work! They have to help the younger kids do their own learning themselves. Also, no younger child wants to be treated as "cute," especially by an older child, as he/she is struggling to master difficult concepts. These sorts of rather obvious guidance do need to be quite explicit for a school ethics-in-action effort to work.

Children who are helping will have many questions: "What's the best way to handle a kid who gets too wild?" "What do I do about a kid who clings to me and wants all my attention?" Helping must be both respectful and gentle if it is to be effective. A fifth grader offered this suggestion, "I never say, 'Do you need help?' because I wouldn't put a kid on the spot like that. Instead I ask, 'Could you show me what you're working on?' then I take it from there."

It is important to reserve time for group discussion about the helping experience. It is also very valuable for the older children to complete written assignments from time to time, in which they must reflect on their ethics-in-action experience. Too, this can be a good way for some children to express privately any concerns or problems they may be having along the way.

Not all children are good at ethics-in-action, certainly, and not all enjoy it. In my opinion, everyone should have to *try* it, but any sort of sustained effort should be voluntary, at least for elementary-school-age children.

There are surprising, sometimes wonderful benefits for these helpers. They may gain new insights and patience through experiencing frustration in trying to help. They may get useful reinforcement in basic skills. Some children (this often happens with boys considered "rough") discover or display a very gentle side of themselves that is a delight for everyone. Many find deep satisfaction and pride, as well as fun, in the helping experience.

EVALUATION ————————————————————————

We shrink from presuming to judge the ethics of others, but need to find ways to measure progress of ethics class efforts. Formal evaluation is necessarily confined to gauging children's progress in *verbal* facility. Improvement in ethical *behavior* is infinitely more elusive and subtle, obviously.

As examples, I have rarely met a child who would not verbally express rejection of stealing or cheating upon entering school and consistently thereafter. Progress in understanding about these behaviors (not to mention actual rejection of them) is therefore hard to gauge. Such other topics as helpful helping and appropriate trust seem too context-dependent to fit measurable objectives.

A sense of having made some difference in behavior will come unexpectedly, if at all:

- I had a fifth grader write in her private (for her and me only) ethics journal the following: "There's one kid whose guts I really hate, and that's ——. But today when a whole bunch of kids started teasing him, I really stood up for him, and I think that was ethical of me and I'm proud of it, but I couldn't tell anybody."

- A third grader made a picture of an event in her recent experience when she was being teased about her doll by two boys, depicting herself as ignoring them rather than teasing back (as she explained in the picture, she *could* have done).

- I overheard a third-grade boy say to two girls as they were lining up, "Hey, you're excluding her just the way we talked about not doing in ethics class last week!" The girls' answer was a prompt, "Oh! You're right," followed by an easy inclusion of the third girl. (Nothing more was said, to my knowledge.)

- Or, children might simply begin to listen more respectfully to one another in class discussion. That in itself is surely an improvement in their ethical behavior!

EVALUATION OBJECTIVES

As for more formal evaluation, I propose two main categories, which I first describe, then present stated as formal objectives:

1. **(a)** Children need to understand the definition of ethics, to be able to express ethical reasons and to distinguish ethical reasons from reasons which may be perfectly good and sensible but are not ethical.

   (b) In identifying ethical reasons, they need also to understand that, often, there may be ethical reasons on both sides of an issue, i.e., ethical reasons may conflict with other ethical reasons. Rather than "right and wrong," choices are likely to be between two (or more) "rights," both worthy.

Objective 1-a: Over the course of a school year, individual children will demonstrate improvement in distinguishing between *ethical* reasons for decisions or actions and reasons which may be good and sensible but are not ethical. (In general, an ethical reason includes some appreciation for principles of justice and beneficence, some reference to rules of conduct which respect others' dignity and sensibility.)

Examples for Objective 1–a

Ethical Reason	Instead Of	Other Reason
Her friend might feel really sad.	…	She could be punished if she did that.
How would you feel if you were in his place?	…	You might get another chance to (whatever the alternative temptation is).
She shouldn't help him, because he might not want to be helped.	…	If she helps him, it would be a big commitment of her time.
He really cared about them.	…	He thought they might reward him.
She didn't want to offend him.	…	She didn't want to get blamed.

Objective 1-b: Over the course of a school year, individual children will demonstrate improvement in articulating ethical reasons for both sides of an issue.

Examples for Objective 1–b

Ethical Reason for One Side of Issue	And	Ethical Reason for Other Side of Issue
His friend trusts him.	…	His friend could get hurt.
She wants to be loyal.	…	She wants to follow the rule.
He did promise.	…	This reason is more important than any promise.
She should tell the truth.	…	Telling the truth could hurt his feelings.

2. There are several specific values which seem appropriate and attainable (or at least accessible) in ethics class. These include

(a) clearer understanding of honesty

(b) respect for individual dignity

(c) rejection of vengeance

(d) increased sensitivity and compassion

(e) rejection of violence

You may find others as well.

Objective 2-a: Over the course of a school year, individual children will show improvement in articulating comprehension of the importance of intention in issues of honesty. (This arises often in contexts of obedience or relating to authority figures. A partial truth, intended to mislead, may not be recognized as a lie.)

Objective 2-b: Over the course of a school year, individual children will show improvement in suggesting behaviors which involve respect for the individual dignity of others.

Objective 2-c: Over the course of a school year, individual children will demonstrate improvement in suggesting such alternatives to vengeance as avoidance, forgiveness, cooperation, or appeal to authority.

Objective 2-d: Over the course of a school year, individual children will demonstrate improvement in articulating sensitivity to others' feelings and compassion for human suffering.

Objective 2-e: Over the course of a school year, individual children will demonstrate improvement in rejecting violence as a good alternative for settling disputes.

In the chart on page 186, I offer story examples which deal directly with each of the objectives. You'll find and use many others. And, of course, there are many other important ethical values to discuss besides those covered in the objectives.

NARRATIVE REPORTS

As for my own evaluation responsibilities, in accordance with the policy and practice at my school, I write formal narrative reports to parents once a year. The objectives stated above are what guide me as I teach and then as I write these reports.

The form I use includes a very brief summary of the ethics curriculum at that grade level for that year (every few years I make adjustments). I have recently used these curriculum statements for the upper grades:

- Fourth-grade ethics curriculum centers on issues of friendship, loyalty, and compassion. Children's literature is used, and students also compose short ethics plays and evaluate them, as well as bringing in issues from their own experience for group discussion. They complete some written assignments.

- The fifth-grade ethics curriculum centers on issues of friendship and autonomy in decision making. Issues of stealing and fairness get attention. Children's literature is used. Although discussion is the main activity, students complete written assignments too.

- Sixth-grade ethics curriculum focuses on personal ethical principles in contexts of friendship and peer pressure. Also, there are debates on ethical issues of contemporary public concern. Students complete regular written assignments and accomplish community service responsibilities within the school.

The curriculum statement is followed by the topic headings, "Response to Ethical Issues," "Ethical Reasoning," "Participation," and "Relationships."

Using this form, I strive to describe behavior I witness in class.

The narrative-report form was devised by ethics department colleagues and me at the Ethical Culture-Fieldston Schools; I am very grateful to the Ethical Culture-Fieldston Schools for permission to include these forms.

Blank narrative-report forms are provided for your use: one for each of the upper grades, containing the sample curriculum statement for that grade and another with space for your own curriculum statement.

In addition to blank forms, I have included a number of sample evaluations. These examples are typical evaluations written for children in my fourth, fifth, and sixth grade classes. The names have been changed.

CONCLUSION

Again, I stress that evaluation in the area of ethics is elusive, almost by definition. The more precise or numerical any measurement of success becomes, the less it may be telling you about your children's actual ethics. Although ethical understandings may be specific, the improvements that you hope for in behavior are of a general nature, extending outside your classroom, over many years, with many individual exceptions and failures. The methods I suggest in this book may result in the kind of incidents I've described, or better ones, for you. The "seeds you sow" may bear fruit twenty years later in a decision you'll never know about. You, your children, and their parents may perceive that their behavior becomes more ethical.

There can be no promises or guarantees. All teaching requires a special kind of heartfelt faith. Connections between your efforts and any measurable results may indeed be fewer in ethics than in other subjects, but that hardly means your efforts are wasted. Teaching ethics to the next generation is the oldest, most universal effort of humankind. I have tried here to offer a method which seems ethical in its respect for children, valid in its precepts, enjoyable, and practical. I am grateful to my school for giving me the opportunity to teach ethics, and I wish it for other teachers.

Objective	Story	Example Situation
1a defining ethics: distinguishing ethical reasons from good reasons	*Between Friends*	Jill must decide whether to go to Boston to see Marla or go to Dede's party. Her previous commitment to Dede is an ethical reason for choosing Dede's party, while her curiosity to see Dede's school is just a good reason for the same choice.
1b recognizing ethical reasons on both sides of an issue	*The Same Sun*	The narrator would have been ethical to change money for the boy in the train station because he needed it, but also ethical not to change money because doing so could have brought the boy real harm.
2a clearer understanding of honesty	*Alan and Naomi*	Alan lies to Shaun by telling him only part of the truth about his helping Naomi.
2b respect for individual dignity	*Thank You, Ma'm*	Mrs. Lucella Bates Washington Jones refrains from asking Roger questions which she suspects would embarass him.
2c rejection of vengeance	*The White Circle*	Tucker is taught the full horror of his own impulse for revenge.
2d increased sensitivity and compassion	*Last Look*	Monica learns how hurt and alone Rhoda had felt, and is therefore more sensitive to the feelings of the next new girl at school.
2e rejection of violence	*On My Honor*	When Joel and Tony started to fight in the river, it led to challenging, with terrible results.

Fourth Grade Ethics Evaluation Example 1

Response to Ethical Issues

Inge's response to ethical issues is very strong—both mature and principled. She is exceptionally secure in her own values and eager to consider their application in all sorts of situations. Her kindness and her good humor are notable.

Ethical Reasoning

Inge is a most agile and articulate reasoner. She is usually the first to make subtle inferences or to see interesting applications of concepts, and she can explain her ideas and insights with perfect clarity (although Inge herself often doubts this and needs encouragement).

Participation

An excellent class participant, Inge is alert and involved in whatever we're doing. She seems to enjoy ethics class. She often initiates questions and comments.

Relationships

Inge gets along very well with her classmates. She has done a wonderful job of helping the younger children through ethics-in-action.

Fourth Grade Ethics Evaluation Example 2

Response to Ethical Issues

Gerardo is unusually sensitive and unusually thoughtful about ethical matters. His interest in them is very strong, consistently. By nature he is cautious about making judgments, but his personal values are clear.

Ethical Reasoning

Gerardo is an effective, logical reasoner who owes it to himself to trust his own powers more. At times, he has misunderstood a question, but more often he is more hesitant than he should be in attacking a problem. He can express his ideas very well in writing or in discussion. I look forward to his developing the confidence to do so more readily.

Participation

Gerardo seems to enjoy ethics class. He is wonderfully focused and attentive, week after week. His contributions to class discussion have been appropriate, insightful, and interesting. As indicated above, his habits of caution and reticence inhibit him from speaking as much as I think he should be.

Relationships

Gerardo gets along well with his classmates. He is notably gentle and polite. He has been very helpful to the younger children through ethics-in-action.

Fifth Grade Ethics Evaluation Example 1

Response to Ethical Issues

Marco is quite thoughtful in his approach to ethical issues. His awareness of them is unusual, as is his fair-mindedness. I appreciate Marco's gentleness.

Ethical Reasoning

Marco's explanations can be wonderfully sharp and succinct. His inferences and perceptions are apt. But his reasoning performance is surprisingly uneven, both orally and in writing—depending on whether he puts any effort into it. He should honor his own fine talent with work.

Participation

Marco is a pleasant, attentive class participant. He seems interested in the topics, and he has had astute contributions to make to class discussion. But he needs to become much more conscientious about completing written assignments.

Relationships

Marco gets along well with his classmates. He is notably kind and courteous. He has been helpful to the younger children through ethics-in-action.

Fifth Grade Ethics Evaluation Example 2

Response to Ethical Issues

Akiko is exceptionally thoughtful, serious, and sensitive in her response to ethical issues, consistently. She seems already to have considered almost any possible topic. Her attitude is one of gentle, good-humored open-mindedness, but her own values seem secure.

Ethical Reasoning

Akiko's reasoning can be startlingly clear. Her comprehension is excellent, then she identifies the "heart" or the "weak link" of an issue. The expression of her ideas is fine, both in writing and orally.

Participation

Akiko is a constructive class participant. Always pleasant and polite, she listens carefully and speaks thoughtfully. She is very conscientious about written assignments.

Relationships

Akiko gets along well with her classmates. She is good at solving problems in small group efforts.

Sixth Grade Ethics Evaluation Example 1

Response to Ethical Issues

Yung has a strong interest in issues of ethics, and basic attitudes of fair-mindedness and kindness to go with it. She seems to have thought quite a bit about ethics on her own initiative.

Ethical Reasoning

Yung's reasoning can be quick and insightful, but it has needed more consistent and thorough attention to written preparation. Recently, this has begun to happen.

Participation

Yung's attitude has usually been pleasant and her participation positive but sporadic. Recently I have noticed more consistent purposefulness and maturity in Yung's approach to ethics.

Relationships

Yung gets along very well with her classmates.

Sixth Grade Ethics Evaluation Example 2

Response to Ethical Issues

Carlos is deeply thoughtful and impressively mature in his response to ethical issues. His personal ethical principles seem very strong, and he seems to enjoy challenging them in all sorts of theoretical situations.

Ethical Reasoning

Carlos is a talented reasoner. His comprehension is excellent, and his comments and questions are keenly insightful. Carlos can be very original in his thinking, but is always clear and appropriate in what he has to say.

Participation

Carlos is an exemplary class participant. He is highly disciplined and alert, listening well and speaking effectively. He is conscientious about written assignments, consistently. His leadership qualities are appreciated by his classmates.

Relationships

Carlos gets along very well with his peers. He has done an outstanding job of helping younger children through ethics-in-action.

Fourth Grade Ethics Evaluation Form

Student: _____   Date: _____

Classroom
  Teacher: _____

Ethics
  Teacher: _____

Curriculum

Fourth-grade ethics curriculum centers on issues of friendship, loyalty, and compassion. Children's literature is used, and students also compose short ethics plays and evaluate them, as well as bringing in issues from their own experience for group discussion. They complete some written assignments.

Response to Ethical Issues

Ethical Reasoning

Participation

Relationships

Fifth Grade Ethics Evaluation Form

Student: _____   Date: _____

Classroom
Teacher: _____

Ethics
Teacher: _____

Curriculum

Fifth-grade ethics curriculum centers on issues of friendship and autonomy in decision making. Issues of stealing and fairness get attention. Children's literature is used. Although discussion is the main activity, students complete written assignments too.

Response to Ethical Issues

Ethical Reasoning

Participation

Relationships

Sixth Grade Ethics Evaluation Form

Student: _____   **Date:** _____

Classroom Teacher: _____   **Ethics Teacher:** _____

Curriculum

Sixth-grade ethics curriculum focuses on personal ethical principles in contexts of friendship and peer pressure. Also, there are debates on ethical issues of contemporary public concern. Students complete regular written assignments and accomplish community service responsibilities within the school.

Response to Ethical Issues

Ethical Reasoning

Participation

Relationships

Ethics Evaluation Form

Student: _____   Grade: _____   Date: _____

Classroom
Teacher: _____   Ethics
Teacher: _____

Curriculum _____

Response to Ethical Issues _____

Ethical Reasoning _____

Participation _____

Relationships _____

RECOMMENDED DISCUSSION BOOKS————

Most of the books listed have been used in ethics class with success. Some books, indicated *, appeared too late for me to have the chance to try them out in my classes, but I suspect they would work very well and therefore recommend them. Suggested grade levels are given.

Avi, *Nothing But the Truth*, Orchard Books, New York, 1991

> * A ninth-grade boy persists in humming along in class when the national anthem is played. The perspectives of his teacher, his parents, school authorities, classmates, and members of the community are expressed, as well as that of the boy himself, as everyone wants "rights," most mean well and try hard to do their best, and everyone loses. This is an unusual, powerful book. (Grade 6)

Bawden, Nina, *The Robbers*, Lothrop, Lee & Shepard, New York, 1979

> Set in present-day London, this book is deeply moral and affecting, and rich in discussion topics. In it, a wealthy boy who has always lived with his grandmother (his mother is dead and his father has been too busy for him) goes to live with his father and new stepmother in the city. There he meets and becomes friends with a poor boy who is struggling with enormous problems. Issues of their friendship and loyalty against his father's selfishness, his grandmother's devotion, and the difference between the two families' values and opportunities are subtly drawn. Among the characters, there is also an interracial marriage, caring for ill family members, a court case, an actual robbery attempt, and an anguished open ending. (You may need to explain the references to English custom as you go along.) (Grade 5 or 6)

Bulla, Clyde Robert, *Dexter*, Thomas Y. Crowell, New York, 1973

> A lonely Missouri farm boy becomes friends with the son of a family who are quite different from everyone else around. He keeps a commitment to care for the friend's pony, without any assurance he'll ever see the friend again. This story nicely brings out issues of how animals should be treated, as well as sensitivity to people who are different, and, most of all, the ethics of commitment in friendship. (Grade 4 or 5)

Byars, Betsy, *Cracker Jackson*, Puffin Books, New York, 1986

> An eleven-year-old boy learns that his beloved former baby-sitter is being battered by her husband, and feels compelled to try to help her. The problems of doing unethical actions for an ethical purpose are well presented. Also there is the need for understanding one's own limitations in the face of enormous problems. This book is very sensitively written and is appropriate for sixth grade discussion. It is quite effectively leavened by humor. (Grade 6)

Cohen, Barbara, *Thank You, Jackie Robinson*, Lothrop, Lee & Shepard Co., New York, 1974

> Sam is a fatherless white boy in New Jersey in 1946 with an exceptional

passion for baseball, especially the Brooklyn Dodgers and most especially Jackie Robinson. His very best friend is a sixty-year-old black man who works at his mother's inn. Ethical issues of race relations, family relationships, honesty, and friendship are subtly and sensitively portrayed. This is a beautiful and very effective book. (Grade 4 or 5)

Cohen, Barbara, *213 Valentines*, Henry Holt and Company, New York, 1991

An African-American fourth grader is chosen for a special gifted and talented program in a school away from his own neighborhood. Class and race prejudice, as well as problems of friendship, loyalty, courage, and open-mindedness are among the topics of this sensitive, humorous, and realistic book. (Grade 4)

DeClements, Barthe, *Five Finger Discount*, Delacorte Press, New York, 1989

A fifth-grade boy whose father is in prison must deal with concern about peers in a new town and school. Issues of stealing, lying, and threatening are dealt with realistically and effectively. However, parts of this book are unnecessarily harsh or inappropriately unethical, and should be edited, in my view. Most of my students tell me that, although they don't really like this book, its ethical issues are so good for discussion that they recommend using it. (Grade 5)

Estes, Eleanor, *The Hundred Dresses*, Harcourt, Brace Jovanovich, New York, 1974

This classic book about children's cruelty and group pressure can be very effective for ethics discussion with fourth graders. Parts that seem dated (it was originally published in 1944) can be explained or edited as it is read aloud. (Grade 4)

Moore, Emily, *Whose Side Are You On?*, Farrar, Straus and Giroux, New York, 1989

A quite enjoyable story, this one is told from the point of view of a believable sixth grader who is struggling with problems of acceptance/rejection with her peers and trust/obedience with the adult world. The setting is present-day middle-class Harlem, and the issues are universal. (Grade 5 or 6)

Naylor, Phyllis Reynolds, *Shiloh*, Atheneum, New York, 1991

* In this gripping, beautiful book, an eleven-year-old West Virginia boy is caught up into lying to his beloved parents and others in his desperate efforts to save a neighbor's dog from abuse. Several of my fourth graders have already read this book on their own and proclaim it their favorite book ever, "especially for the ethics!" (Grade 4, 5, or 6)

Parks, Rosa, *Rosa Parks: My Story*, with Jim Haskins, Dial Books, New York, 1992

* The true story of an authentic American hero is told simply and effectively. Certain chapters, especially the one explaining the bus boycott, could be well read aloud for learning and discussion. (Grade 4, 5, or 6)

Paulsen, Gary, *The Crossing*, Orchard Books, New York, 1987

> This is an unusual and powerful book, which should *not* be used for younger than sixth grade, in my opinion. It tells the story of a solitary, starving Mexican boy who meets an American Army sergeant broken by his (Vietnam) war experiences. The time is the present and the place is the border town of Juarez. Issues of truth, lying, and trust are subtly depicted. The realistic portrayal of desperate poverty is very important. (Grade 6)

Speare, Elizabeth George, *The Sign of the Beaver*, Houghton Mifflin, Boston, 1983

> This rich adventure/history novel is not as full of ethics discussion issues as other books, but the basic problems it presents are deeper than many, and very engaging to upper-elementary students. In eighteenth century Maine, how can a white colonist boy and a Native American boy learn to help and respect one another as friends? (Grade 4, 5, or 6)

Steig, William, *The Real Thief*, Farrar, Straus & Giroux, New York, 1973

> This beautifully written book is about intense feelings and universal childhood experiences as much as it is about ethical concepts, and it can engender great discussions with fourth graders. Gawain the goose is wrongfully accused of a crime actually done by his friend, Derek the mouse. Issues of accusation, guilt, courage, friendship, envy, forgiveness, and redemption are all involved, and the ending is happy. A lesson plan for this book is included in *Exploring Ethics through Children's Literature, Book 1*. (Grade 4)

Tolan, Stephanie S., *Sophie and the Sidewalk Man*, Four Winds Press, New York, 1992

> Sophie has been saving her money for a very special toy, a small stuffed animal. There is also the incentive of competition in a favorite-toy school pageant. But a homeless man, obviously hungry and sad, is there outside the toy store, sitting on the sidewalk, every day, and Sophie can't stop worrying about him. Is there any way to help? Complicated issues are handled sensitively and realistically here. (Grade 4)

Yep, Laurence, *The Star Fisher*, Morrow Junior Books, New York, 1991

> * This is a beautiful and unusual story (based on experiences of the author's own family) of a Chinese-American family moving from Ohio to West Virginia in the 1920s to open a laundry. The protagonist is a fourteen-year-old girl yearning for acceptance by her peers and for the success of her family. There is the resonating myth of the star fisher, caught between the two worlds of sky and earth, and there are many subtly drawn ethical issues. (Grade 6)

SHORT STORIES

Ashley, Bernard, "Lenny's Red Letter Day," anthologized in *Junior Great Books*, Series Five, Second Semester, Volume Two, The Great Books Foundation, Chicago, 1987

This story deals with the urgent topic of distinguishing between pity and friendship. The pride of an outcast boy, the issue of false suspicion, and powerful surprises are all presented in a very few pages. (Grade 5 or 6)

Thomas, Maria, "Abdullah and Mariam," in *Come to Africa and Save Your Marriage and Other Stories*, Soho Press, Inc., 1987

This is a beautiful, poignant story about dignity, courage, and devotion in a devout Muslim couple in present-day east Africa. Students find it challenging, but I think it is worth the effort because it affords sympathetic identification with a culture which, otherwise, is often misunderstood. (Grade 6)

Wilbur, Richard, "A Game of Catch," anthologized in *Junior Great Books*, Series 6, Volume 1, 1975 (and other editions), The Great Books Foundation, Chicago

This is a quick, subtle, powerful story about the excruciating tensions of exclusion/inclusion among three boys. Issues of personal responsibility are also crucial. (Grade 5 or 6)

BACKGROUND READING IN ETHICS

BOOKS

Aristotle, *Nicomachean Ethics*, translated by Terence Irwin, Hackett Publishing Company, Indianapolis, 1985 (also transl. W.D. Ross, Charlie Scribner's Sons, 1955; J.A.K. Thomson, Penguin Books, 1955)

Bok, Sissela, *Lying: Moral Choice in Public and Private Life*, Pantheon Books, New York, 1978

Carter, C., editor, *Scepticism and Moral Principles*, New University Press, Inc., Evanston, Ill., 1973

Cohen, Dorothy, *The Learning Child*, Vintage Books, New York, 1973

✳ Coles, Robert, *The Call of Stories*, Houghton Mifflin Company, Boston, 1989
———, *The Moral Life of Children*, Atlantic Monthly Press, New York, 1986

DeVries, Rheta with Lawrence Kohlberg, *Programs of Early Education—The Constructivist View*, Longman, New York, 1987

Foot, Philippa, *Virtues and Vices*, University of California Press, Berkeley and Los Angeles, 1978, 1981

✳ Frankena, William K., *Ethics*, Prentice-Hall, Englewood Cliffs, New Jersey, 1963

✳ Gilligan, Carol, *In a Different Voice*, Harvard University Press, Cambridge, Mass., 1982

Gowans, Christopher W., editor, *Moral Dilemmas*, Oxford University Press, New York, 1987

Harding, Carol, editor, *Moral Dilemmas, Philosophical and Psychological Issues in the Development of Moral Reasoning*, Precedent Publishing, Inc., Chicago, 1985

Hare, R. M., *Essays on the Moral Concepts*, University of California Press, Berkeley and Los Angeles, 1973

Hume, David, *An Enquiry Concerning the Principles of Morals*, L. A. Selby-Bigge, Edit., Clarendon Press, Oxford, 1961

———, *A Treatise of Human Nature*, (Mossner, Ernest C., editor) Penguin Books, New York, 1969

Kagan, Jerome, *The Nature of the Child*, Basic Books, Inc., Publishers, New York, 1984

Kagan, Jerome and Sharon Lamb, editors, *The Emergence of Morality in Young Children*, The University of Chicago Press, Chicago, 1987

Kant, Immanuel, *Groundwork for the Metaphysics of Morals*, L. W. Beck, transl., The Liberal Arts Press, Inc., New York, 1950; also transl. James W. Ellington, Hackett Publishing Company, Inc., Indianapolis, 1981

Kegan, Robert, *The Evolving Self*, Harvard University Press, Cambridge, Mass., 1982

Kekes, John, *Moral Tradition and Individuality*, Princeton University Press, Princeton, N.J., 1989

Kohlberg, Lawrence, *Child Psychology and Childhood Education*, Longman, Inc., White Plains, New York, 1987

———, *The Philosophy of Moral Development*, Harper and Row, Publishers, San Francisco, 1981

Kohn, Alfie, *The Brighter Side of Human Nature—Altruism and Empathy in Everyday Life*, Basic Books, Inc., Publishers, New York, 1990

Larmore, Charles E., *Patterns of Moral Complexity*, Cambridge University Press, Cambridge, New York, and others, 1987

Lickona, Thomas, *Educating for Character*, Bantam Books, New York 1991

———, *Raising Good Children*, Bantam Books, New York, 1983

Lipman, Matthew et al., *Philosophy in the Classroom*, Universal Diversified Services, Inc., West Caldwell, N.J., 1977

MacIntyre, Alasdair, *After Virtue*, University of Notre Dame Press, Notre Dame, Indiana, 1984

———, *A Short History of Ethics*, Collier Books, New York, 1966

Matthews, Gareth B., *Philosophy and the Young Child*, Harvard University Press, Cambridge, Mass., 1980

Midgley, Mary, *Can't We Make Moral Judgements?*, St. Martin's Press, New York, 1991

Noddings, Nel, *Caring: A Feminine Approach to Ethics and Moral Education*, University of California Press, Berkeley and Los Angeles, 1984

Nucci, Larry P., editor, *Moral Development and Character Education: A Dialogue*, McCutchan Publishing Corporation, Berkeley, California, 1989

Paley, Vivian Gussin, *You Can't Say You Can't Play*, Harvard University Press, Cambridge, 1992

Plato, *Meno, Euthyphro, Apology, Crito, Phaedo*, many editions available

Purpel, David & Kevin Ryan, editors, *Moral Education...It Comes with the Territory*, McCutchan Publishing Corporation, Berkeley, Calif., 1976

Radest, Howard B., *Can We Teach Ethics?*, Praeger, New York, 1989

Rawls, John, *A Theory of Justice*, The Belknap Press of Harvard University Publications, Cambridge, 1971

Reimer, Joseph, and Diana P. Paolitto, and Richard H. Hersh, *Promoting Moral Growth*, Second Edition, Longman, New York, 1983

Sandel, Michael J., *Liberalism and the Limits of Justice*, Cambridge University Press, New York, 1982

Schulman, Michael and Eva Mekler, *Bringing Up a Moral Child*, Addison-Wesley Publishing Company, Inc., Reading, Mass., 1985

Stein, Harry, *Ethics (and Other Liabilities)*, St. Martin's Press, New York, 1982 (paperback edition, 1983)

Toulmin, Stephen, *The Place of Reason in Ethics*, University of Chicago Press, Chicago, 1950, 1986

Williams, Bernard, *Ethics and the Limits of Philosophy*, Harvard University Press, Cambridge, Mass., 1985

PERIODICALS

American Psychologist, June 1990, "The Use of Stories in Moral Development: New Psychological Reasons for an Old Education Method," by Paul C. Vitz

Ethics, An International Journal of Social Political and Legal Philosophy, The University of Chicago Press, Chicago

Ethics in Education, Ontario Institute for Studies in Education, Toronto, Ontario

Harvard Educational Review (Reprint No. 13) "Stage Theories of Cognitive and Moral Development: Criticism and Application," Harvard University Press, Cambridge, Mass., 1978

The Journal of Moral Education, The Social Morality Council, Carfax Publishing Co., Abingdon, England

Journal of Social Issues, Susan Opotow, issue editor, 1990, Vol. 46 No. 1, "Moral Exclusion and Injustice"

Moral Education Forum, Hunter College, City University of New York, New York

The New York Review of Books, Volume XXXVIII, Number 11, "Nietsche's Immoralism" by Philippa Foot; Volume XXXIX, Number 16, "Justice for Women!" by Martha Nussbaum (also many other issues of this journal)